OXFORD WORLD'S CLASSICS

THREE EARLY MODERN UTOPIAS

UTOPIAS have existed almost since the beginnings of literature, but some eras have produced more utopian literature than others. The early modern period was one such time. The geographical and scientific discoveries of the age, as well as its profound social conflicts, provided a context in which the fusion of ideas about the ideal with representations of 'other' fictitious communities became a natural mode of conceiving how things might be different in a world elsewhere. But early modern utopias rarely offered 'simple' solutions to the problems that they confronted. Their writers frequently offered representations of other worlds not in order to answer questions about the social, cultural, and political *mores* of their own times, but rather to raise the issues in their readers' minds. In other words very few early modern utopias are merely blueprints for ideal societies: their meanings emerge only through the juxtaposition of the utopia represented with the writer's own world. In different ways this is true of all three of the utopias reprinted in this volume: Thomas More's *Utopia* (1516), which addresses the social problems of early sixteenth-century England; Francis Bacon's *New Atlantis* (1627), which foregrounds England's shortcomings in the nurture of scientific endeavour; and Henry Neville's *The Isle of Pines* (1668), which engages with issues of colonialism and sexual propriety. These three texts illustrate the range of the utopian imagination in the early modern period, and the different uses to which it could be put.

SUSAN BRUCE is Lecturer in the English Department of Keele University. She is the author of articles on More, Bacon, Rochester, and Swift, and the editor of *The Icon Critical Guide to King Lear*.

OXFORD WORLD'S CLASSICS

*For over 100 years Oxford World's Classics have brought
readers closer to the world's great literature. Now with over 700
titles—from the 4,000-year-old myths of Mesopotamia to the
twentieth century's greatest novels—the series makes available
lesser-known as well as celebrated writing.*

*The pocket-sized hardbacks of the early years contained
introductions by Virginia Woolf, T. S. Eliot, Graham Greene,
and other literary figures which enriched the experience of reading.
Today the series is recognized for its fine scholarship and
reliability in texts that span world literature, drama and poetry,
religion, philosophy and politics. Each edition includes perceptive
commentary and essential background information to meet the
changing needs of readers.*

THE WORLD'S CLASSICS

THOMAS MORE

Utopia

FRANCIS BACON

New Atlantis

HENRY NEVILLE

The Isle of Pines

Edited with an Introduction and Notes by
SUSAN BRUCE

OXFORD
UNIVERSITY PRESS

OXFORD

UNIVERSITY PRESS

Great Clarendon Street, Oxford OX2 6DP

Oxford University Press is a department of the University of Oxford.
It furthers the University's objective of excellence in research, scholarship,
and education by publishing worldwide in

Oxford New York

Athens Auckland Bangkok Bogotá Buenos Aires Calcutta
Cape Town Chennai Dar es Salaam Delhi Florence Hong Kong Istanbul
Karachi Kuala Lumpur Madrid Melbourne Mexico City Mumbai
Nairobi Paris São Paulo Singapore Taipei Tokyo Toronto Warsaw

with associated companies in Berlin Ibadan

Oxford is a registered trade mark of Oxford University Press
in the UK and in certain other countries

Published in the United States
by Oxford University Press Inc., New York

Introduction, Note on the Texts, Select Bibliographies, Chronologies © Susan Bruce 1999
Chronology of Francis Bacon © Brian Vickers 1996

The moral rights of the author have been asserted

Database right Oxford University Press (maker)

First published as an Oxford World's Classics paperback 1999

British Library Cataloguing in Publication Data

Data available

Library of Congress Cataloging in Publication Data

Data available

ISBN–13: 978–0–19–283885–8
ISBN–10: 0–19–283885–7

9

Typeset by RefineCatch Limited, Bungay, Suffolk
Printed in Great Britain by
Clays Ltd, St Ives plc

CONTENTS

ACKNOWLEDGEMENTS

Like other editors, I have consulted other editions of the texts in producing my own. I am especially indebted to J. H. Lupton's and to J. Churton Collins's editions of *Utopia*, to J. Weinberger's and Brian Vickers's editions of *New Atlantis* and to Worthington Chauncey Ford's edition of *The Isle of Pines* for the Club of Odd Volumes. Many individuals have assisted more directly in the production of this volume, and to all of them I am very grateful. Neil Rhodes encouraged me, some years ago now, to propose the anthology to Oxford World's Classics. John Rogers assisted me with one of the explanatory notes to Utopian attitudes to the more obscure aspects of medieval philosophy. Dima Abdulrahim helped me on those occasions where expertise in Arabic was required; Marguerite Palmer helped me to ascertain the meaning of a Dutch sentence. Sue Wiseman was kind enough to help me to track down early versions of Neville's pamphlets; Mishtooni Bose helped me to find a translation of a letter. Tim Lustig has been supportive in many different ways throughout the time I have been working on this anthology, as have Daniel and Luke Lustig-Bruce, in their inimitable and much appreciated fashions. Both Sue and Tim also read and commented on my introduction to *The Isle Of Pines*, as did Roger Pooley and Julie Sanders; Bridget Orr was kind enough to listen to some early ideas. I should also like to thank Judith Luna of Oxford University Press for her efficiency and helpfulness, the copy-editor, Jeff New, for his careful reading of the typescript, and for his excellent suggestions for improvements, some of which I have incorporated in the notes on the texts, and Brian Vickers, editor of the Oxford Authors *Francis Bacon*, for allowing me to base the text of the *New Atlantis*, and the chronology of Francis Bacon, on his edition. Perhaps my greatest debt of gratitude is due to Alison Sharrock of the Classics Department of Keele University, who extended her time (with extraordinary generosity) in helping me with classical allusions in the *New Atlantis*, and more especially *Utopia*, and whose suggestions for new connotations of 'Abraxa', 'Philarch', and 'Syphogrant' I have included in the notes to *Utopia*.

INTRODUCTION

I

Historical Origins: The Early Modern Utopia and the 'Age of Discovery'

All three of the utopias reprinted in this volume engage at some level with a discourse of origins. Just as Utopus civilizes his people, bringing them to 'that excellent perfection . . . wherein they now go beyond all the people of the world' (p. 50), so Solamona, in Bacon's *New Atlantis*, acts as the original 'lawgiver' of his nation, Bensalem, devising for his people the edicts which will regulate their behaviour in perpetuity and thus establish Bensalem as the wisest—and hence in Bacon's terms the most powerful—nation in the world. George Pine too, at least on the surface of Neville's short narrative, endeavours before he dies to lay the foundations (however unspecific) of good government, appointing one ruler and 'exhorting him to use justice and sincerity' (p. 201) among his peers. And just as each text represents the genesis of its utopia in the form of an originating individual whose legacy persists in the very nature of the community that he ruled, so too each is insistent on the separation of its nation from its immediate neighbours, and from the rest of the known world. The Isle of Pines is isolated in terms of its geographical position; similarly removed from Europe in geographical terms, Utopia and Bensalem are further distanced from the outside world by the respective actions of their founding fathers. Utopus turns what was a peninsula into an island, severing Utopia from the mainland in an action which has been read as a kind of birth fantasy;[1] Solamona establishes laws forbidding the entry of strangers and restricting the travel of native Bensalemites, whose visits to other lands are henceforth strictly regulated by the state.

In one very obvious respect the isolation of early modern utopias fulfils a necessary narrative function. The writers of such texts felt impelled to offer a plausible explanation for the fact that the

---

[1] See Louis Marin, *Utopiques: jeux d'espaces* (Paris: Minuit, 1973), 145–6.

imaginary lands they described were unknown to the audiences to whom they described them, and to posit an unknown nation in the middle of the Indian Ocean or off the coast of the Americas is self-evidently more credible than it would be to situate such a community in a village in the Alps, or an island in the middle of the Mediterranean sea. The opportunities for narrative plausibility here were vastly increased by the explosion of knowledge about the globe which took place over these years: underlying the construction of the early modern utopia was the sense of discovery and possibility afforded by the Renaissance voyages of exploration. The Portuguese had explored much of the coastline of Africa during the fifteenth century, but it was the turn of the century which saw the real explosion in 'discovery', as European countries competed with one another to find faster ways of tapping into the immense riches (gold, spices, and, progressively and appallingly, slaves) of Asia and Africa. And with the advent of the printing press, the opportunities for the dissemination of 'news' of the discoveries were limited only by literacy: printed records of the explorations were, in a very short space of time, everywhere available to those who could read.

That the texts in this volume are all to some degree a product of this exploratory context is undeniable. More explicitly makes his traveller a sailor with Amerigo Vespucci: Raphael Hythloday has, he says, accompanied Vespucci on three of the voyages 'of those four that be now in print' (p. 12). 'We sailed from Peru' (p. 152), begins the *New Atlantis*, whose opening rehearses those of the travel narratives which, in part, served as its sources. Similarly, in its detailed transcription of the voyages undertaken by its two narrators, *The Isle of Pines* likewise replicates the style of the early modern travel narrative (although Neville's community engages more with anxieties about colonialism than it does with the excitement of discovery). Even the fact that the title-pages of these texts announce their own novelty ('the new isle of Utopia'; the 'New' Atlantis; the 'new and further discovery of the Isle of Pines')[2] bespeaks their indebtedness to the travel narratives, which often advertised their contents in their titles as 'new'. And in their common appeal to the 'new', both the utopia and the travel narrative betray their origins in the early

---

[2] In one version of the text: for the publishing history of *The Isle of Pines* see Part II of the Introduction.

modern (rather, than say, the medieval) period. For previous ages 'novelty' had been an indicator of the fictional, the truth of a narrative gauged instead by the degree of its conformity to ancient authorities; now the 'new' was coming instead to signify fact instead of fiction, truth instead of falsehood.[3]

Generic Origins: Earlier Representations of Ideal Worlds

The relations between the early modern utopia and the travel narrative are many, and apparently obvious. But assumptions of the 'obvious' can sometimes serve to mask more fundamental questions. In our case, two such questions might be these. First, why fiction? Why do so many writers of early modern utopias construct their ideal worlds in the form of fictional narratives? Secondly, and apparently paradoxically, why truth? Why do these early modern utopianists try so hard to convince their readers of the reality of their island, the 'truth' of the description that they offer them? Why, in other words, do these writers first feel that they must represent their ideal worlds in a fictional form, and then take pains to convince their readership of the literal (not metaphorical or allegorical) truth of that representation? The real resonance of these questions emerges more fully if we compare the early modern utopia with the ideal worlds which pre- and post-date it. Thomas More invented the word 'utopia', as well as the genre it has since come to denote: the genre, stated very simply, of fictional works which claim truly to describe a community posited at some level as ideal. To represent an ideal world, however, was not in itself a novel literary act. Biblical precedents existed in the story of Moses taking his people to the promised land, in the pre-lapsarian state of Adam and Eve, and in prophecies of the second coming, which were later to give rise to forms of millenarianism. From another 'high' culture had emerged Plato's *Republic*; from many different 'low' ones came fantasies of lands of plenty: the 'Lands of Cockaygne', where larks fly into one's mouth ready cooked, and the rivers flow with wine. Many of these texts were influential on early modern utopias. More's *Utopia*, for instance, conducts a kind of dialogue with classical meditations on ideal commonwealths: with

[3] For this argument, see Michael McKeon, *The Origins of the English Novel, 1600–1740* (Baltimore: Johns Hopkins University Press, 1988), 47.

Aristotle's *Politics*, for instance, and, in particular, with Plato's *Republic*, as well as with his *Timaeus, Critias,* and *Laws,* with which Bacon also engages in the *New Atlantis.* Another type of model of an ideal world was to be found in the dialogues of the Greek satirist Lucian. More had translated, with Erasmus, some of these dialogues, including *Menippus,* in which a representation of a fictional world is posed, playfully, as the answer to problems elaborated earlier in the text. And travel narratives too, had classical antecedents: in Pliny's *Natural History,* for instance, in which a number of different customs and communities are described.

Most of these may loosely be described as 'utopian', if by such we mean to indicate their various gestures towards a better world. Yet their degree of difference from the early modern texts we are talking about here can be measured by the nature of the truth claims that each, implicitly or explicitly, makes. Biblical narratives, for instance, and the ideal world discourses which developed out of those narratives, claim literal or prophetic truth: they are not posited as fictional. Lands of Cockaygne, conversely, make no claim to truth at all, except insofar as their dreams of plenty indicate their authors' rueful recognition of the insufficiencies of the natural world. Texts such as Plato's *Republic* may appear to be the closest to the utopia in respect of the truth claims each type of text establishes. But one aspect of the *Republic*'s difference from the early modern utopia can be apprehended when one considers how emphatically, even emblematically, embedded in reality the early modern utopia generally is. Many early modern utopias, Benedict Anderson has pointed out, not only claimed to exist in a locatable point on the globe, but illustrated this location with a bogus map: 'how unimaginable it would be to place Plato's Republic on any map, sham or real', he remarks.[4]

Two Definitions of the Utopian Genre

Early modern utopias, then, even as they embraced fiction as their mode of representation, insisted on the location in real space of the communities that they described. So too they rejected any temporal relocation, refusing to displace their ideals into the past (as do

[4] Benedict Anderson, *Imagined Communities: Reflections on the Origin and Spread of Nationalism* (London: Verso, 1983), 68.

Golden Age narratives) or project them into the future (as does millennial literature or today's science fiction). Cognate with this insistence on spatial and temporal truth is the utopia's insistence on a credible reality in its representation both of nature and of humanity, a feature which at least one recent critic, J. C. Davis, has seen as the defining characteristic of the utopian genre. Davis has argued that ideal world narratives can be classified according to the way in which they negotiate the problem of supply and demand; the problem, that is, of balancing a finite amount of materials (food, lodging, or women, for example) with a potentially infinite amount of desire for those materials. Davis divides ideal world narratives into five types, each characterized by its particular mode of negotiating this gap between supply and demand. The Land of Cockaygne, he argues, assumes unlimited abundance in order to fulfil unlimited desire. The Arcadia fuses a less excessive natural abundance with a representation of a humanity less acquisitive and more easily satisfied than 'real' human beings would be. The Perfect Moral Commonwealth realizes its ideal through an idealization of the nature of humanity. In Millennial literature parity between desire and available material wealth is effected by a *deus ex machina*, whose intervention transforms both man and nature. But for Davis, what distinguishes the utopia from other kinds of ideal world narrative is its refusal of these solutions to the perennial and trans-historical problem of supply and demand. In utopia, Davis argues, people are as potentially transgressive as they are in the real world, their desires as potentially subversive to collective well-being (no change in humanity); in utopia, the availability of material satisfactions is as limited as it is in reality (no change in nature). The utopian solution to the problems of reality, according to Davis, is to idealize neither man nor nature, but organization: the utopianist devises bureaucratic and institutional systems in order to contain desire and transgression, and thus to apportion a limited supply of material satisfactions.[5]

J. C. Davis's definition is very astute, and allows us to make clear distinctions between different kinds of ideal world narratives. It admirably clarifies the degree to which the utopia insists on 'human' solutions to 'human' problems; it enables us to raise useful questions

[5] J. C. Davis, *Utopia and the Ideal Society: A Study of English Utopian Writing, 1516–1700* (Cambridge: CUP, 1984), 9

about individual utopian narratives. But an emphasis on the utopian *idealization* of social organization can also mislead: the degree to which social organization—or indeed almost anything else—is 'idealized' in utopias is often far from transparent. The *New Atlantis*, certainly, idealizes the organization of academic learning into institutions of scientific inquiry, but *Utopia* and *The Isle of Pines* may well undermine almost everything they ostensibly represent as ideal. In those two texts, indeed, claims to the idealism of the communities they describe can, on closer examination disappear (like Gonzalo's utopia in Shakespeare's *The Tempest*) into 'nothing'.[6] The question of how 'ideal' a utopian community is really intended to be recurs frequently in our reading of utopian narratives (despite the everyday meaning of the word 'utopia', which takes for granted the exemplary character of the imagined community described).

Thus far among critics it is Louis Marin, in *Utopiques: jeux d'espaces*, who has offered the most influential answer to such questions as these, and to their logical extension: what is the relation between the 'real' world out of which the author of a utopia writes, and the fictional—and purportedly ideal—world which he or she creates in the text? For Marin, whose intellectual roots lie in the Marxism of Althusser and Macherey, such questions can only be answered if we first think through the nature of our own relation to the 'real' world itself. That real world, and our relation to it, Marin believes, can never be apprehended by us clearly and thoroughly. Rather, we all experience it through the workings of ideology, which occludes social contradictions and 'explains' injustices in the real world in the interests of the dominant class. Some individuals may see through, at least partially, the haze of ideology to perceive to some degree the contradictions it obscures, but it is impossible to own a complete understanding of one's social present—of the 'real' world—for to do so would mean to step outside the history through which all of us are constructed.

What, then, is the relation between the utopia and the real world? For Marin, it is a very close one. Utopia for Marin is not 'other' to the 'real' world with which it purports to contrast itself: the two are not opposites, even if they present themselves as such in the

[6] William Shakespeare, *The Tempest*, ed. Stephen Orgel (Oxford: OUP, 1987), II. i. 145–79.

text(s). Rather, the utopia is a reconstruction of its author's reality, which displaces aspects of its own world into the fictional world it represents, and in so doing foregrounds the social and economic contradictions lived by its writer and his contemporaries. Such contradictions are betrayed in the utopia in the form of ruptures underlying its apparently smooth and seamless surface. In this respect, the utopia is a critique of dominant ideology, offering to its readers an imaginary or fictive solution to the social contradictions of its own time. But utopia's critique, according to Marin, can never be total, for utopia too is a product of history and immersed in it, unable to stand outside it. Thus utopia's critique must itself be ideological: utopia, for Marin, is an ideological critique of the dominant ideology.

From Origins of the Utopia to the Utopia as Origins: The Utopia as a Precursor of the Novel

Another approach to trying to make sense of the odd way in which early modern utopias negotiate the path between truth and fiction might be to understand the utopian narrative in terms similar to those recently used to explain the origins of a later form of prose narrative, the novel. In an influential argument, as complex as it is elegant, Michael McKeon claims that the novel's eventual domination over other forms of literature arises from its ability to 'formulate, and to explain, a set of problems that are central to early modern experience'.[7] It is impossible to do McKeon's argument justice in the limited space available here, but, very briefly, his claims go something like this: the problems that the novel arises to explain are divisible into two main types. The first manifests itself through the way in which early modern writers seem uncertain about how to separate 'fact' from 'fiction', 'true lives' from romance, 'history' from 'literature', an uncertainty which, according to McKeon, denotes a major cultural shift in solutions to the problem of 'how to tell the truth in narrative'. A second set of problems, McKeon argues, betrays a crisis of uncertainty regarding the relation of the external social order to the internal moral state of its members. Responses to those questions (about truth on the one hand and

---

[7] See McKeon, *Origins*, 20–2 for the summary of his argument.

virtue on the other) followed two trajectories, both dialectical in nature. Insofar as truth is concerned, McKeon argues, the period moves from siting truth in traditional authorities (such as classical writers, for instance), through an empiricist challenge to this dependance on ancient authority which argues instead that truth is to be found in the immediately observable (such as travel narratives, for example), to a sceptical challenge to that empirical view, which returns, in part, to the original dependance on traditional authority. These epistemological developments, McKeon claims, have a political counterpart: the period begins with an 'aristocratic ideology', which is challenged by a 'progressive ideology', which is in turn challenged by a 'conservative critique', which returns, in part, to some of the opinions expressed in the original, aristocratic, ideology.

Now to invoke McKeon's argument as a way of perceiving the kinds of questions raised by the utopias in this volume is in some respects a dubious move, at least, and especially, as far as *Utopia* itself is concerned. For McKeon sees these changes beginning (at least most dramatically and extensively) in 1600, whereas More's text was written almost a century before. It will nevertheless be apparent that his argument has much to say about *Utopia*, which so conspicuously raises questions concerning authority and truth, social behaviour and individual virtue, and so systematically juxtaposes very different epistemological and ideological 'answers' to those questions. A couple of examples will suffice to illustrate this claim.

One might read in the England that always hovers around the borders of *Utopia* an essentially aristocratic ideology. One might see the Utopians themselves as the embodiment of a progressive critique of this ideology. And one might then argue that that progressive critique is itself ultimately challenged in the figure of More himself, whose interventions within the text cast conservative doubt on the progressive solutions Utopian society would seem to offer to the aristocratic social evils Hythloday so fervently denounces. Alternatively, one might read in the text a dialectical approach to questions of truth and authority. Dependence on traditional authority is explicitly challenged in *Utopia* in Hythloday's scornful rejection of the European belief that true wisdom resides in the authority of one's 'forefathers and ancestors', and in his parodic rendition of the basis of their argument: 'it were a very dangerous matter if a man in any point should be found wiser than his forefathers were' (p. 17). In this view, *Utopia*'s claim to newness, its elaborate supporting apparatus of letters, maps, alphabets, and other attestations to the empirical truth of the island, serves as the empirical critique of this outdated dependance on the authority of the ancients: 'now in our time divers lands be found which to the old geographers were unknown,' Giles remarks in his prefatory letter (p. 126). That empirical challenge to the authority of the ancients, however, is itself contained in the text by the ultimate exposure of Utopia as a hoax, which exerts a sceptical check on the empirical claims of the 'new' geographers, and in so doing reaffirms, to some degree, the authority of the old.

These are brief—and somewhat literal—examples of ways in which *Utopia* itself could be read as an early forerunner of the novel, or at least as a text which engages very directly with some of the epistemological and social questions which the novel has recently been understood to confront and to formulate. Similar questions might be asked of the *New Atlantis* and *The Isle of Pines*, and also of the texts together: might it be possible, for example, to see the *New Atlantis* as an essentially empirical critique of an aristocratic ideology? To what degree might *The Isle of Pines* represent a sceptical negation of an empirical ideal? These are difficult questions, and they have no easy answers. Nor, indeed, do questions which are apparently more simple: questions, for instance, about the way in which narratorial point of view affects the 'meaning' of these texts; whether 'plot' takes on an increasingly important role as we move from *Utopia* through the *New Atlantis* to *The Isle of Pines*; whether the texts are more—and perhaps increasingly—concerned with the individuals who visit these utopias than with the societies the texts purport to describe.

Early prose narratives such as Swift's *Gulliver's Travels* and Defoe's *Robinson Crusoe* are indubitably indebted to narratives such as *The Isle of Pines*: the relation between the two latter texts has long been recognized, even if the more general relation of the early modern utopia to the novel is still far from clear, and a matter of debate. But whatever this relation is, it seems true to say that if McKeon is right in arguing that the novel's hegemony arose through its 'unrivalled power to formulate, and to explain, a set of problems that are central to early modern experience', the utopia is also grappling with some of the same problems, and, if not explaining them, encouraging its readers to attempt to understand them.

II

Utopia

Thomas More's was a life of paradoxes, even of contradictions, which find their continued expression in the conflicting views of those who write about the man and his work even today. No historical consensus has emerged on More. Some revere him as a saint (he was canonized in 1935); others condemn him as a religious fanatic who persecuted heretics and condemned several of them to death. He has been understood as a medieval traditionalist, unshaken in his defence of the Catholic church against the Protestant onslaught of Luther and his peers; and as a modern reformist, a prominent member of the humanist circle which was at the time the seat of liberal learning in Europe. He was both public statesman (famous as a counsellor to Henry VIII and responsible for enacting some of the severest of Tudor legal punishments), and private man (his household held up as a model of domestic happiness, his daughters educated to a degree extraordinary for the time, beyond the level of many men). All of these aspects of his personality and life have at various times been brought to bear on interpretations of *Utopia*, More's most famous work, and perhaps his only literary masterpiece.

More began writing *Utopia* whilst serving on a state delegation to the Low Countries in 1515. According to his great friend, the Dutch humanist Erasmus, he first composed Book 2 of *Utopia* (concerning the island of Utopia itself), writing Book 1 (a dialogue about the ills of England) later, when Book 2 was substantially complete. Quite why he chose to compose the books in this order; whether he conceived the bipartite structure of *Utopia* from the outset; what consequences this division into two books and the order of their composition have for our understanding of the work: all these have been matters of debate. It is certain that More was, at the time of composition, debating within himself the advisability of acting as a statesman to Henry VIII, and likely, therefore, that the conversation in Book 1 regarding the same matter had for More at the time a very personal resonance. It is also self-evident that More's visit to the Low Countries directly influenced *Utopia*: More mentions that visit, as well as Peter Giles (one of the humanists he met whilst serving on this delegation) explicitly in his narrative. But other, deeper consequences of the addition of Book 1 to Book 2 remain enigmatic, and the relation of the two books is still one of *Utopia*'s many teasing problems. Does the criticism of England in Book 1 act to impress upon readers the ideal nature of the country described in Book 2, for instance? Or does it do the opposite, subverting the apparent ideal by making explicit criticisms of its untenability? To attempt to provide definitive answers to questions such as these is beyond the scope of this Introduction. But I hope that in the pages that follow I will at least be able to indicate why they remain so pressing.

Like More's life, *Utopia* itself is a tissue of paradox and contradiction, and since its first publication in 1516, More's purpose in its creation has been a perennial problem for its readers. *Utopia* is the most slippery of texts: in no other literary work is the question of authorial intention at once more pressing and more unanswerable. Its playful juxtaposition of the real with the imaginary; the nature of Utopian society itself; the incongruence between 'ideal' Utopian practices and what we know of More's own life and beliefs; the relation between Books 1 and 2 of the text: all these things encourage *Utopia*'s readers to ask themselves what More meant by this text, and simultaneously preclude attempts to answer that question with any certainty. The text has generated diametrically opposed interpretations from its critics, ranging from the dubious claim that Utopia describes a real historical community to the assertion that it is only a literary game; and from readings which maintain that it is a vision of an ideal Catholic society to those which see it as a proto-Communist text. More recent are the interpretations of those who have attempted with the help of literary theory to find ways of fusing the text's ludic qualities with the seam of social critique that also runs through it, but before these contributions, most readings of the text essentially fell into two camps. On the one side were those who saw it as a grand joke at the expense of its readers; on the other stood those who claimed that the discourse of social critique within *Utopia* is at some level seriously intended. To what degree does *Utopia* offer ammunition for these variant strands of interpretation?

A summary of the manifest content of the text is sufficient to illustrate why the impulse to read *Utopia* as a serious critique is so tempting. The book purports to relate the story of More's meeting in Antwerp with a traveller, Raphael Hythloday, to whom he is introduced by his friend Peter Giles. The three men start talking, and enter into the prolonged debate on the social evils of sixteenth-century England which is the content of Book 1. In the course of this debate, Hythloday launches an impassioned attack on a number of abuses, especially on the English use of the death penalty and on the desperate poverty and degradation which was the lot of so many at the time. He is most concerned with the plight of the peasants. Dispossessed of their livelihoods through the enclosure of common land by rapacious landlords eager to profit from the wool trade, sixteenth-century English peasants had become economic refugees from their places of origin, and were driven into destitution. The unemployment created by this agricultural upheaval was swelled by the disbanding of private feudal armies, whose soldiers were released from their duties without alternative occupations to maintain them. In this context, Hythloday argues, theft and beggary are neither a matter of choice nor a consequence of innate immorality within the individual, but the necessary recourse of those from whom all choice has been taken away. To sentence petty thieves to death, he argues, is wrong, capital punishment being both impractical (because fear of it encourages a thief to kill his victim in order to preclude the threat of exposure to the law), and unethical (in that it transgresses God's commandment not to kill).

In the course of this debate, Hythloday invokes Plato's *Republic* (one of the main literary inspirations for *Utopia*) to argue that the only way to overcome these problems is to eradicate what he claims is their fundamental cause: private property. '[S]o long as [property] shall continue,' he claims, 'so long shall remain among the most and best part of men the heavy and inevitable burden of poverty and wretchedness' (p. 45). Thus is introduced the description of Utopia itself, invoked by Hythloday as the 'answer' to the problems raised in the preceding dialogues. The three men break for dinner, and Book 2 of *Utopia* then begins. With the exception of a brief intervention by More at the conclusion of the text, Book 2 consists entirely of Hythloday's description of the commonwealth of Utopia: its social organization, the daily life of its people, its governors, laws, and religions. And on the surface at least, Utopia stands as the opposite of the England Hythloday has attacked. Where England has crime, Utopia has order; where England has injustice, Utopia has equity; where England has hugely rich and desperately poor, Utopia has neither riches nor poverty. Instead, it has communist equality, in which 'all things be common to every man', and where no individual lacks anything so long as the larger community has enough (p. 119). At the close of Hythloday's description of Utopia, More concludes the text by leading Hythloday into supper, and 'thus endeth the afternoon's talk of Raphael Hythloday concerning the . . . Island of Utopia' (p. 123).

It is important to recognize that the eradication of private property is the single most important aspect of Utopia. Utopian communism is 'the principal foundation of all [Utopian] ordinances' (p. 123), from which all else in Utopian society follows. And it is in part because of the absolute centrality to the text of this debate about the ethics and consequences of property ownership that critics have felt it imperative to decide for their own audiences the 'meaning' of *Utopia*. For critics of the right it is irksome that one of the most canonical texts in English literature appears to express so profound and explicit a critique of the economic system underlying all Western societies. Critics of the left have traditionally experienced the opposite impulse: the German Marxist and one-time secretary to Karl Marx, Karl Kautsky, for example, celebrated *Utopia* as a communist manifesto *avant la lettre*. From what we have said so far it is clear how *Utopia* might lend itself to such an interpretation. What, though, limits this reading, and makes it dubious that More intended *Utopia* to be read simply as a manifesto?

There are many answers to that question, but we might start with the most obvious: the warning to the naive reader that *Utopia* offers in its names. 'Utopia' itself, of course, derived from the Greek '*ou*' ('non-') and '*topos*' ('place'), means 'no-place' (with a possible pun on '*eu*' ('good'): good-place'), and almost all the names in the text play similar kinds of jokes on the reader. 'Anyder' ('waterless') is the principal river of Utopia's main town Amaurote ('dim city'), for instance; like the Utopians, the Achorians are the people of no-place, and the Polylerites inhabit the land of much nonsense. Most significant of all, Hythloday's name signifies 'peddlar of nonsense', 'expert in trifles', or perhaps, according to Richard Halpern (who believes that traditional translations of 'Hythloday' exaggerate the irony of his discourse), 'skilled in pleasant speech'.[8]

This salutary warning to those who would read the text as a straightforward critique of More's England and as an unproblematically serious proposal for an alternative social organization is not confined only to the names in *Utopia*. The text is punctuated with similar jokes, littered with traps into which the unwary reader may fall. To take just one example, let us examine the discussion of the Polylerites in Book 1. The Polylerites, Hythloday maintains, have devised the best alternative to the death penalty, using bonded labour to punish their criminals instead of capital punishment. The bondmen (or 'serving-men', as Robinson calls them) are marked by their clothing, which is of a particular colour worn by no one else, by their short haircuts, and by the excision of the tip of one ear (p. 29). Consider the following passage, where Hythloday relates what would happen should a bondman escape:

Neither they can have any hope at all to scape away by fleeing. For how should a man that in no part of his apparel is like other men fly privily and unknown, unless he would run away naked? Howbeit, so also fleeing he should be descried by the rounding of his head and his ear mark. (p. 30)

If the Polylerites saw a naked man running across the countryside, would they really need to pay attention to his haircut, or stop him in order to examine his ears?

Hythloday's discussion of the Polylerites can also be used to illustrate another way in which the apparently serious proposals communicated by *Utopia* are not all that they might at first seem. Ostensibly, as we have said, the Polylerites are invoked by Hythloday to exemplify a society which has developed a successful alternative to the death penalty. But the conclusion of the anecdote about them

---

[8] See Richard Halpern, *The Poetics of Primitive Accumulation: English Renaissance Culture and the Genealogy of Capital* (Ithaca: Cornell University Press, 1991), 142–3.

renders dubious that claim. For the bondmen to receive money, recounts Hythloday,

is death, as well to the giver as to the receiver. And no less jeopardy it is for a free man to receive money of a serving man . . . and likewise for serving men to touch weapons. The serving men . . . be . . . known . . . by their . . . badges which to cast away is death, as it is also to be seen out of . . . their own shire, or to talk with a serving man of another shire. And it is no less danger to them for to intend to run away than to do it indeed. Yea, and to conceal such an enterprise in a serving man it is death, in a free man servitude. (p. 29)

In contradiction to what Hythloday implies in opening the discussion, the Polylerites have not eradicated the death penalty. All that they have done is displace it, rendering it less visible.

It could be argued that whatever the relation of the conclusion of the example to Hythloday's original claim, the Polylerite practice is still vastly more humane than the profligate use of the death penalty which obtained in More's England. Such an argument is valid, but it cannot eradicate the inconsistency at the heart of the anecdote. This kind of inconsistency, moreover, wherein an initial claim to liberty is curtailed by its subsequent elaboration in the text, is a recurrent feature of *Utopia*. It was Stephen Greenblatt who first drew attention to this characteristic of the text. Greenblatt examines the way in which the Utopian workday (supposedly only six hours) expands, on closer attention to the text, to fill most daylight hours, thus ending up very similar to the labouring day of the English peasantry in the early sixteenth century. He notes too that a similar movement inhabits the text's account of Utopian travel, which 'begins with almost unlimited license and ends with almost total restriction', since the Utopians who do not attend lectures in their 'free' time work at their 'own occupations' instead. This move, he argues, is ubiquitous in the text: 'freedoms', Greenblatt claims, 'are heralded, only to shrink in the course of the description.'[9] Indeed, this uncertainty about how far liberties in the text actually extend is replayed even on the level of the text's sentences: as Elizabeth McCutcheon has pointed out, More's Latin original makes

---

[9] See Stephen Greenblatt, *Renaissance Self-Fashioning* (Chicago: University of Chicago Press, 1980), 40–1.

repeated use of litotes, a figure of speech which affirms something by denying its opposite, as in the phrases, 'not uncommon' and 'not unlike'.[10]

In its jokes, in 'the steady constriction of an initially limitless freedom', as Greenblatt puts it, in a rhetoric which frequently constitutes Utopian practices not so much by what they are as by what they are not, *Utopia* makes it very difficult for a reader to say with any certainty how seriously Utopian practices are intended to be taken. Yet another way in which More undermines our security in the idealism of the text is in the relation which obtains between *Utopia* and the 'real world'. Utopia and England, for example, ostensibly invoked in the text as each other's opposite, are in many ways very similar: like the British Isles, Utopia is an island; its main town and river resemble London and the Thames, as contemporary commentators were quick to note. On closer investigation Utopia becomes more a distorted reflection of the 'real' England than its antithesis; the relation between the two more obscure than an initial reading might suggest. Similar instabilities inhabit the representation of individuals in the text. Hythloday, of course, is invented, but Peter Giles, like More himself, was an actual person, as were the writers and recipients—Erasmus and Busleyden, for example—of the dedicatory letters that surround the text itself. (For more information on the apparatus surrounding *Utopia*, see the Note on the Texts.) Yet recognition of the distinction between the fictional Hythloday and the 'real' More can, if we are not careful, lead the unwary reader into another of the text's traps, for the opposition which More constructs between 'himself' and Hythloday becomes increasingly unstable the more knowledge about More one brings to *Utopia*. Hythloday, for example, claims to have worked as a page in the household of Cardinal Morton (also a real historical figure); in fact, More himself had held this position. Hythloday expresses his unwillingness to work as a counsellor to princes; More too, although he served as a statesman and counsellor to Henry VIII, had had his own doubts about the advisability of pursuing such a career.

Perhaps the 'More-within-the-text' and Hythloday are not

[10] See Elizabeth McCutcheon, 'Denying the Contrary: More's Use of Litotes in the *Utopia*', in R. S. Sylvester and G. P. Marc'hadour (eds.), *Essential Articles for the Study of Thomas More* (Hamden, Conn.: Archon Books, 1977).

'different' characters, then, but both representations of different aspects of More-the-author? This claim, however, is equally contentious. Hythloday extols the virtues of a society which (for example) banishes lawyers, allows women priests, tolerates the expression of pagan beliefs, encourages euthanasia, and permits not only divorce but subsequent remarriage. It is hard to square admiration for such practices as these with the beliefs of the real-life More, a lawyer himself, as well as a devout Catholic who wrote furiously against the reformist tracts of Luther and his fellow Protestants, who participated in the burning of heretics, and who eventually lost his life through his conviction that the King's divorce from Catherine of Aragon was wrong. But perhaps the text's ultimate jest is embedded in its conclusion, when 'More' (the textual character) intervenes to undermine all that More (the actual person) has offered us as food for thought through the discourse of Hythloday. 'Thus when Raphael had made an end of his tale,' says More, '. . . many things came to my mind which in the manners and laws of that people seemed to be . . . founded of no good reason'; these unreasonable customs and laws, he says, include 'their chivalry', 'their sacrifices and their religions', and other Utopian laws and ordinances; 'yea and chiefly,' he goes on:

in . . . the principal foundation of all their ordinances, that is to say, in the community of their . . . living without any . . . money (by the which thing only all nobility, magnificence, worship, honour, and majesty, the true ornaments and honours . . . of a commonwealth, utterly be overthrown . . .) (p. 123).

What 'More' admires in Utopian customs is left uncertain at the book's conclusion; what is made explicit is that he finds the most radical aspect of Utopia, and the base on which all of its qualities depend, Utopian communism, to be the most unreasonable of all of the social correctives which Hythloday has proposed in the course of his discourse. The argument initiated in Book 1 about the shortcomings of English society and the best possible solution to them is only exacerbated by the text's conclusion; *Utopia* preserves, even to its last lines, an ambivalence which it never resolves.

Utopian ambivalence has by now been extensively documented in literary criticism, and today it would be an ill-informed reader who would propose that *Utopia* is presented as a serious or straight-forward representation of a better world. Yet that said, it seems important to insist that it is equally mistaken to understand the text solely as a joke. It is not self-evidently true that Utopia's subor-dination of individual choice and happiness to the good of the community is a misguided ideal, even if it is one transparently not pursued by late-twentieth-century Western societies. And although Utopia may appear authoritarian, perhaps even totalitarian, it is worth remembering that it is not nearly so repressive as early mod-ern England was, where there was little freedom of speech; where poverty severely delimited any choice for the vast majority of the population; where torture of suspected traitors was commonly prac-tised by the state; and where one might be hanged for petty theft, or hanged, drawn and quartered for offences against the crown. I am in agreement with Richard Halpern here, who maintains that, although there is some truth in C. S. Lewis's account of *Utopia* as a *jeu d'esprit*, to read the text purely as a game is to attempt to depolitize the work, to 'trivialize [it] and stifle debate'.[11] It is hard, even with the knowledge of all the text's myriad forms of playfulness in mind, to ignore the impassioned sense of injustice with which Hythloday denounces English poverty in Book 1; or the equally impassioned sense of conviction with which the concluding paragraphs of his description of Utopia in Book 2 are infused; hard too to read *Utopia* and believe that the author of the text was immune to the sense of social injustice which he communicates so effectively through the words of his fictitious traveller.

Perhaps the most convincing answers to the perennial question of the relation in *Utopia* between social critique and the playful, or pleasurable qualities of the text have been offered by critics who utilize the insights of literary theory to inform the kinds of question that they ask of the text. Such insights allow Greenblatt, for example, in comparing *Utopia* with Holbein's painting *The Ambas-sadors*, to argue that the book's 'subtle displacements, distortions, and shifts of perspective are the closest equivalent in Renaissance prose to the anamorphic virtuosity of Holbein's art': *Utopia*, Greenblatt claims, presents two distinct worlds that occupy the same space

---

[11] Halpern, *Poetics of Primitive Accumulation*, 141.

while insisting on the impossibility of their doing so'.[12] They allow Halpern to argue that 'England occupies the position of the unconscious with respect to Utopia',[13] and to analyse the text in terms of the logic of its desires and repressions. But even sophisticated analyses such as these cannot hope to provide answers to all the enigmas in the text regarding More's intentions, nor can they provide definitive solutions to the more general problems about social rights and wrongs that Utopia so seriously, if so ludicly, plays out. And this, ultimately, may be part of the text's point. As More leads Hythloday in to supper for the second and the last time he tells him that they 'would choose another time to weigh and examine the same matters and to talk with him more at large therein' (p. 123). Perhaps one thing that More wished *Utopia* to do is to invite us into the debate which the book so self-consciously fails to conclude, encouraging us to do as More and Hythloday do, beyond the confines of the text's enigmatic ending, in the future to which its final lines direct us. It may be that we too are being asked to weigh and examine the questions which *Utopia* raises, many of which are as pressing today as they were for More in 1516; to continue to talk about the possibilities of other, and perhaps better, worlds; and in so doing to acknowledge, perhaps, the shortcomings of our own.

New Atlantis

Like Thomas More, Francis Bacon was a lawyer, a statesman, and an intellectual. In the early 1580s he became a barrister and an MP, and over the next three decades experienced a rapid rise to power, becoming Lord Chancellor (the highest position in the land) in 1618. Shortly afterwards, in 1621, his public life ended when he was accused of (and admitted) taking bribes, committed briefly to the Tower of London, expelled from the court, and fined £40,000. This ignominious end to his public career blighted his reputation for centuries after, at least so far as Bacon the man was concerned. But it should not influence our reception of Bacon the intellectual, who produced, over the course of his life, a vast body of work. Much of this work (such as *The Advancement of Learning*, the *Novum*

[12] Greenblatt, *Renaissance Self-Fashioning*, 22.
[13] Halpern, *Poetics of Primitive Accumulation*, 144.

Organum, and the *Sylva Sylvarum, or a Natural History*, to which the *New Atlantis* was appended) was an attempt to codify and systematize scientific enquiry. Other works, such as his *Essays* (for which he is today best remembered), and various letters to monarchs, statesmen, and courtiers, range over other subjects: moral qualities, for instance, such as truth, envy, and love, or political matters, such as sedition, empire, and kingdoms. If science was his main interest, then, he was also intensely interested in the politics of his age, serving two monarchs, and being an admirer of Machiavelli. It was the conflation of these two interests, in science on the one hand and politics on the other, I want to argue here, that led Bacon to produce his single work of fiction, the *New Atlantis*.

In his essay 'Of Travel', Bacon remarks that 'travel, in the younger sort, is a part of education; in the elder, a part of experience'.[14] Lamenting the propensity of travellers to keep records at sea where there is nothing to be observed, and to neglect them on land where there is much more to be recorded, Bacon proposes that travel diaries be brought into general use, and offers a list of what the diarist should observe: the churches, monuments, and courts of the countries that he visits; their fortifications and harbours, libraries and lectures; their markets and gardens, processions, feasts, and executions.

For Bacon here, the purpose of travel is to amass knowledge, and to amass that knowledge in a methodical manner. In this respect, the *New Atlantis* seems to offer a fictional model of Bacon's ideal travel narrative and his ideal traveller. The unnamed narrator of the text is concerned methodically to record everything that he and his fellows see in Bensalem (the name of Bacon's utopian nation). From their arrival in the Bensalemite harbour, through their quarantine in the 'Strangers' House', to their attendance at a Bensalemite feast and procession, everything of note is dutifully set down by the narrator, who punctuates his account of these events with reports of the conversations he has had with various individuals. The first of these is the Governor of the Strangers' House, who informs the travellers of some Bensalemite laws, explains to them how the islanders heard of Christianity, and tells them of the history of Bensalem and its original 'lawgiver', Solamona. The second is Joabin, a Jew, who

---

[14] Francis Bacon, 'Of Travel' in *Francis Bacon: A Critical Edition of the Major Works*, ed. Brian Vickers (Oxford: Oxford University Press, 1996), 374.

provides information regarding Bensalemite sexual and marital customs. The third and last is one of the 'Fathers' of Salomon's House, with whom the narrator is granted an audience. In this final conversation the Father tells the narrator about Salomon's House, Bensalem's most notable institution, and the work that goes on in it. This discourse constitutes the remaining pages of the *New Atlantis*, and makes up almost a third of the text. It lists the numerous experiments undertaken in Salomon's House, and the different institutions which it possesses in order to enable these experiments to take place; after the relation of this information the text ends, abruptly, with the words 'The rest was not perfected'.

The relative space afforded to the description of Salomon's House is illustrative of the importance which Bacon attached to the role which science should play in an ideal society and, by extension, in modern life. Bacon's historical place in the formulation of that role has, however, been a matter of debate over the centuries. For many years lauded as one of the 'fathers' of modern science, his achievement compared to those of figures such as Galileo and Kepler, Bacon's status as a 'scientist' was later reassessed, and—to draw a broad generalization from a complex debate—interest in his work shifted from his scientific legacy to his power as a rhetorician. Brian Vickers, for example, noted in 1968 that studies of Bacon's contribution to science had shown him to be derivative, contradictory, and either unaware of many of the new scientific discoveries of his age or dismissive of them. 'If we can no longer estimate Bacon the scientist very highly,' Vickers concluded, 'justice has certainly yet to be done to him as a writer.'[15] For Vickers and others, it was Bacon's literary art, his rhetorical power, which marked his place in our cultural history. More recently, new contributions to the history of ideas have re-emphasized Bacon's legacy to science, but from a perspective whose fundamental presuppositions differ enormously from those held by endorsers of either of these earlier accounts of Bacon's place in our cultural history. To this third account we will return later.

However we view his scientific legacy, two things are undeniable: that Bacon himself conceived of the reform of the natural sciences as the great project of his life; and that the *New Atlantis* is intended

[15] Brian Vickers, *Francis Bacon and Renaissance Prose* (Cambridge: CUP, 1968), 2.

to further this aim. Throughout the text, Bacon's conviction of the benefits which, if properly managed, science can confer on humanity, is pervasive. From the opening of the narrative, when the Bensalemites refuse—on the orders of the city's 'Conservator of Health'—to board the European ship for fear of infection, to the sailors' quarantine in the 'Strangers House', where their sick are treated with citrus fruit and pills, Bacon's narrative offers a vignette of a society in which scientific knowledge (in this case, of medicine) is not only profound but methodical, organized into institutions. It is not, in other words, merely in the description of Salomon's House that science pervades the *New Atlantis*. Let us take, as an example, Bacon's single direct allusion to *Utopia*, which occurs in the conversation with Joabin. 'I have read in a book of one of your men,' says Joabin,

of a Feigned Commonwealth, where the married couple are permitted, before they contract, to see one another naked. This they dislike; for they think it a scorn to give a refusal after so familiar knowledge. But because of many hidden defects in men and women's bodies, they have a more civil way; for they have near every town a couple of pools . . . where it is permitted to one of the friends of the man, and another of the friends of the woman, to see them severally bathe naked. (pp. 174–5)

Why do the Bensalemites revise the practice they lift from *Utopia*? Perhaps because in doing so they shift the purpose of the custom. In More, the practice ensures that future lack of desire will not impair the emotional bond necessary to a lasting marriage, for in Utopia marriage is the bedrock of civil stability. In Bensalem the role of marriage lies not so much in the disciplinary function that the family can play, as in the production of the main commodity upon which the power of the nation depends: children. The 'propagation' (Bacon's term) of healthy children might well be inhibited by 'defects' of either (potential) parent's body were these not exposed prior to their union. So to guard against this eventuality, the subjective gaze of the intended spouse (who may deliberately or unconsciously ignore the presence of such 'defects' in the body of his or her beloved) is replaced in Bensalem by the objective examination of an impartial observer (who, it is assumed, will not).

We see here a shift from the subjective to the objective, from desire to observation, and in acknowledging this shift we can recognize how fundamental to the *New Atlantis* the discourse of science actually is: in moving to the detailed description of Salomon's House, Bacon is making explicit what has hitherto been implicit throughout the text. It is, then, unsurprising that the text has frequently been understood to be one whose purpose is singular and self-evident: to represent a society in which scientific knowledge is properly nurtured and in so doing to illustrate the benefits of such investment. This was certainly the way in which many early readers understood the *New Atlantis*. One of these was William Rawley, Bacon's secretary, who prefaced its first publication with these words:

This fable my Lord devised, to the end that he might exhibit therein a model or description of a college instituted for the interpreting of nature and the producing of great and marvellous works for the benefit of men, under the name of Salomon's House, or the College of the Six Days' Works. (p. 151)

Later, the text was credited with precisely this influence. Widely reprinted in the years following its first publication, it was cited more than once in the mid-seventeenth century as a model for the Royal Society. It was not, of course, the only such model. Some academies of science, such as the Accademia dei Lincei in Rome, pre-dated Bacon's narrative, and other individuals shared Bacon's vision of the benefits of investment in the natural sciences: Tommaso Campanella, for instance, wrote a utopia very similar to the *New Atlantis*, which was published some three years before it.

Contemporary readers of the *New Atlantis*, then, saw its purpose and influence as being that of providing a blueprint for a new scientific institution, and to this aspect of the text we will return shortly. In describing the narrative as a fable, however, Rawley implicitly raises another aspect of Bacon's work: its literary nature. A fable is a literary vehicle for communicating a distinct message through illustration of the consequences of a given action or actions; like a parable, it is intended to teach its audience some kind of lesson. To assume that this 'lesson' is that a scientific academy is beneficial to the society that is foresighted enough to support it, however, is problematic: such an account does not explain adequately some of the problems of the *New Atlantis*.

In fact, it is possible to claim that illustrating the benefits of science is precisely what the *New Atlantis* does *not* do. With the exception of the discourse about disease which we have discussed above, there is almost nothing in the text which illustrates how the great works produced by the Fathers of Salomon's House ameliorate the lives of 'men', of ordinary people. A juxtaposition of the *New Atlantis* with *Utopia*, in which we hear so much about the lives of Utopian citizens, makes this transparent, and also serves to foreground the extent to which Bacon neglects to describe the very institutions which he elsewhere claims it to be the first duty of the traveller to ascertain. We learn virtually nothing, for instance, of Bensalemite courts, nothing of their warehouses, markets, or executions. Elsewhere in his writings Bacon states emphatically that what is most important to report are the government, councils, magistrates, laws and practices of warfare of the countries that one visits.[16] This, essentially, is the kind of information which *Utopia* takes pains to elaborate, yet in the *New Atlantis* we learn almost nothing of any of this (aside from the fact that Bensalem, unlike Utopia, is a monarchy). Why is Bacon reluctant to provide this information, and in what ways, if at all, does this contribute to his 'end' in creating this utopia, and to the 'lesson' that this 'fable' is intended to teach us?

For those who believe that the *New Atlantis* is, as Rawley maintains, primarily a model for a scientific institution, the answer to these questions lies in the text's self-advertised incompleteness. Rawley himself suggests that Bacon intended to offer his readers a fuller picture of the 'best state or mould of a commonwealth' (p. 151); his failure to do so, Rawley maintains, was a result of his being distracted by other, more pressing scholarly concerns. Yet this answer seems less convincing when we consider that the *New Atlantis*'s concluding claim to incompletion ('The rest was not perfected') is mirrored within the narrative by other, more worrying, lacunae. Conversations repeatedly end abruptly when the narrator's interlocutors are 'commanded away in haste' (p. 175) by Bensalemite officials for purposes never revealed; these conversations are not resumed, no matter how

---

[16] Francis Bacon, 'Advice to the Earl of Rutland on His Travels', in Brian Vickers, ed., *Francis Bacon: A Critical Edition of the Major Works* (Oxford: Oxford University Press, 1996), 79.

ostentatiously incomplete they appear. Bensalem is, furthermore, an extremely secretive society. Its officials repeatedly impress on the narrator (and hence also the reader) that they are only permitted to divulge to foreigners some aspects of Bensalemite society, and that others must remain undisclosed. Most secret of all are the Fathers of Salomon's House, about whom we learn almost nothing, and who remain segregated even from the rest of the Bensalemite population (p. 175).

Different kinds of incompletion in the text appear, in short, to be not accidental but designed. And these explicit refusals to gratify narratorial (or readerly) curiosity exist alongside other, equally enigmatic difficulties. The text's very names provoke questions. Why is the country called Bensalem and the text *New Atlantis*, for example? What is the relation between the original lawgiver of the island, 'Solamona', the biblical King 'Solomon', and the name of the island's most significant institution, 'Salomon's House'? Why is the narrator finally given leave to publish the account of Salomon's House when throughout the text we—as he—have been led to believe that it is the most secret of all of Bensalem's secretive institutions? Why is one of the narrator's main informants not a native Bensalemite but a Jew—hardly a trustworthy figure in the iconography of early modern English texts, as a glance at Barabas in Marlowe's *The Jew of Malta* or Shylock in Shakespeare's *The Merchant of Venice* would indicate? To these and other such questions the *New Atlantis* offers no certain answers—and, importantly, neither does an interpretation of the text which sees its purpose merely to be the illustration of an ideal scientific institution. How, then, might we account for these difficulties, and square them with Bacon's evident conviction that the nurture of scientific inquiry is not merely desirable, but necessary? In order to do this we need to look again not only at the *New Atlantis*, but also at the nature of the discourse of science itself.

As we have seen, of the two main accounts of Bacon's relation to science, one saw him as one of the 'fathers' of modern science, while the other argued that he was not a scientist in any recognizably modern sense of the term. In the past two decades, however, a third claim has been made: one which sees Bacon's works as fundamental to the construction of modern scientific thought, but which is both more critical of Bacon and more sceptical of science than are either of the two earlier positions. Broadly speaking, while the first two positions see modern science as primarily a discourse of knowledge, the latter is more interested in the power that a discourse of 'pure' knowledge may act to occlude or obscure. Feminist writers such as Evelyn Fox Keller and Sandra Harding, and Foucauldian critics such as Denise Albanese have claimed that knowledge cannot be divorced from power, and that an understanding of the fundamental connections between power and knowledge is indispensable to an understanding of Bacon's writings. In making these claims, such critics have been able to point not only to the underlying presence of power within science's supposedly objective discourse of knowledge, but also to the frequency with which Bacon himself links the two factors in his writings. 'Those twin objects, human Knowledge and human Power, really do meet one,' Bacon insists elsewhere;[17] the connection between the two is more implicit, but undoubtedly present, in the Father's description of the purpose of Salomon's House: 'the knowledge of Causes, and secret motions of things; and the enlarging of the bounds of Human Empire, to the effecting of all things possible' (p. 177). With this connection in mind, we can return to the question of the purpose and function of the secrecy which Bensalem and the *New Atlantis* so studiously preserve. For this secrecy is indubitably inscribed in the text in a discourse of power. It is encoded in laws; it appears to operate at least once in the service of repression; it always operates in service of the power of the Bensalemite nation. Consider the nature of some of the things that we, like the narrator, are kept from knowing. We are not allowed to know how the 'vulgar sort of mariners are contained from being discovered at land' in Bensalem's secret expeditions to other countries (p. 168). We are denied information about how Bensalem organizes the mechanics of its cultural espionage, nor are we told what has happened to the other 'strangers' who have lighted upon Bensalemite shores: to the Europeans who have found their way to Bensalem in the past, for instance (p. 159), or to the other Jews of Bensalem, apparently more numerous in times gone by (p. 172).

There is too much we do not know about Bensalem and too many

---

[17] *The Great Instauration*, in *The Works of Francis Bacon*, ed. J. A. Spedding, R. L. Ellis, and D. D. Heath (London, 1857–74), iv. 32.

occasions when the limit of our knowledge is impressed on us by the text. This being the case, we might return to the notion of the ideal traveller with which we began. How ideal can the narrator of the *New Atlantis* really be, given his repeated failure to ask the questions of his Bensalemite interlocutors that readers have (recently at least) felt so pressing and insistent? Why is the narrator blind to the potentially sinister nature of Bensalem's repeated refusal to reveal itself fully to him? Why does he never wonder why one of his most loquacious informers is a Jew, and not find it odd that someone supposedly marginal to Bensalemite society is also, apparently, a privileged participant in Bensalemite policy, being, like the governor, 'commanded away in haste' for unspecified official purposes at key moments in his conversation (p. 175)?

More and more systematically, the text establishes a split between its narrator and its reader, whose respective experiences of Bensalem appear to be so radically different. Indeed, the narrator's refusal to question Bensalemite secrecy itself provokes in the reader the curiosity which the narrator never betrays: we, in short, are continually encouraged to suspect unspecified dangers of which the narrator appears to be almost entirely unaware. So perhaps the 'message' of the *New Atlantis* is more complex than it might at first seem. We have had no time here to consider the possible influence on the text of another, growing, political concern for early modern nations: empire. But the 'enlarging' of empire is one of the principal motivations for the work of Salomon's House, and although in that instance 'empire' is invoked as a common cause of all humanity, the same was not true of the race for actual empires beginning at the time of Bacon's writing, which involved intense competition both between European powers, and between them and the peoples that they conquered, and frequently killed, in the seventeenth century and after.

Does the *New Atlantis* suggest that its English readers should nurture investigation in the natural sciences? Yes, it does. But it may also illustrate the conviction that such investigation should be nurtured because scientific knowledge is indivisible from political power, and political power is a competitive reality. Bacon sees scientific empiricism as being fundamental to the goal of political empire, and it is the relation between empire and empiricism, power and knowledge, which he wants his reader not merely intellectually to consider, but emotionally to feel. Perhaps it is for this reason that Bacon chose a literary vehicle for the communication of what he had to say. The *New Atlantis* is indeed a kind of fable: a parable whose implications only emerge to the sceptical reader, who is unable to inhabit the position embodied in the unquestioning trust of the narrator himself. In encouraging us to ask the questions for which the text explicitly refuses to provide answers, the *New Atlantis* may alert its readers to the political necessity of attaining the knowledge that bestows on its owners such power. The narrator fails—in stark contrast to the Bensalemites—to understand the manner and degree in which knowledge and power are intertwined. We should not, the text may be telling us, make the same mistake.

The Isle of Pines

Henry Neville (sometimes spelt 'Nevile') was, like his father and grandfather before him, and indeed like Thomas More and Francis Bacon, influential in the highly complex politics of his age. He entered parliament after the regicide of Charles I, and remained an MP throughout the period of Oliver Cromwell's Commonwealth and into the Restoration of the monarchy, writing, over these years, a number of tracts and pamphlets. All these were, in various ways and with various degrees of directness, interventions in the political debates of his time. These debates were highly complex, the basic opposition between monarchism and republicanism being compli-cated by the fact that there were in the period many different brands of republicanism, as well as by the fact that alliances frequently formed between factions which might appear at first sight to be antithetical: religious groups such as Puritans and nonconformists, for example, frequently made common cause with republicans. Neville himself, for instance, was friendly with at least one promin-ent Puritan, even though he was at one point charged with atheism (for, allegedly, preferring Cicero to the Bible).

This complex political and intellectual background often makes the tracts and pamphlets produced during the period very difficult to interpret. This is not, perhaps, the case with some of Neville's writings—of his translation of Machiavelli's works, self-evidently, or of his best-known work, *Plato Redivivus*, a defence of some of the principles of James Harrington's Oceana (itself one of the most important works of republican political theory produced in the period, on which Neville may well have had an influence). Other pamphlets Neville wrote, however, are more difficult to interpret. Some (including, I think, *The Isle of Pines*) are satires, whose targets are no longer as transparent as they may once have been. Such satires, moreover, frequently operate by fusing political critique with sexual salaciousness and sexual anxieties, in ways which only recently have been acknowledged and taken seriously.

For these reasons, and also because of the complicated publishing history of *The Isle of Pines*, the meaning of this text has, until very recently, eluded many of its readers. *The Isle of Pines* consists of two narratives. One is of the story of an Englishman, George Pine, who discovered the island; the other frames Pine's tale, and purports to be written by Cornelius Van Sloetten, a Dutch sailor who happened on Pine's descendants many years later. These two narratives were published separately at first, in pamphlet form; shortly after their publication a third pamphlet was issued, which inserted Pine's tale within Van Sloetten's. Few copies remain of these early texts, the pamphlet being an ephemeral form; most which survive offer only one part of the complete whole. Another reason for the text's comparative oblivion over the past 300 years is also, no doubt, its salacious nature. Even the person who edited the only complete reprint this century, Worthington Chauncey Ford, felt it necessary to apologize for this aspect of *The Isle of Pines*. Pointing out that early readers of the text had noticed that 'pines' is an anagram of 'penis', and proposing in addition that 'Sloetten' may suggest the word 'slut', Ford concluded that 'such an interpretation reduces our tract to a screaming farce'.[18]

The assumption that the text's interest in matters sexual renders it insignificant is not one which would be shared by literary critics today. Indeed, it is for its complex rehearsal of questions concerning the matters which most deeply preoccupy many of today's critics— gender and sexuality, but also race, class, nation, and colonialism— that the text holds considerable interest. Some of these concerns are

[18] Worthington Chauncey Ford, *The Isle of Pines: An Essay in Bibliography* (Boston: The Club of Odd Volumes, 1920), 39.

transparent enough in Pine's narrative alone, in which the English-man tells of his shipwreck on an uninhabited island somewhere near Madagascar with four women: his master's daughter, two maid-servants, and a black slave. Pine's tale explains how he proceeded to people the island, producing by the time of his death at eighty 1,789 children, and how he organized his descendants into tribes named after their respective mothers. Finally, Pine tells us, he gives the narrative to his eldest son to be transmitted for posterity.

Insofar as Pine's own narrative is concerned, then, the text might be read (and indeed has been read) as a fantasy of absolute sexual liberty, a wish-fulfilment of individual phallic and paternal tran-scendence. Pine is a man with four women at his sole disposal: no threat here from any other man, no competition for this embarrass-ment of sexual riches. Male potency in this narrative collapses class boundaries as effectively as it does shame: Pine sleeps with the two maidservants first, in private and then openly; his master's daughter 'Sarah English', observing their intercourse 'was content also to do as we did' (p. 198). Fulfilment of such fantasies of sexual transgression—polygamy, voyeurism, cross-class intercourse—does not end here. Pine's black slave Philippa, 'seeing what we did, longed also for her share', and with the consent of the other women she seduces Pine, who 'satisfied [himself] with her, as well as with one of the rest' (p. 198). Miscegenation and orgiastic sexual indul-gence are thus added to the list of the taboos broken by the text; in the remainder of Pine's narrative incest quietly joins this catalogue of transgressions, since Pine's children must sleep with their half-siblings to produce their own issue. Male sexual fantasy in the text, moreover, extends beyond 'simple' gratification of unlimited male desire, since in addition it acts to assuage one of the fears which underlies the construction of patriarchy: the uncertainty, that is, of paternity. Neville organizes his narrative so as to suggest the eradication of doubt about Pine's paternal status: Pine begins to sleep with 'his' women after he has been on the island for four months, and thus, unlike other men, can be possessed of certain knowledge that the children which issue from his women are his own.

If a fantasy of absolute sexual liberation coupled with absolute certainty about paternity is one generative impulse of Pine's narrative, a fantasy of absolute colonial freedom to control the island settled is another. Absence of sexual competition from other men is mirrored in the text by the absence of colonial competition from other European powers and of resistance from native populations: this is a vision of a place which one can overrun without the unpleasant necessity of at best exploiting native peoples or killing them, and at worst being killed by them instead, or driven out or massacred by one's fellow Europeans. In this sense, Pine's tale reads like a travel narrative from which all labour has been expunged. The natural fertility of the island precludes the labour of husbandry; its lack of native peoples precludes the labour of defence; the absence of other men precludes the labour—if such it can be called—of courtship. Even childbirth (the one kind of labour indispensable to the production of the particular kind of commodity—people—around which this narrative is so centred) is downplayed in the text, the women being all 'soon well again' after their deliveries, and only one experiencing any difficulty (apparently because she was overweight) (p. 198). In this respect, the text bears more similarity to a Land of Cockaygne or an Arcadia than it does to a utopia proper (for this distinction, see the first section of this introduction). This is a place where natural abundance, not systems or institutions, generates the happiness of the community; a place where food (in the realistic shape of something like a dodo) is there for the taking, and where mossy banks and trees provide all the shelter that one needs.

This is perhaps the commonest reading of *The Isle of Pines*, which has usually, when it has been discussed at all, been interpreted as a narrative of phallic wish-fulfilment: a kind of 'pornotopia'. Some of those who read the text this way, however, have read only Pine's narrative; others have assumed that the main function of Van Sloetten's tale is to provide a plausible explanation for the return of Pine's narrative to England. It is, however, a great mistake to divorce Pine's narrative from the frame in which it eventually appeared, or to underestimate the significance of Van Sloetten's tale, which offers us the consequences, as it were, of Pine's 'history'; the present context through the lens of which we must read the narrative of Pine's past. In his narrative, Van Sloetten tells us of his arrival on the island and his entertainment there by Pine's grandson William, who in turn relates the tale of the community's collapse after his grandfather's death. The population 'fell to whoredoms, incests and adultery; so that what my grandfather was forced to do for necessity, they did for wantonness' (p. 201), says William; in consequence, William explains, the then ruler of the island (Pine's son Henry), institutes extreme punishments for transgressions, and appoints one official from each tribe of Pine's descendents to ensure the observation of his decrees. William's story told, the Dutch visitors tour the island and map it. As they are about to leave, William Pine requests the assistance of the Dutch in fighting off a rebellion (p. 207); with William's help the Dutch capture the rebel leader (who is subsequently killed), and resume their journey to the East Indies. The remainder of Van Sloetten's narrative relates his travels to Calicut and Camboia and his journey home.

What, then, are we to make of the text as a complete work? What we might initially have understood as a fantasy of sexual and colonial wish-fulfilment—a utopia of peaceful plenty—emerges as its opposite: a story of degeneration, a dystopia of absolute disorder and rebellion. Even the text's title embodies this dichotomy: 'Pines' may be an anagram of 'penis', but 'pine' also signified 'punishment', 'suffering' (especially the suffering of hell), and (as a verb) 'to lose one's vitality or vigour', as well as 'to languish with desire' (as it still does). William Pine's appeal to 'necessity' as a justification of his grandfather's conduct begins to seem like a hollow explanation of the difference between Pine's conflict and that of his offspring, especially when we recognize the degree to which those things that are valorized in Pine's narrative are shown to be defective in Van Sloetten's. In Pine's account his offspring by his black slave is 'a fine white girl'; in Van Sloetten's, it is a series of rapacious and rebellious black men (both episodes of degeneration are instigated by the offspring of Pine and his slave). From Pine's point of view, his community is a kind of extended patriarchal family; in Van Sloetten's, it is an emergent monarchy, Pine's grandson being 'Prince' William Pine (Neville himself was a staunch republican). By the time that Cornelius Van Sloetten arrives in the Isle of Pines, he meets not a 'nation' of 'English Pines' (the grand finale of Pine's narrative) but a fragmented tribal society, fraught with internecine divisions, a society which would be coded quite clearly for a seventeenth-century reader as barbarous: 'No use of metal, corn, or wine, or oil; | No occupation; all men idle, all.'[19]

No one can say with any certainty why Neville wrote a sequel to his initial narrative, or why he then published them both together. But it is possible that he did so in order to preclude interpreting *The Isle of Pines* merely as pornotopia, as simple wish-fulfilment. For, episodic and fragmented as the narrative sometimes seems, there exist in it indications of deeper conceptual links between the two halves of the text, from minor details (such as the axe Pine originally takes from the ship, replaced by Cornelius Van Sloetten) to much more significant indicators of narrative congruence. At the end of the pamphlet, for instance, an apparently inconsequential description of the 'Brachmans' (Brahmins) of Calicut emerges as crucially linked to the narrative of Pine himself, as Van Sloetten details what anthropologists now recognize as a particular cultural mechanism for bypassing uncertainty about paternity whilst preserving patrilineal inheritance systems, property being passed from the father to his sister's sons (with whom the father knows he shares blood, or genes), rather than to his own children (whose relation to him he must take on faith and not knowledge).

But perhaps the most significant factor of all for our understanding of the relation of the two narratives is the nationalities of the narrators in it. It is not coincidental that Pine is English and Van Sloetten Dutch. The Dutch and the English had for more than half a century been involved in competition for dominance of the spice trade of the East Indies. The English East India company was established in 1600 (two years after George Pine embarks on his voyage), the Dutch East India Company in 1602. In the succeeding decades competition between the two nations had become ever more intense, escalating by the mid-seventeenth century into the Anglo-Dutch Wars which re-erupted periodically over succeeding decades.

One way to understand *The Isle of Pines* might be to view it as a moral tale, an exemplary narrative which tries to illustrate how the Dutch and the English might make common cause in joint colonial endeavour. Another, quite opposite, reading might attempt to insert the narrative into the history which provides its most immediate

---

[19] William Shakespeare, *The Tempest*, ed. Stephen Orgel (Oxford: Oxford University Press, 1987), II. i. 158–9.

backdrop in a very different way, extracting from it a rather different moral tale. When George Pine arrives on the island, he essentially goes to sleep, devoting his life to pleasure and to idleness. When the Dutch arrive on the island, they engage in the labour which Pine evades, mapping the island, charting it, and working out exactly where it lies. One only has to compare Pine's behaviour with that of the Dutch to realize how far short he might be thought to fall of the ideal colonist.

The real significance of those alternative responses to the discovery of an unknown island may be clearer when we look at its location. Those familiar with More's *Utopia* might be forgiven for fighting shy of taking too seriously another utopia's references to the details of the voyages of its protagonists, and to the location of the island it describes. But in the case of *The Isle of Pines* we should suspend our scepticism concerning the information the text offers us on the location of its island. The Isle of Pines, we are told in Van Sloetten's narrative, is situated at 76 degrees longitude, 20 degrees latitude. This places it some distance north-east of Madagascar, in the centre of the Indian Ocean (almost directly due south of the tip of India and almost directly due west of Java), and thus an ideal spot from which to dominate the age's most lucrative and desirable of prizes: the spice trade of the East Indies. *The Isle of Pines*, in short, may have been written not to indulge fantasies about sexual excess, but to provide an explanation for Dutch ascendancy in the area—or perhaps to suggest another utopia altogether. What might have been had George Pine's hedonism been replaced by Utopian industry or by the Bensalemite desire for knowledge? What would it have meant to British interests in the area had a different kind of English colonist—say, Robinson Crusoe—been shipwrecked on this particular island around 1600, when the English East India Company was first established? Neville could not have formulated precisely this last question, for *The Isle of Pines* was a precursor of *Robinson Crusoe*—as many, indeed, have noted—and not the other way round. But I strongly suspect that English labour, not English sexuality, is the utopian ideal to which this text is ultimately pointing. It is just that English labour is notable in this text only by its absence: like utopia itself, it just isn't there.

NOTE ON THE TEXTS

Utopia

The Latin text of More's *Utopia* was first published in Louvain in 1516. Three further editions followed within the next two years: one in 1517 (published in Paris) and two in 1518 (published in Basel). The text was first translated into English by Ralph Robinson in 1551. A second, revised edition of Robinson's translation followed in 1556. It is this 1556 edition I have used for the text in this volume. I have modernized spelling and put in inverted commas and paragraphs (the 1556 edition has neither), but have kept as much as possible of Robinson's punctuation. Robinson's translation is generally accurate, if more verbose than More's original; in the notes I have drawn the reader's attention to occasional inaccuracies.

In its early editions the text of *Utopia* itself appeared with a variety of supporting materials: maps, the Utopian alphabet, poems and letters written by and to different members of the humanist circle of which More was a part. These ancillary materials all participated, in various ways, in the hoax that was *Utopia*, mentioning conversations with Hythloday, for example, or speculating on the location of the island. Different editions of the text published different selections of this material, so I have chosen here to reproduce the entirety of Robinson's 1556 edition in order to show readers what an early edition would have looked like, and to illustrate the way in which early editions of *Utopia* were, to some degree at least, a collaborative enterprise. An appendix reproduces most of the ancillary materials which appeared in other early editions of the text but not in the 1556 edition: notes to all of these indicate the edition in which they first appeared.

This 'collaborative authorship' also applies to the marginalia in Robinson's edition. The majority of these are ascribed (in various places) to Peter Giles and to Erasmus; Robinson appears to be responsible for some of them.

Note on the Texts

New Atlantis

The *New Atlantis* was first published by William Rawley, Bacon's secretary, in 1627, the year following Bacon's death, and appeared at the end of the volume containing Bacon's *Sylva Sylvarum: Or, A Natural History*. The text in this volume is taken from Brian Vickers's, edition for The Oxford Authors series. I have modernized spelling in a couple of instances.

The Isle of Pines

The publishing history of *The Isle of Pines* is very complex. George Pine's narrative was published first, in June 1668. Cornelius Van Sloetten's narrative was published shortly after, in July, without Pine's narrative included in it—a frame, so to speak, lacking the picture it should enclose. Later in July, or early in August, a new version of the text appeared, again in pamphlet form, conflating the two earlier pamphlets into one and in so doing properly inserting Pine's narrative into the frame provided by Van Sloetten. As my copy-text I have used Worthington Chauncey Ford's edition of *The Isle of Pines* (Boston: The Club of Odd Volumes, 1920). Neville's punctuation, which Worthington Chauncey Ford preserves, is haphazard in the extreme. I have throughout silently regularized, preserving the slack punctuation only when to regularize would involve choosing one potential meaning over another. I have silently amended the occasional typographical error, but have retained inconsistencies in names (Pines/Pine, Sparkes/Sparks).

SELECT BIBLIOGRAPHY

Thomas More, Utopia

There is a huge amount of material on More: the following list mentions only a few of the most influential writings on the man and on *Utopia*.

Other Editions

The standard edition of the text is that edited by J. H. Hexter and Edward J. Surtz in volume IV of *The Yale Edition of the Complete Works of St Thomas More* (New Haven: Yale University Press, 1965). Hexter's introduction to the text in this edition is itself an important interpretation of the text. There are two other widely available translations of *Utopia* on the market. One is Paul Turner's Penguin Classics edition (Harmondsworth: Penguin, 1965). This is colloquial and readable, but its Anglicization of the names in the text (Hythloday, for example, becomes 'Nonsenso') undermines the serious aspect of *Utopia*. The other translation is Robert M. Adams's for the Norton Critical Edition of *Utopia* (New York: Norton, 1975), which is indebted to Robinson's. Adams's translation is also reproduced in slightly different form in the Cambridge Texts in the History of Political Thought edition, edited by George M. Logan and Robert M. Adams (Cambridge: CUP, 1989), which has comprehensive notes, especially with regard to the philosophical and classical aspects of *Utopia*. Two early editions of the text remain very useful: J. H. Lupton's 1895 scholarly edition (Oxford: Oxford University Press), and J. Churton Collins's *Sir Thomas More's Utopia*, which is aimed more at a student audience (Oxford: Clarendon Press, 1904). Both of these reprint Robinson's translation in its first (1551) edition; Lupton's has the Latin on facing pages. Both have extremely comprehensive notes and introductions, which remain informative and readable.

Biographies

More's son-in-law William Roper wrote the first *Life of Sir Thomas More*, reprinted in *Two Early Tudor Lives*, ed. Richard S. Sylvester and Davis P. Harding (New Haven: Yale University Press, 1962). Anthony Kenny's *Thomas More* (Oxford: Oxford University Press, 1983), in the Past Masters series, provides a readable and short introduction to More's life and major works. R. W. Chambers's *Thomas More* (London: Bedford Historical Series, 1935) has been very influential this century; it sees More in the light of his medievalism, his Christianity, and his Englishness. Alastair Fox's *Thomas More: History and Providence* (Oxford: Basil Blackwell, 1982) is not exactly a biography, although its organization follows the trajectory of More's life: Fox is interested in the tensions between reaction and radicalism in More's personality, which he sees expressed in More's writings from the beginning of his career. For information on More as a public figure, see J. A. Guy, *The Public Career of Sir Thomas More* (New Haven: Yale University Press, 1980).

Utopia: *Sources and Contexts*

As the notes will indicate, More alluded to, and argued with, a number of classical sources in the *Utopia*. The most important of these are Plato's *Republic* and his *Laws*, both of which are readily available in a number of different English translations. (See also below, under 'Other Utopian Literature'.) George M. Logan's *The Meaning of More's Utopia* (Princeton: Princeton University Press, 1983) discusses many of the relations between *Utopia* and its classical sources in a consideration of the nature of its political thought; Quentin Skinner's *The Foundations of Modern Political Thought* (Cambridge: CUP, 1978) is a detailed introduction to the political philosophy of More's age. See also his 'Sir Thomas More's *Utopia* and the Language of Renaissance Humanism', in Anthony Pagden (ed.), *The Languages of Political Theory in Early-Modern Europe* (Cambridge: CUP, 1987). For background regarding the familial history of More's time, see Lawrence Stone, *The Family, Sex and Marriage in England 1500–1800* (Weidenfeld and Nicolson, 1977; abridged edn. Harmondsworth: Penguin, 1979).

Utopia: *Interpretations*

The debates about *Utopia* for the greater part of the twentieth century centred around its Communist or Catholic implications. Karl Kautsky's *Thomas More and His Utopia* trans. H. J. Stenning (New York: International Publisher Co., 1927), was the first to see Utopia as a proto-Communist community; Chambers's biography (for details of which see above) saw its moral as a Christian one. Russell Ames's *Citizen Thomas More and His Utopia* (Princeton: Princeton University Press, 1949) was, like Kautsky, influenced by Marxist and socialist theory, while J. H. Hexter's *More's Utopia: The Biography of an Idea* (Princeton: Princeton University Press, 1952), attempted to mediate between the interpretations of the political left and right by proposing that a Christian humanist perspective generated *Utopia*, and that its main target is the sin of pride. See also Hexter's *The Vision of Politics on the Eve of the Reformation: More,*

Machiavelli and Seyssel (London: Allen Lane, 1973). Extracts from all except the last of these are reprinted in the Norton edition of the text (for details of which see above), as is an extract from C. S. Lewis's *English Literature in the Sixteenth Century, Excluding Drama* (Oxford: The Clarendon Press, 1954), which characterized *Utopia* as a *jeu d'esprit*, and Elizabeth McCutcheon's 'Litotes: Denying the Contrary', which first appeared in the journal *Moreana*, 31–2 (1971), 116–21, and which is reprinted in R. S. Sylvester and G. P. Marc'hadour, (eds.), *Essential Articles For the Study of Thomas More* (Hamden, Conn.: Archon Books, 1977). The journal *Moreana* itself is not very useful: it is hagiographical in its approach to More and his writings, and the articles which it prints are generally, although not always, uncritical. For a succinct discussion of approaches to *Utopia* prior to the publication of the Yale edition, see Quentin Skinner's review, 'More's *Utopia*', *Past and Present*, 38 (1967), 153–68.

The most influential account of *Utopia* in recent years has been Louis Marin's, in his *Utopiques jeux d'espaces* (Paris: Minuit, 1973). For a brief synopsis of Marin's general approach see the introduction to the present volume. To a greater or lesser degree, all of the following discussions of the text utilize the insights of Louis Marin: Stephen Greenblatt, *Renaissance Self-Fashioning From More to Shakespeare* (Chicago: University of Chicago Press, 1980); Christopher Kendrick, 'More's *Utopia* and Uneven Development', *boundary* 2. 13.2–3 (1985), 233–66; Richard Halpern, *The Poetics of Primitive Accumulation: English Renaissance Culture and the Genealogy of Capital* (Ithaca: Cornell University Press, 1991). All are well worth reading.

A selection of other works of interest to the student of *Utopia* might include: Arthur Blaim, 'The Text and Genre Pattern: More's *Utopia* and the Structure of Early Utopian Fiction', *Essays in Poetics*, 6 (1981), 18–53; John Freeman, 'Discourse in More's *Utopia*: Alibi/Pretext/Postscript', *ELH* 59 (1992), 289–311; A. R Heiserman, 'Satire in the *Utopia*', *PMLA* 78 (1963) 163–74; A. Kenyon, 'The Problem of Freedom and Moral Behaviour in Thomas More's *Utopia*', *Journal of the History of Philosophy*, 21 (1983), 349–73; John N. Perlette, 'Of Sites and Parasites: The Centrality of the Marginal Anecdote in Book 1 of More's *Utopia*', *ELH* 54 (1987), 321–52.

Francis Bacon, New Atlantis

Other Editions

The standard edition of the *New Atlantis* appears in volume 3 of *The Works of Francis Bacon*, ed. J. A. Spedding, R. L. Ellis, and D. D. Heath

Select Bibliography

(London, 1857–74). J. M. Robertson's edition of the *Philosophical Works of Francis Bacon* (New York: Routledge, 1905) reproduces from the Spedding/Ellis edition a selection of the most important works, including the *New Atlantis*. *Francis Bacon: A Critical Edition of the Major Works*, ed. Brian Vickers (Oxford: Oxford University Press, 1996), also includes a good selection of material. J. Weinberger's edition of the *New Atlantis* contains a few textual inaccuracies, but includes a stimulating and unusual introduction to the text which is well worth reading: see J. Weinberger (ed.), *The Great Instauration and New Atlantis* (Arlington Heights, Ill.: Harlan Davidson, 1980).

Biographies and General Studies

William Rawley's short *Life of Bacon* (in Robertson, above) was the first biography of Bacon; John Aubrey also has an essay on Bacon in his *Brief Lives*, ed. Oliver Lawson Dick (Harmonsworth: Penguin, 1987). A voluminous account of *The Life and Letters of Bacon* was published, in seven volumes, by James Spedding between 1861 and 1874. Anthony Quinton has a short chapter on Bacon's life in his *Francis Bacon* for the Past Masters series (Oxford: Oxford University Press, 1980), and a clear account of the major presuppositions behind Bacon's thinking, and the shifts in his reputation through the ages. Another good general account is provided by Mary Hesse in *A Critical History of Western Philosophy*, ed. D. J. O'Connor (London, 1964).

General Criticism, and Criticism of the New Atlantis

There are a number of accounts of Bacon's contribution to scientific thought. Paolo Rossi's *Francis Bacon: From Magic to Science*, trans. S. Rabinovitch, (London: 1968) treats his separation of science and religion. Antonio Perez-Ramos's *Francis Bacon's Idea of Science and the Maker's Knowledge Tradition* (Oxford: Clarendon Press, 1988) is perhaps the most influential modern treatment of the subject. For discussions of the gendered nature of Bacon's discourse on science see: Evelyn Fox Keller, *Reflections on Science and Gender* (New Haven: Yale University Press, 1984); Sandra Harding, *The Science Question in Feminism* (Ithaca: Cornell University Press, 1986); and Carolyn Merchant, *The Death of Nature: Women, Ecology and the Scientific Revolution* (San Francisco: Harper and Row, 1983). Brian Vickers's *Essential Articles for the Study of Francis Bacon* (Connecticut: Archon Books, 1968) includes two good introductions to Bacon's scientific project: 'Francis Bacon's Philosophy of Science', by Mary Hesse, and 'Bacon's Man of Science', by Moody E. Prior. *Essential Articles* also includes three essays on Bacon's power as a rhetorician. Other works treating of this aspect of his writing are: Stanley Fish's *Self-Consuming Artifacts: The Experience of Seventeenth-Century Literature* (Berkeley: University of California Press, 1972); Lisa Jardine's *Francis Bacon: Discovery and the Art of Discourse* (Cambridge: CUP, 1974); Brian Vickers's *Francis Bacon and Renaissance Prose* (Cambridge: CUP, 1968); and W. A. Sessions (ed.), *Francis Bacon's Legacy of Texts* (New York, 1990). On rhetoric and power, see Victoria Kahn, *Machiavellian Rhetoric from the Counter-Reformation to Milton* (Princeton: Princeton University Press, 1994). On Bacon as a politician, see the chapter on Bacon in John Michael Archer's *Sovereignty and Intelligence: Spying and Court Culture in the English Renaissance* (Stanford: Stanford University Press, 1993). Finally, in *Francis Bacon: History, Politics and Science, 1561–1626* (Cambridge: CUP, 1993) W. H. G. Wormald addresses Bacon's conception of the relationship between nature and policy.

On the *New Atlantis* itself, the best contemporary article I know of is Denise Albanese, 'The *New Atlantis* and the Uses of Utopia', *ELH* 57 (1990), 503–28. Also interesting is J. Weinberger's introduction to the text in his edition (see above). See also his 'Science and Rule in Bacon's Utopia: An Introduction to the Reading of the *New Atlantis*', *American Political Science Review*, 70: 3, 7 (1976), 865–85. The following remain informative studies of the text and/or its relation to other early modern utopias: J. Bierman, 'Science and Society in the *New Atlantis*', *PMLA* 78 (1963), 492–500; E. Blodgett, 'Campanella and the *New Atlantis*', *PMLA* 46 (1931), 763–80; R. L. Colie, 'Cornelius Drebbel and Salomon de Caus: Two Jacobean Models for Salomon's House', *Huntingdon Library Quarterly*, 18 (1954), 245–60.

Henry Neville, The Isle of Pines

Very little has been written on Henry Neville; still less on *The Isle of Pines*. Readers should be aware that some of the material on *The Isle of Pines* is written by people who have only read Pine's narrative, and not Van Sloetten's.

Other Editions

Two editions have been issued in English this century. The first is Worthington Chauncey Ford's edition of the complete text, in his *The Isle of Pines: An Essay in Bibliography* (Boston: The Club of Odd Volumes, 1920). This was a very limited edition, and is hard to come by. The other, easier to find, is in Philip Henderson's *Shorter Novels: Seventeenth*

Century (London: Dent, 1967), which prints only Pine's narrative, and has misled some readers into thinking that this is the complete text.

Background and Criticism

A good introduction to English republicanism, which includes some material on Neville, is offered by Blair Worden in J. H. Burns (ed.), *The Cambridge History of Political Thought* (Cambridge: CUP, 1991). Also relevant in this volume is J. P. Sommerville's introduction to 'Absolutism and Royalism', and especially the section on patriarchalism. For more information on patriarchalism in the period, see Gordon J. Schochet's *Patriarchalism in Political Thought* (Oxford: Blackwell, 1975); for more on republicanism, see Perez Zagorin's *History of Political Thought in the English Revolution* (London: Routledge, 1954); and for more on popular politics, see David Underdown's *Revel, Riot and Rebellion* (Oxford: Clarendon Press, 1985).

C. Robbins edited a reprint of Neville's best known tract, *Plato Redivivus*, in *Two English Republican Tracts* (Cambridge: CUP, 1969). Christopher Hill has some pages on Neville and his relation to the republican thinking of James Harrington in *The Experience of Defeat* (Harmondsworth: Penguin, 1984), but mentions *The Isle of Pines* only to describe it as 'a jovial glorification of polygamy'. This assumption that the text is a masculine fantasy is also held by James Holstun in his *A Rational Millennium: Puritan Utopias of Seventeenth-Century England and America* (Oxford: Oxford University Press, 1987), and by Michael McKeon in *The Origins of the English Novel 1600–1740* (Baltimore: Johns Hopkins University Press, 1988). By far the best essay on the text that I know of, which argues against the commonly held assumption that *The Isle of Pines* is merely pornography, is Susan Wiseman's '"Adam, the Father of all Flesh", Porno-Political Rhetoric and Political Theory In and After the English Civil War', which appeared in the special issue of *Prose Studies* devoted to 'Pamphlet Wars and Prose in the English Revolution' (*Prose Studies*, 14 (1991), 134–57.

Other Utopian Literature

There is a vast range of texts which either are utopias or have utopian leanings: I list here only a few, which are either precursors of the early modern utopias included in this volume, or other examples of early modern utopian discourse. Two classical sources are Ovid on the Golden Age, in *Metamorphoses*, Book I; and Plato's *Republic*. Augustine's *City of God* may well have influenced More's *Utopia*. Michel de Montaigne, 'Of the

Caniballes', influenced Shakespeare's *The Tempest*, and can be found in good selections of Montaigne's *Essays*. Tomaso Campanella's *La Città del Sole* (*City of the Son*) is most closely related to, and possibly an influence on, Bacon's *New Atlantis*. Neville may have had a hand in James Harrington's *Oceana*—see *The Commonwealth of Oceana and A System of Politics*, ed. J. G. A. Pocock (Cambridge: CUP, 1992).

On the Utopian Genre

Definitions of the utopian genre range from the extremely general to the very particular. Frank E. and Fritzie P. Manuel's *Utopian Thought in the Western World* (Oxford: Basil Blackwell, 1979) includes in its definition almost any printed text which invokes the possibility of a better world. Robert C. Elliot's *The Shape of Utopia: Studies in a Literary Genre* (Chicago: Chicago University Press, 1970) argues that utopia is a 'secularization of the myth of the Golden Age', which 'entails a negative appraisal of present conditions' and is inseparable from satire (p. 24). Elliott's emphasis on the importance of reason and will in the construction of the utopia is adopted and elaborated by J. C. Davis, whose theory regarding the nature of the utopian genre is described at more length in the introduction to the present volume. See J. C. Davis, 'The History of Utopia: The Chronology of Nowhere', in Peter Alexander and Roger Gill (eds.), *Utopias* (London: Duckworth, 1984), 1–18, and, at greater length, in his *Utopia and the Ideal Society: a Study of English Utopian Writing, 1516–1700* (Cambridge: CUP, 1981). Darko Suvin argues that the utopia is a 'verbal artifact' located in this world, characterized by its manner of functioning as a literature of historical and cognitive estrangement. See Darko Suvin, 'On the Poetics of the Science Fiction Genre', in Mark Rose (ed.), *Science Fiction: A Collection of Critical Essays* (Englewood Cliffs, NJ: Prentice-Hall, 1956), 57–71, and his *Metamorphoses of Science Fiction* (New Haven: Yale University Press, 1979). 'Estrangement' is also a crucial term in Peter Ruppert's *Reader in a Strange Land* (Athens and London: University of Georgia Press, 1986); for Ruppert, utopian literature 'works' by initiating a hermeneutical dialectic between reader and text. The most influential modern critic of utopian literature is Louis Marin, whose claims are, like Davis's, detailed briefly in the introduction to this volume. See Louis Marin, *Utopiques, jeux d'espaces* (Paris: Minuit, 1973). Marin's 'Theses on Ideology and Utopia' are translated by Fredric Jameson in *Minnesota Review*, 6 (Spring 1976), 71–5, who also reviewed *Utopiques* in his 'Of Islands and Trenches: Neutralization and the Production of Utopian Discourse', *Diacritics* (June 1977), 2–21.

Select Bibliography

Further Reading in Oxford World's Classics

An Anthology of Elizabethan Prose Fiction, ed. Paul Salzman.

An Anthology of Seventeenth-Century Prose Fiction, ed. Paul Salzman.

Aphra Behn, *Oroonoko and Other Writings*, ed. Paul Salzman.

John Bunyan, *Grace Abounding and Other Spiritual Autobiographies*, ed. John Stachniewski with Anita Pacheco.

—— *The Pilgrim's Progress*, ed. N. H. Keeble.

Plato, *Republic*, trans. and ed. Robin Waterfield.

William Shakespeare, *The Tempest*, ed. Stephen Orgel.

Sir Philip Sidney, *The Countess of Pembroke's Arcadia* (*The Old Arcadia*), ed. Katherine Duncan-Jones.

CHRONOLOGIES OF THE AUTHORS

Thomas More

1478　6 or 7 February: born in Milk Street, Cheapside, London, second child and eldest son of Agnes, daughter of Thomas Graunger, and John More, gentleman and later (1520) judge of the King's Bench.

1483　Edward IV dies; Richard III usurps throne. Luther born.

c.1485　Attends St Anthony's School at Threadneedle Street, London, where fellow pupils include John Colet and William Latimer. Richard III defeated and killed at Bosworth Field; Henry VII becomes King.

1490　Apprenticed to the Lord Chancellor and Archbishop of Canterbury, John Morton (later Cardinal Morton), where he serves as a page for two years.

1492　Sent by Morton to Canterbury Hall, Oxford (later Christchurch), where his Greek studies are tutored by Thomas Linacre. Christopher Columbus discovers the New World.

1493　The Pope publishes a bull dividing the New World between Spain and Portugal.

1494　Enters New Inn (affiliated to Lincoln's Inn) to train as a lawyer.

1495　Parliament passes act against vagabonds and beggars.

1496　12 February: admitted student of Lincoln's Inn.

1497　Defeat of Cornish rebels at Blackheath, with huge loss of life.

1499　Meets Erasmus, then 30 years old. According to Roper, More considers priesthood, living as a brother (but without having taken vows) of London Charterhouse (the Carthusians, a very strict order; More wears a hair shirt and scourges himself). After about four years he decides against priesthood. Voyages of Amerigo Vespucci begin.

1500　Called to the Bar. Erasmus's *Adagia* published.

1501　Made reader at Furnivall's Inn. Lectures on Augustine's *De Civitate Dei* (*City of God*)

1504/5　Marries Jane Colt of Newhall in Essex. Summoned as burgess to

Parliament, where on several occasions he resists King Henry VII's demands for new subsidies; in revenge (according to Roper) More's father is fined by the King and imprisoned in the Tower of London. More travels abroad. Accounts of Vespucci's voyages begin to appear in print.

1505　Daughter Margeret born. Erasmus visits More as his guest.

1506　Daughter Elizabeth born. Publication of More's translation (with Erasmus) into Latin of Lucian's dialogues *Cynicus*, *Philopseudes*, and *Menippus*.

1507　Daughter Cicely born.

1508　Visits Universities of Paris and Louvain.

1509　Son John born. Death of Henry VII and accession to the throne of Henry VIII who marries his deceased brother's wife, Catherine of Aragon. Beginnings of the slave trade. Erasmus writes *The Praise of Folly*.

1510　More made Under-Sheriff of London, at a salary of about £400 p.a. Publishes translation of Gherascho's *Life* of Pico della Mirandola and some other pieces.

1511　Jane Colt dies. More married again, to Alice Middleton, widow with one daughter, one month after Colt's death. Made Bencher of his Inn and called as reader there.

1512　Serves in Parliament as minister for London. War with France begins.

1513–18　Writes *History of Richard III*.

1515　15 May: sent on delegation to Bruges to negotiate on behalf of the King in a dispute concerning the wool trade. Continues to Antwerp. Whilst serving on this delegation, meets Peter Giles and composes Book 2 of the *Utopia*.

1516　Composes Book 1 of the *Utopia*. December: first edition of *Utopia* published at Louvain.

1517　Made Master of Requests and member of the Privy Council. Second edition of *Utopia* published at Paris. Luther publishes *Ninety-Five Theses Against Indulgences*, and the Reformation can be said to have begun. Sixty people hanged by Wolsey after riots in London.

1518　March and November: third and fourth editions of *Utopia* published at Basel. More's *Epigrams* published.

1520　Attends Henry VIII at the Field of the Cloth of Gold. Luther publishes *De Captivate Babylonica* and other works and is excommunicated.

1521　Made Under-Treasurer and knighted. Ralph Robinson, *Utopia*'s future translator, born of relatively poor parents in Lincolnshire.

1522　Luther translates New Testament into German.

1523　Moves to Chelsea. Made Speaker of the House of Commons. Attacks Luther.

1524(2?)　Writes *Four Last Things*.

1525　Made Chancellor of the Duchy of Lancaster. Tyndale translates New Testament into English. Luther writes 'On the Bondage of the Will'.

1527　September: Henry VIII asks More's advice on propriety of dissolving marriage with Catherine of Aragon. More can see no reason why the marriage should be annulled. Holbein paints portrait of More.

1529　Conducts negotiations at Treaty of Cambrai. Made Lord High Chancellor. Publishes *A Dialogue Concerning Heresies*, attacking Luther and Tyndale. Publishes *Supplication of the Souls*.

1531　Henry VIII named Supreme Head of the Church of England.

1532　16 May: resigns from office over the 'Submission of the Clergy', a bill which allowed the Crown to veto ecclesiastical legislation. In resigning, he may also have been attempting to avoid confrontation with Henry VIII over divorce with Catherine of Aragon.

1533　Publishes *Apology, Confutation of Tyndale's Answer, Deballation of Salem and Bizane, Answer to John Frith*. Thomas Cranmer, Archbishop of Canterbury, allows divorce between Henry and Catherine. Henry marries Anne Boleyn in defiance of the Pope and is excommunicated. Birth of Elizabeth, later Elizabeth I.

1534　March: Act of Succession passed, legitimizing issue of Henry and Anne Boleyn and bastardizing Mary (daughter of Henry and Catherine of Aragon). 1 July: More refuses to take Oath of Supremacy, which would ratify the Act of Succession and acknowledge Henry VIII as Supreme Head of the Church of England. Committed to the Tower of London. Writes *A Dialogue of Comfort Against Tribulation, The Sadness of Christ*. Second edition of Tyndale's translation of the New Testament.

1535　1 July: Tried. 6 July: beheaded.

1536　Ralph Robinson, having been educated at Grantham and

Stamford grammar schools, enters Corpus Christi College, Oxford.

1542   Robinson, who graduated in 1540, becomes a fellow of Corpus Christi College.

1544   Robinson applies for degree of MA. Some time after he leaves Oxford for London and obtains livery of Goldsmith's company. Enters service of William Cecil, Lord Burleigh.

1551   First edition of his English translation of *Utopia* published. May: Robinson appeals to Cecil for an increase in income.

1556   Second, revised edition of Robinson's translation of *Utopia*.

c.1572   By this time Robinson is impoverished and appealing to Cecil once again for an increase of income. Thereafter nothing is known of him.

Francis Bacon

1561   22 January: born at York House, the Strand, the younger of Sir Nicholas Bacon's two sons by his marriage to Lady Ann Bacon (née Cooke), his second wife (there being four sons from the first marriage).

1564   New Royal Charter bestowed on English Merchant Adventurers company.

1565   Royal College of Physicians, London, allowed to carry out human dissections.

1570   First modern atlas (with 53 maps) published by Abraham Ortelius.

1573   5 April: goes up to Trinity College, Cambridge. Francis Drake sees the Pacific Ocean for the first time.

1575   March: leaves Cambridge.

1576   27 June: is entered at Gray's Inn; admitted 21 November, but in September had accompanied Sir Amias Paulet, English ambassador to France.

1577   Richard Eden publishes his *History of Travel in the East and West Indies*.

1579   20 March: returns from France. Trinity Term, admitted to Gray's Inn.

1581   Elected to Parliament as member for Bossiney, Cornwall.

1582   27 June: admitted as Utter Barrister of Gray's Inn. Richard Hakluyt's accounts of voyages begin to be published.

1584 23 November: MP for Weymouth and Melcombe Regis.

1586 29 October: MP for Taunton. Becomes a Bencher of Gray's Inn.

1587 Lent Term, elected Reader at Gray's Inn. Privy Council consults him on legal matters.

1588 August: appointed to government committee examining recusants. December: appointed to select committee of lawyers to review parliamentary statutes.

1589 4 February: MP for Liverpool. Asked to prepare official document justifying the Queen's religious policies. 29 October: granted reversion of Clerkship of Star Chamber.

1591 Easter Term, first appearance as pleader in court.

1592 Galileo publishes *Della Scienze Mechanica* (on raising weights). Plague kills 15,000 people in London, with further outbreaks in following years.

1593 19 February: MP for Middlesex. 2 and 8 March: speaks against the Queen's demand for additional taxes, and loses royal favour.

1595 Mercator's atlas published.

1596 Appointed Queen's Counsel Extraordinary (honorific title). Galileo invents thermometer.

1597 February: first edition of *Essays* (ten essays), with *Colours of Good and Evil*, and *Religious Meditations*. 18 October: MP for Ipswich; speaks against enclosures.

1598 Tycho Brahe publishes account of his discoveries, with a description of the instruments he has used.

1599 March: acts as prosecuting counsel in trial of Essex over Irish debacle. The Italian naturalist Ulissi Aldrovani publishes an account of his studies of birds.

1600 24 October: Double Reader at Gray's Inn. William Gilbert publishes *De Magnete* (on magnetism and electricity).

1601 19 February: acts as state prosecutor in trial of Essex for rebellion. Commanded by the Queen to write *A Declaration of the Practises and Treasons attempted and committed by Robert late Earl of Essex*. 27 October: MP for Ipswich. November: introduces bill for repealing superfluous laws.

1603 24 March: death of Queen Elizabeth, accession of King James I. 23 July: Bacon knighted by James, along with 300 others. Publishes (anonymously) *A Brief Discourse, touching the Happy Union of the Kingdoms of England, and Scotland*. Member of the ecclesiastical commission.

1604   March: MP for Ipswich. June: publishes *Sir Francis Bacon His Apology, in certain imputations concerning the late Earl of Essex,* and (anonymously) *Certain Considerations touching the better Pacification and Edification of the Church of England,* which is suppressed by the Bishop of London. 18 August: appointed King's Counsel. Kepler publishes his *Optics.*

1605   October: publishes *The Two Books of Francis Bacon. Of the proficience and advancement of Learning, divine and human* (reprinted 1629).

1606   10 May: marries Alice Barnham, daughter of a wealthy London alderman.

1607   17 February: makes important speeches in Parliament supporting union of the kingdoms and naturalization of Scottish citizens. 25 June: appointed Solicitor-General.

1608   Becomes Clerk of the Star Chamber. Appointed Treasurer of Gray's Inn.

1609   Publishes *De Sapientia Veterum.*

1610   February: MP for Ipswich. June: speaks in defence of the royal prerogative.

1611   Marco de Dominis offers a scientific account of the phenomenon of the rainbow.

1612   November: publishes enlarged edition of the *Essays* (thirty-eight essays).

1613   26 October: appointed Attorney-General.

1614   January: publishes *The Charge of Sir Francis Bacon, Knight, His Majesty's Attorney-general, touching Duells* . . . April: MP for Cambridge University.

1616   25 May: acts as state prosecutor against the Earl and Countess of Somerset over the poisoning of Sir Thomas Overbury. 9 June: appointed Privy Counsellor.

1617   7 March: appointed Lord Keeper of the Seal; reforms workings of Chancery.

1618   January: appointed Lord Chancellor. 12 July: created Baron Verulam. Royal College of Physicians issues *Pharmacopoeia Londinensis.*

1619   October: involved in prosecution of the Earl of Suffolk for illegal exaction.

1620   12 October: publishes in part *Instauratio Magna*: Preface, 'Plan of the Work', and Part II, *Novum Organum* (two books only). This volume includes *Parasceve ad Historiam Naturalem et Experimentalem.* November: involved in prosecution of Sir Henry Yelverton, Attorney-General, for unlawfully amending the charter of the City of London.

1621   27 January: created Viscount St Alban. 3 May: sentenced by the House of Lords on charge of taking bribes. Dismissed from office as Lord Chancellor, fined £40,000, and temporarily imprisoned; but retains other titles and is given a limited pardon. Retires to Gorhambury.

1622   March publishes *The Historie of the Reign of King Henry the Seventh.* November: publishes *Historia Naturalis et Experimentalis . . .* , Part I: *Historia Ventorum.*

1623   January: publishes Part II: *Historia Vitae et Mortis.* October: publishes *De Dignitate & Augmentis Scientiarum Libri IX.*

1624   March: composes treatise concerning a war with Spain. December: publishes *Apophthegms New and Old* and *The Translation of Certain Psalms into English verse.*

1625   27 March: death of King James; accession of King Charles I. April: publishes third edition of the *Essays or Counsels, Civil and Moral . . . Newly enlarged* (fifty-eight essays). 19 December: makes last will and testament.

1626   9 April: dies at Highgate, having caught a chill experimenting with the effect of refrigeration on preserving food. Santorio Santorio measures human temperature with thermometer for the first time; Jardin des Plantes created in Paris.

1627   Publication of *Sylva Sylvarum: or A Natural History*, to which is appended the *New Atlantis.*

Henry Neville

1620   Born in Berkshire, second son of Sir Henry Neville and Elizabeth, daughter of Sir John Smith of Kent.

1621   English attempt to colonize Newfoundland and Nova Scotia. Dutch West India Company chartered.

1623   Dutch massacre English factors in Moluccas.

1624   James I dissolves Parliament.

1625   James I dies. Charles I succeeds. Colonial office established in London.

1629   Charles dissolves Parliament.

1634   English settle at Malabar. Pilgrims leave in *The Mayflower* to found Plymouth colony.

1635   Enters Merton College, Oxford. Later moves to University College, Oxford. Leaves without a degree. Dutch occupy English Virgin Islands.

1636   Dutch settle in Sri Lanka.

1642   English Revolution begins. Portuguese cede Gold Coast to Dutch.

1645   Neville returns to England from a trip to the continent. Recruits soldiers for Parliament in Abingdon. Dutch occupy St Helena.

1646   English Revolution ends with victory of Cromwell.

1647   Publishes *The Parliament of Ladies* and *The Ladies a Second Time Assembled in Parliament*.

1649   Sits on Goldsmiths Hall committee on delinquents. Charles I beheaded.

1650   Publishes *News from the New Exchange, or the Commonwealth of Ladies*. Accord between English and Dutch over North American colonies.

1651   Neville made member of the Council of State. Becomes friendly with staunch republicans such as James Harrington and grows suspicious of Oliver Cromwell's commitment to republicanism. Thomas Hobbes's *Leviathan* published. English Navigation Act, aimed against the Dutch, gives English ships monopolies in foreign trade. Dutch settle Cape of Good Hope.

1652   War with the Netherlands. English defeat Dutch at Folkestone. Filmer's *Observations concerning the Original of Government* published.

1653   Oliver Cromwell becomes Lord Protector. English defeat Dutch again, in various battles.

1654   Neville banished from London by Oliver Cromwell. Treaty of Westminster ends Anglo–Dutch War; Dutch recognize 1651 Navigation Act.

1655   Cromwell dissolves Parliament.

1656   Harrington's *Oceana* published.

1657   Cromwell rejects title of King; creates House of Lords.

1658   Cromwell dies. Succeeded by son Richard as Lord Protector, who resigns following year.

<table>
<tr><td></td><td>30 December: Neville returned to Parliament as MP for Reading.</td></tr>
</table>

1659   16 February: charged unsuccessfully with atheism and blasphemy in an attempt to exclude him from Parliament. 21 Febrary: argues against armed intervention in war between Sweden and Denmark. Becomes member of Harrington's Rota Club. Publishes *Shuffling, Cutting and Dealing in a Game of Piquet*.

1660   Parliament invites Charles II to return to England, and dissolves itself. Dutch peasants (Boers) settle in South Africa. Royal African Company founded.

1661   Coronation of Charles II.

1663   October: Neville arrested on suspicion of involvement in the Yorkshire rising. Imprisoned in the Tower but released for want of evidence. Moves shortly after to Silver Street near Bloomsbury market.

1664   British seizure of New Netherlands; New Amsterdam renamed New York.

1666   France and the Netherlands declare war on England.

1667   Peace of Breda between the Netherlands, France, and England. Milton starts to publish *Paradise Lost*.

1668   Neville publishes *The Isle of Pines*, first in two separate pamphlets, then as a combined pamphlet.

1672   Britain declares war on the Netherlands.

1675   Neville publishes translation of a selection of Machiavelli's works.

1680   Extinction of the dodo.

1681   Neville publishes *Plato Redivivus, or a Dialogue concerning Government*.

1685   Charles II dies, succeeded by brother James II.

1688   James II abdicates; William (of Orange) and Mary crowned. Aphra Behn publishes *Oroonoko*.

1694   20 September: Neville dies; buried in parish church of Warfield, Berkshire.

A frutefull

pleasaunt, & wittie worke,
of the beste state of a publique
weale, and of the newe yle, called Utopia: written in Latine, by the right wor-
thie and famous Syr Thomas More
knyght, and translated into Englishe by
Raphe Robynson, sometime fellowe
of Corpus Christi College in Ox-
forde, and nowe by him at this se-
conde edition newlie perused and corrected, and
also with diuers no-
tes in the margent
augmented.

Imprinted at London, by
Abraham Vele, dwellinge in
Pauls churchyarde, at the signe
of the Lambe.

The Title page of the 1556 edition of Robinson's translation of *Utopia*.

The Translator to the Gentle Reader

Thou shalt understand, gentle reader, that though this work of *Utopia* in English come now the second time forth in print, yet was it never my mind nor intent that it should ever have been imprinted at all, as who for no such purpose took upon me at the first the translation thereof; but did it only at the request of a friend, for his own private use, upon hope that he would have kept it secret to himself alone.* Whom though I knew to be a man indeed, both very witty and also skilful, yet was I certain that in the knowledge of the Latin tongue he was not so well seen as to be able to judge of the fineness or coarseness of my translation. Wherefore I went the more slightly through with it, propounding to myself therein rather to please my said friend's judgement than mine own. To the meanness of whose learning I thought it my part to submit and attemper my style. Lightly, therefore, I overran the whole work, and in short time, with more haste than good speed,* I brought it to an end. But, as the Latin proverb sayeth: 'The hasty bitch bringeth forth blind whelps.'* For when this my work was finished, the rudeness thereof showed it to be done in post-haste. Howbeit, rude and base though it were, yet fortune so ruled the matter that to imprinting it came, and that partly against my will.

Howbeit, not being able in this behalf to resist the pithy persuasions of my friends, and perceiving therefore none other remedy, but that forth it should, I comforted myself for the time only with this notable saying of Terence:*

> *Ita vita est hominum, quasi quum ludas tesseris.*
> *Si illud, quod est maxume opus iactu non cadit:*
> *Illud, quod cecidit forte, id arte ut corrigas.*

In which verses the poet likeneth or compareth the life of man to a dice-playing or a game at the tables. Meaning therein, if that chance rise not which is most for the player's advantage, that then the chance, which fortune hath sent, ought so cunningly to be played, as may be to the player least damage. By the which worthy similitude surely the witty poet giveth us to understand, that though in any of our acts and doings (as oft chanceth) we happen to fail and miss of our good pretensed purpose, so that the success and our intent prove things far odd; yet so we ought with witty circumspection to handle the matter, that no evil or incommodity, as far forth as may be, and as in us lieth, do thereof ensue. According to the which counsel, though I am indeed in comparison of an expert gamester and a cunning player but a very bungler, yet have I in this by chance, that on my side unawares hath fallen, so (I suppose) behaved myself that, as doubtless it might have been of me much more cunningly handled, had I forethought so much or doubted any such sequel at the beginning of my play, so I am sure it had been much worse than it is if I had not in the end looked somewhat earnestly to my game. For though this work came not from me so fine, so perfect, and so exact yet at first, as surely for my small learning it should have done if I had then meant the publishing thereof in print; yet I trust I have now in this second edition taken about it such pains that very few great faults and notable errors are in it to be found. Now, therefore, most gentle reader, the meanness of this simple translation, and the faults that be therein (as I fear much there be some), I doubt not but thou wilt, in just consideration of the premisses, gently and favourably wink at them. So doing thou shalt minister unto me good cause to think my labour and pains herein not altogether bestowed in vain. *Vale*!

Thomas More to Peter Giles sendeth greeting*

I am almost ashamed, right well beloved Peter Giles, to send unto you this book of the Utopian commonwealth wellnigh after a year's space, which I am sure you looked for within a month and a half. And no marvel. For you knew well enough that I was already disburdened of all the labour and study belonging to the invention in this work, and that I had no need at all to trouble my brains about the disposition or conveyance of the matter, and therefore had herein nothing else to do, but only to rehearse those things which you and I together heard Master Raphael* tell and declare. Wherefore there was no cause why I should study to set forth the matter with eloquence, forasmuch as his talk could not be fine and eloquent, being first not studied for, but sudden and unpremeditate, and then, as you know, of a man better seen in the Greek language than in the Latin tongue. And my writing, the nigher it should approach to his homely, plain, and simple speech, so much the nigher should it go to the truth, which is the only mark whereunto I do and ought to direct all my travail and study herein. I grant and confess, friend Peter, myself discharged of so much labour, having all these things ready done to my hand, that almost there was nothing left for me to do. Else either the invention or the disposition of this matter might have required of a wit neither base neither at all unlearned, both some time and leisure, and also some study. But if it were requisite and necessary that the matter should also have been written eloquently and not alone truly, of a surety that thing could I have performed by no time nor study. But now seeing all these cares, stays, and lets were taken away, wherein else so much labour and study should have been employed, and that there remained no other thing for me to do but only to write plainly the matter as I heard it spoken, that indeed was a thing light and easy to be done.

*Truth loveth simplicity and plainness.**

Howbeit, to the dispatching of this so little business, my other cares and troubles did leave almost less than no leisure. Whiles I do daily bestow my time about law matters, some to plead, some to hear, some as an arbitrator with mine award to determine, some as an umpire or a judge, with my sentence finally to discuss; whiles I go one way to see and visit my friend, another way about mine own private affairs; whiles I spend almost all the day abroad among others, and the residue at home among mine own; I leave to myself, I mean to my book, no time. For when I am come home I must commune with my wife, chat with my children, and talk with my servants. All the which things I reckon and account among business forasmuch as they must of necessity be done, and done must they needs be, unless a man will be stranger in his own

The author's business and lets.

house. And in any wise a man must so fashion and order his conditions and so appoint and dispose himself that he be merry, jocund, and pleasant among them whom either nature hath provided or chance hath made or he himself hath chosen to be the fellows and companions of his life, so that with too much gentle behaviour and familiarity he do not mar them, and by too much sufferance of his servants make them his masters. Among these things now rehearsed stealeth away the day, the month, the year. When do I write then? And all this while have I spoken no word of sleep, neither yet of meat, which among a great number doth waste no less time than doth sleep, wherein almost half the lifetime of man creepeth away. I therefore do win and get only that time which I steal from sleep and meat.

Meat and sleep great wasters of time.

Which time, because it is very little, and yet somewhat it is, therefore have I once at the last, though it be long first, finished *Utopia*, and have sent it to you, friend Peter, to read and peruse, to the intent that if anything have escaped me you might put me in remembrance of it. For though in this behalf I do not greatly mistrust myself (which would God I were somewhat in wit and learning, as I am not all of the worst and dullest memory), yet have I not so great trust and confidence in it that I think nothing could fall out of my mind. For John Clement, my boy,* who, as you know, was there present with us, whom I suffer to be away from no talk wherein may be any profit or goodness (for out of this young-bladed and new-shot-up corn, which hath already begun to spring up both in Latin and Greek learning, I look for plentiful increase at length of goodly ripe grain), he, I say hath brought me into a great doubt. For whereas Hythloday* (unless my memory fail me) said that the bridge of Amaurote which goeth over the river of Anyder is five hundred paces, that is to say half a mile, in length, my John saith that two hundred of those paces must be plucked away, for that the river containeth there not above three hundred paces in breadth. I pray you heartily call the matter to your remembrance. For if you agree with him I also will say as you say and confess myself deceived. But if you cannot remember the thing, then surely I will write as I have

John Clement.

done and as mine own remembrance serveth me. For as I will take good heed that there be in my book nothing false, so if there be anything doubtful I will rather tell a lie than make a lie, because I had rather be good than wily. *A diversity between making a lie and telling a lie.*

Howbeit, this matter may easily be remedied if you will take the pains to ask the question of Raphael himself by word of mouth, if he be now with you, or else by your letters. Which you must needs do for another doubt also that hath chanced, through whose fault I cannot tell, whether through mine or yours or Raphael's. For neither we remembered to inquire of him, nor he to tell us, in what part of the new world Utopia is situate. The which thing I had rather have spent no small sum of money than that it should thus have escaped us, as well for that I am ashamed to be ignorant in what sea that island standeth whereof I wrote so long a treatise, as also because there be with us certain men, and especially one virtuous and godly man and a professor of divinity, who is exceeding desirous to go unto Utopia, not for a vain and curious desire to see news, but to the intent he may further and increase our religion which is there already luckily begun. And that he may the better accomplish and perform this his good intent he is minded to procure that he may be sent thither by the high Bishop; yea, and that he himself may be made Bishop of Utopia, being nothing scrupulous herein that he must obtain this bishopric with suit. For he counteth that a godly suit which proceedeth not of the desire of honour or lucre, but only of a godly zeal. Wherefore I most earnestly desire you, friend Peter, to talk with Hythloday, if you can, face to face, or else to write your letters to him, and so to work in this matter that in this my book there may neither anything be found which is untrue, neither anything be lacking which is true. And I think verily it shall be well done, that you show unto him the book itself. For if I have missed or failed in any point, or if any fault have escaped me, no man can so well correct and amend it as he can; and yet that can he not do unless he peruse and read over my book written. Moreover, by this means shall you perceive whether he be well willing and content that I should undertake to put this work in writing. For if he be minded to publish and

In what part of the world Utopia standeth is unknown.

It is thought of some, here is unfeignedly meant the late famous vicar of Croydon in Surrey.*

A godly suit.

put forth his own labours and travels himself, perchance he would be loath, and so would I also, that in publishing the Utopian weal-public I should prevent him and take from him the flower and grace of the novelty of this his history.

The unkind judgements of men.

Howbeit, to say the very truth, I am not yet fully determined with myself whether I will put forth my book or no. For the natures of men be so diverse, the phantasies of some so wayward, their minds so unkind, their judgements so corrupt, that they which lead a merry and a jocund life, following their own sensual pleasures and carnal lusts, may seem to be in a much better state or case than they that vex and unquiet themselves with cares and study for the putting forth and publishing of something, that may be either profit or pleasure to others, which others nevertheless will disdainfully, scornfully, and unkindly accept the same. The most part of all be unlearned. And a great number hath learning in contempt. The rude and barbarous alloweth nothing but that which is very barbarous indeed. If it be one that hath a little smack of learning, he rejecteth as homely gear and common ware whatsoever is not stuffed full of old moth-eaten terms and that be worn out of use. Some there be that have pleasure only in old rusty antiquities. And some only in their own doings. One is so sour, so crabbed, and so unpleasant, that he can away with no mirth nor sport. Another is so narrow between the shoulders, that he can bear no jests nor taunts. Some silly poor souls be so afeard that at every snappish word their nose shall be bitten off, that they stand in no less dread of every quick and sharp word than he that is bitten of a mad dog feareth water. Some be so mutable and wavering, that every hour they be in a new mind, saying one thing sitting and another thing standing. Another sort sitteth upon their ale-benches, and there among their cups they give judgement of the wits of writers, and with great authority they condemn, even as pleaseth them, every writer according to his writing, in most spiteful manner mocking, louting, and flouting them, being themselves in the mean season safe and, as saith the proverb, 'out of all danger of gunshot'.* For why, they be so smug and smooth, that they have not so much as one hair of an honest man whereby one may take hold of them. There be, moreover, some so unkind and ungentle, that, though they take great pleasure and delectation in the work, yet for all that they cannot find in their hearts to love the author thereof nor to afford him a good word, being much like uncourteous, unthankful, and churlish guests, *A fit* which when they have with good and dainty meat well filled *similitude.* their bellies, depart home, giving no thanks to the feast maker. Go your ways now, and make a costly feast at your own charges for guests so dainty mouthed, so divers in taste, and besides that of so unkind and unthankful natures.

But nevertheless, friend Peter, do, I pray you, with Hythloday as I willed you before. And as for this matter I shall be at my liberty afterwards to take new advisement. Howbeit, seeing I have taken great pains and labour in writing the matter, if it may stand with his mind and pleasure I will, as touching the edition of publishing of the book, follow the counsel and advice of my friends and specially yours. Thus fare you well, right heartily beloved friend Peter, with your gentle wife, and love me as you have ever done, for I love you better than ever I did.

The First Book of the Communication of Raphael Hythloday,* Concerning the Best State of a Commonwealth

The most victorious and triumphant King of England, Henry the eighth of that name, in all royal virtues a Prince most peerless, had of late in controversy with Charles, the right high and mighty king of Castile,* weighty matters, and of great importance. For the debatement and final determination whereof the king's majesty sent me ambassador into Flanders, joined in commission with Cuthbert Tunstall, a man doubtless out of comparison and whom the King's majesty of late, to the great rejoicing of all men, did prefer to the office of Master of the Rolls.* But of this man's praises I will say nothing, not because I do fear that small credence shall be given to the testimony that cometh out of a friend's mouth; but because his virtue and learning be greater, and of more excellence than that I am able to praise them, and also in all places so famous, and so perfectly well known, that they need not nor ought not of me to be praised, unless I would seem to show and set forth the brightness of the sun with a candle, as the proverb saith.*

Cuthbert Tunstall.

There met us at Bruges (for thus it was before agreed) they whom their prince had for that matter appointed commissioners: excellent men all. The chief and the head of them was the Margrave (as they call him) of Bruges, a right honourable man: but the wisest and the best spoken of them was George Temsice, Provost of Cassel, a man not only by learning but also by nature of singular eloquence, and in the laws profoundly learned;* but in reasoning and debating of matters, what by his natural wit and what by daily exercise, surely he had few fellows.* After that we had once or twice met, and upon certain points or articles could not fully and thoroughly agree, they for a certain space took their leave of us and departed to Brussels, there to know their prince's pleasure. I, in the meantime (for so my business lay), went straight thence to Antwerp.

Whilst I was there abiding, often times among other, but

which to me was more welcome than any other, did visit me
one Peter Giles,* a citizen of Antwerp; a man there in his country of honest reputation, and also preferred to high promotions, worthy truly of the highest. For it is hard to say whether
the young man be in learning or in honesty more excellent. For
he is both of wonderful virtuous conditions, and also singularly well learned, and towards all sorts of people exceeding
gentle; but towards his friends so kind-hearted, so loving, so
faithful, so trusty, and of so earnest affection, that it were very
hard in any place to find a man that with him in all points of
friendship may be compared. No man can be more lowly or
courteous. No man useth less simulation or dissimulation; in
no man is more prudent simplicity. Besides this, he is in his
talk and communication so merry and pleasant, yea and that
without harm, that, through his gentle entertainment and his
sweet and delectable communication, in me was greatly abated
and diminished the fervent desire that I had to see my native
country, my wife, and my children, whom then I did much
long and covet to see, because that at that time I had been more
than four months from them.

Upon a certain day when I had heard the divine service in
our Lady's Church* (which is the fairest, the most gorgeous,
and curious church of building in all the city, and also most
frequented of people) and, the service being done, was ready
to go home to my lodging, I chanced to espy this foresaid
Peter talking with a certain stranger, a man well stricken in
age,* with a black sun-burned face, a long beard, and a cloak
cast homely about his shoulders, whom, by his favour and
apparel, forthwith I judged to be a mariner. But the said Peter
seeing me he came unto me, and saluted me. And as I was
about to answer him: 'See you this man?' sayeth he (and therewith he pointed to the man that I saw him talking with before).
'I was minded', quoth he, 'to bring him straight home to
you.'

'He should have been very welcome to me,' said I, 'for your
sake.'

'Nay,' quoth he, 'for his own sake if you knew him, for there
is no man this day living that can tell you of so many strange

and unknown peoples and countries as this man can. And I know well that you be very desirous to hear of such news.'

'Then I conjectured not far amiss,' quoth I, 'for even at the first sight, I judged him to be a mariner.'

'Nay,' quoth he, 'there ye were greatly deceived. He hath sailed indeed, not as the mariner Palinurus, but as the expert and prudent prince Ulysses; yea, rather as the ancient and sage

*Raphael
Hythloday.*

philosopher Plato.* For this same Raphael Hythloday (for this is his name) is very well learned in the Latin tongue, but profound and excellent in the Greek language, wherein he ever bestowed more study than in the Latin, because he had given himself wholly to the study of philosophy; whereof he knew that there is nothing extant in Latin that is to any purpose, saving a few of Seneca's and Cicero's doings.* His patrimony that he was born unto he left to his brethren (for he is a Portugall born),* and for the desire that he had to see and know the far countries of the world, he joined himself in company with Amerigo Vespucci, and in the three last voyages of those four that be now in print, and abroad in every man's hands,* he continued still in his company, saving that in the last voyage he came not home again with him. For he made such means and shift, what by entreatance, and what by importune suit, that he got licence of Master Amerigo (though it were sore against his will) to be one of the twenty-four which in the end of the last voyage were left in the country of Gulike.* He was therefore left behind for his mind's sake,* as one that took more thought and care for travelling than dying, having customarily in his mouth these sayings:* "He that hath no grave is covered with the sky," and, "The way to heaven out of all places is of like length and distance". Which fantasy of his (if God had not been his better friend) he had surely bought full dear. But after the departing of Master Vespucci, when he had travelled through and about many countries with five of his companions Gulikians, at the last by marvellous chance he arrived in Taprobane,* from whence he went to Calicut,* where he chanced to find certain of his country ships, wherein he returned again into his country, nothing less than looked for.'*

All this when Peter had told me, I thanked him for his gentle

kindness that he had vouchsafed to bring me to the speech
of that man whose communication he thought should be to
me pleasant and acceptable. And therewith I turned me to
Raphael. And when we had hailed each other and had spoken
those common words that be customably spoken at the first
meeting and acquaintance of strangers, we went thence to my
house, and there in my garden, upon a bench covered with
green turves, we sat down talking together.

There he told us, how that after the departing of Vespucci,
he and his fellows that tarried behind in Gulike began by little
and little, through fair and gentle speech, to win the love and
favour of the people of that country, insomuch that within
short space they did dwell amongst them not only harmless,
but also occupying with them very familiarly. He told us also
that they were in high reputation and favour with a certain
great man (whose name and country is now quite out of my
remembrance) which of his mere liberality did bear the costs
and charges of him and his five companions. And besides that
gave them a trusty guide to conduct them in their journey
(which by water was in boats and by land in wagons) and to
bring them to other princes with very friendly commendations. Thus after many days' journeys, he said, they found
towns and cities and weal-publics, full of people, governed by
good and wholesome laws.

'For under the line equinoctial, and on both sides of the
same, as far as the sun doth extend his course, lieth', quoth he,
'great and wide deserts and wildernesses, parched, burned,
and dried up with continual and intolerable heat. All things
be hideous, terrible, loathsome, and unpleasant to behold; all
things out of fashion and comeliness, inhabited with wild
beasts and serpents, or at the least wise with people that be no
less savage, wild, and noisome than the very beasts themselves
be. But a little farther beyond that, all things begin by little and
little to wax pleasant: the air soft, temperate, and gentle; the
ground covered with green grass; less wildness in the beasts.
At the last shall ye come again to people, cities, and towns
wherein is continual intercourse and occupying of merchandise and chaffare, not only among themselves and with their

borderers, but also with merchants of far countries, both by land and water. There I had occasion', said he, 'to go to many countries on every side. For there was no ship ready to any voyage or journey, but I and my fellows were into it very gladly received.'

Ships of strange fashions.

The ships that they found first were made plain, flat, and broad in the bottom, trough-wise. The sails were made of great rushes, or of wickers, and in some places of leather. Afterwards they found ships with ridged keels and sails of canvas, yea, and shortly after, having all things like ours. The shipmen also very expert and cunning, both in the sea and in the weather. But he said that he found great favour and friendship among them for teaching them the feat and the use of the lodestone, which to them before that time was unknown.* And therefore they were wont to be very timorous and fearful upon the sea, nor to venture upon it, but only in the summer time. But now they have such a confidence in that stone, that they fear not stormy winter: in so doing farther from care than danger. Insomuch that it is greatly to be doubted lest that thing, through their own foolish hardiness, shall turn them to evil and harm, which at the first was supposed should be to them good and commodious.

The lodestone.

But what he told us that he saw in every country where he came, it were very long to declare. Neither it is my purpose at this time to make rehearsal thereof. But peradventure in another place I will speak of it, chiefly such things as shall be profitable to be known, as in special be those decrees and ordinances that he marked to be well and wisely provided and enacted among such peoples as do live together in a civil policy and good order. For of such things did we busily inquire and demand of him, and he likewise very willingly told us of the same. But as for monsters, because they be no news, of them we were nothing inquisitive. For nothing is more easy to be found than be barking *Scyllas*, ravening *Celaenos*, and *Laestrygons*, devourers of people, and suchlike great and incredible monsters.* But to find citizens ruled by good and wholesome laws, that is an exceeding rare and hard thing. But as he marked many fond and foolish laws in those new-found lands, so he rehearsed divers acts and constitutions whereby these our cities, nations, countries, and kingdoms may take example to amend their faults, enormities, and errors. Whereof in another place, as I said, I will entreat.

Now at this time I am determined to rehearse only that he told us of the manners, customs, laws, and ordinances of the Utopians. But first I will repeat our former communication by the occasion and (as I might say) the drift whereof he was brought into the mention of that weal-public. For when Raphael had very prudently touched divers things that be amiss, some here and some there, yea, very many on both parts; and again had spoken of such wise laws and prudent decrees as be established and used both here among us and also there among them, as a man so perfect and expert in the laws and customs of every several country, as though into what place soever he came guestwise, there he had led all his life: then Peter, much marvelling at the man: 'Surely, Master Raphael,' quoth he, 'I wonder greatly why you get you not into some king's court. For I am sure there is no prince living that would not be very glad of you, as a man not only able highly to delight him with your profound learning, and this your knowledge of countries and peoples, but also meet to instruct him with examples and help him with counsel. And thus doing, you shall bring yourself in a very good case, and also be of ability to help all your friends and kinsfolk.'

'As concerning my friends and kinsfolk,' quoth he, 'I pass not greatly for them. For I think I have sufficiently done my part towards them already. For these things that other men do not depart from until they be old and sick, yea, which they be then very loath to leave when they can no longer keep, those very same things did I, being not only lusty and in good health, but also in the flower of my youth, divide among my friends and kinsfolks. Which I think with this my liberality ought to hold them contented, and not to require nor to look that besides this: I should for their sakes give myself in bondage unto kings.'

'Nay, God forbid that,' quoth Peter. 'It is not my mind that you should be in bondage to kings, but as a retainer to them at your pleasure.* Which surely I think is the nighest way that you can devise how to bestow your time fruitfully, not only for the private commodity of your friends and for the general profit of all sorts of people, but also for the advancement of yourself to a much wealthier state and condition than you be now in.'

'To a wealthier condition,' quoth Raphael, 'by that means that my mind standeth clean against?* Now I live at liberty after mine own mind and pleasure, which I think very few of these great states and peers of realms can say. Yea, and there be enough of them that sue for great men's friendships, and therefore think it no great hurt if they have not me, nor three or four such other as I am.'

'Well, I perceive plainly, friend Raphael,' quoth I, 'that you be desirous neither of riches nor of power. And truly I have in no less reverence and estimation a man of your mind than any of them all that be so high in power and authority. But you shall do as it becometh you: yea, and according to this wisdom, to this high and free courage of yours, if you can find in your heart so to appoint and dispose yourself that you may apply your wit and diligence to the profit of the weal-public, though it be somewhat to your own pain and hindrance. And this shall you never so well do, nor with so great profit perform, as if you be of some great prince's council, and put into his head (as I doubt not but you will) honest opinions and virtuous persuasions. For from the prince, as from a perpetual well-spring, cometh among the people the flood of all that is good or evil. But in you is so perfect learning that without any experience, and again so great experience that without any learning, you may well be any king's counsellor.'

'You be twice deceived, Master More,' quoth he, 'first in me and again in the thing itself. For neither is in me that ability that you force upon me, and if it were never so much, yet in disquieting mine own quietness I should nothing further the weal-public. For, first of all, the most part of all princes have more delight in warlike matters and feats of chivalry (the knowledge whereof I neither have nor desire) than in the good feats of peace, and employ much more study how by right or by wrong to enlarge their dominions, than how well and peaceably to rule, and govern that they have already. Moreover, they that be counsellors to kings, every one of them either is of himself so wise indeed that he needeth not, or else he thinketh himself so wise that he will not, allow another man's counsel, saving that they do shamefully and flatteringly give assent to the fond and foolish sayings of certain great men. Whose favours, because they be in high authority with their prince, by assentation and flattery they labour to obtain. And verily it is naturally given to all men to esteem their own inventions best. So both the raven and the ape think their own young ones fairest.* Then if a man in such a company, where some disdain and have despite at other men's inventions, and some count their own best; if among such men, I say, a man should bring forth anything that he hath read done in times past or that he hath seen done in other places, there the hearers fare as though the whole existimation of their wisdom were in jeopardy to be overthrown, and that ever after they should be counted for very dizzards, unless they could in other men's inventions pick out matter to reprehend and find fault at. If all other poor *Trip takers.** helps fail, then this is their extreme refuge: "These things", say they, "pleased our forefathers and ancestors; would God we could be so wise as they were." And, as though they had wittily concluded the matter, and with this answer stopped every man's mouth, they sit down again. As who should say it were a very dangerous matter if a man in any point should be found wiser than his forefathers were. And yet be we content to suffer the best and wittiest of their decrees to lie unexecuted: but if in anything a better order might have been taken than by them was, there we take fast hold, finding therein many faults. Many times have I chanced upon such proud, lewd, over- *Partial* thwart, and wayward judgements, yea, and once in England.' *judgements.*

'I pray you, sir,' quoth I, 'have you been in our country?'

'Yea forsooth,' quoth he, 'and there I tarried for the space of four or five months together, not long after the insurrection that the western Englishmen made against their king, which by their own miserable and pitiful slaughter was suppressed and ended.* In the mean season I was much bound and beholden to the right reverend father, John Morton,

Archbishop and Cardinal of Canterbury, and at that time also Lord Chancellor of England: a man, Master Peter (for Master More knoweth already that I will say),* not more honourable for his authority than for his prudence and virtue. He was of a mean stature, and though stricken in age, yet bare he his body upright. In his face did shine such an amiable reverence as was pleasant to behold. Gentle in communication, yet earnest, and sage, he had great delight many times with rough speech to his suitors, to prove, but without harm, what prompt wit and what bold spirit were in every man. In the which, as in a virtue much agreeing with his nature, so that therewith were not joined impudency, he took great delectation.* And the same person, as apt and meet to have an administration in the weal-public, he did lovingly embrace. In his speech he was fine, eloquent, and pithy. In the law he had profound knowledge, in wit he was incomparable, and in memory wonderful excellent. These qualities, which in him were by nature singular, he by learning and use had made perfect. The King put much trust in his counsel, the weal-public also, in a manner, leaned unto him when I was there. For even in the chief of his youth he was taken from school into the court, and there passed all his time in much trouble and business, being continually tumbled and tossed in the waves of divers misfortunes and adversities. And so by many and great dangers he learned the experience of the world, which so being learned cannot easily be forgotten.

'It chanced on a certain day, when I sat at his table, there was also a certain layman cunning in the laws of your realm. Who, I cannot tell whereof taking occasion, began diligently and earnestly to praise that strait and rigorous justice which at that time was there executed upon felons, who, as he said, were for the most part twenty hanged together upon one gallows.* And, seeing so few escaped punishment, he said he could not choose but greatly wonder and marvel, how and by what evil luck it should so come to pass that thieves, nevertheless, were in every place so rife and so rank. "Nay, sir," quoth I (for I durst boldly speak my mind before the Cardinal), "marvel nothing hereat: for this punishment of thieves passeth the limits of justice, and is also very hurtful to the weal-public. For it is too extreme and cruel a punishment for theft, and yet not sufficient to refrain and withhold men from theft. For simple theft* is not so great an offence that it ought to be punished with death. Neither there is any punishment so horrible that it can keep them from stealing which have no other craft whereby to get their living. Therefore in this point not you only, but also the most part of the world, be like evil schoolmasters, which be readier to beat than to teach their scholars. For great and horrible punishments be appointed for thieves. Whereas much rather provision should have been made, that there were some means whereby they might get their living, so that no man should be driven to this extreme necessity, first to steal and then to die." "Yes," quoth he, "this matter is well enough provided for already. There be handicrafts, there is husbandry to get their living by, if they would not willingly be nought." "Nay," quoth I, "you shall not scape so: for, first of all, I will speak nothing of them that come home out of the wars maimed and lame, as not long ago out of Blackheath field, and a little before that out of the wars in France:* such, I say, as put their lives in jeopardy for the weal-public's or the king's sake, and by reason of weakness and lameness be not able to occupy their old crafts, and be too aged to learn new: of them I will speak nothing, forasmuch as wars have their ordinary recourse. But let us consider those things that chance daily before our eyes.

Of laws not made according to equity.

By what means there might be fewer thieves and robbers.

'"First, there is a great number of gentlemen which cannot be content to live idle themselves (like dors), of that which others have laboured for: their tenants, I mean, whom they poll and shave to the quick by raising their rents* (for this only point of frugality do they use, men else, through their lavish and prodigal spending, able to bring themselves to very beggary); these gentlemen, I say, do not only live in idleness themselves, but also carry about with them at their tails a great flock or train of idle and loitering serving men,* which never learned any craft whereby to get their livings. These men, as soon as their master is dead, or be sick themselves, be incontinent thrust out of doors. For gentlemen had rather keep idle persons than sick men, and many times the dead man's heir is not able to maintain so great a house and keep so many serving

Idleness the mother of thieves.

Landlords by the way checked for rent-raising.

Of idle serving men come thieves.

men as his father did. Then in the mean season they that be thus destitute of service either starve for hunger or manfully play the thieves. For what would you have them to do? When they have wandered abroad so long until they have worn threadbare their apparel and also appaired their health, then gentlemen, because of their pale and sickly faces and patched coats, will not take them into service. And husbandmen dare not set them a-work; knowing well enough that he is nothing meet to do true and faithful service to a poor man with a spade and a mattock for small wages and hard fare, which, being daintily and tenderly pampered up in idleness and pleasure, was wont with a sword and a buckler by his side to jet through the street with a bragging look and to think himself too good to be any man's mate."

'"Nay, by Saint Mary, Sir," quoth the lawyer, "not so. For this kind of men must we make most of. For in them, as men of stouter stomachs, bolder spirits, and manlier courages than handicraftsmen and ploughmen be, doth consist the whole power, strength, and puissance of our army when we must fight in battle."

'"Forsooth, sir, as well you might say", quoth I, "that for war's sake you must cherish thieves. For surely you shall never lack thieves while you have them. No, nor thieves be not the most false and faint-hearted soldiers, nor soldiers be not the cowardliest thieves: so well these two crafts agree together. But this fault, though it be much used among you, yet is it not peculiar to you only, but common also almost to all nations. Yet France besides this is troubled and infected with a much sorer plague.* The whole realm is filled and besieged with hired soldiers in peace time (if that be peace). Which be brought in under the same colour and pretence that hath persuaded you to keep these idle serving men. For these wise fools and very archdolts thought the wealth of the whole country herein to consist, if there were ever in a readiness a strong and sure garrison, specially of old practised soldiers, for they put no trust at all in men unexercised. And therefore they must be forced to seek for war, to the end they may ever have practised soldiers and cunning manslayers, lest that (as it is prettily said

Between soldiers and thieves small diversity.

of Sallust*) their hands and their minds, through idleness or lack of exercise, should wax dull. But how pernicious and pestilent a thing it is to maintain such beasts the Frenchmen by their own harms have learned, and the examples of the Romans, Carthaginians, Syrians, and of many other countries do manifestly declare.* For not only the empire but also the fields and cities of all these, by divers occasions have been overrunned and destroyed of their own armies beforehand had in a readiness.* Now how unnecessary a thing this is, hereby it may appear: that the French soldiers, which from their youth have been practised and inured in feats of arms, do not crack nor advance themselves to have very often got the upper hand and mastery of your new-made and unpractised soldiers.* But in this point I will not use many words, lest perchance I may seem to flatter you. No, nor those same handicraftsmen of yours in cities, nor yet the rude and uplandish ploughmen of the country, are not supposed to be greatly afraid of your gentlemen's idle serving men, unless it be such as be not of body or stature correspondent to their strength and courage, or else whose bold stomachs be discouraged through poverty. Thus you may see that it is not to be feared lest they should be effeminated, if they were brought up in good crafts and laboursome works whereby to get their livings, whose stout and sturdy bodies (for gentlemen vouchsafe to corrupt and spill none but picked and chosen men*) now, either by reason of rest and idleness be brought to weakness, or else by too easy and womanly exercises be made feeble and unable to endure hardness. Truly, howsoever the case standeth, this, me thinketh, is nothing available to the weal-public, for war sake, which you never have but when you will yourselves, to keep and maintain an innumerable flock of that sort of men, that be so troublesome and noyous in peace, whereof you ought to have a thousand times more regard, than of war. But yet this is not only the necessary cause of stealing. There is another, which, as I suppose, is proper and peculiar to you Englishmen alone."

' "What is that?" quoth the Cardinal.

' "Forsooth, my lord," quoth I, "your sheep that were wont

What inconvenience cometh by continual garrisons of soldiers.

to be so meek and tame and so small eaters, now, as I hear say,
be become so great devourers and so wild, that they eat up and
swallow down the very men themselves.* They consume, destroy, and devour whole fields, houses, and cities. For look in
what parts of the realm doth grow the finest and therefore
dearest wool, there noblemen and gentlemen, yea and certain
abbots, holy men no doubt,* not contenting themselves with the
yearly revenues and profits that were wont to grow to their
forefathers and predecessors of their lands, nor being content
that they live in rest and pleasure, nothing profiting, yea, much
annoying the weal-public, leave no ground for tillage: they
enclose all into pastures; they throw down houses; they
pluck down towns, and leave nothing standing but only the
church to be made a sheep-house. And as though you lost
no small quantity of ground by forests, chases, lands, and

parks, those good holy men turn all dwelling places and all
glebeland into desolation and wilderness. Therefore that one
covetous and insatiable cormorant* and very plague of its
native country may compass about and enclose many thousand acres of ground together within one pale or hedge, the
husbandmen be thrust out of their own, or else either by
covin and fraud or by violent oppression they be put besides
it, or by wrongs and injuries they be so wearied, that they
be compelled to sell all. By one means, therefore, or by
other, either by hook or crook, they must needs depart away,
poor, silly, wretched souls, men, women, husbands, wives,
fatherless children, widows, woeful mothers, with their
young babes, and their whole household small in substance
and much in number, as husbandry requireth many hands.
Away they trudge, I say, out of their known and accustomed
houses, finding no place to rest in. All their household stuff,
which is very little worth though it might well abide the

*The decay of
husbandry
causeth
beggary,
which is the
mother of
vagabonds
and thieves.*

sale,* yet being suddenly thrust out they be constrained to
sell it for a thing of nought. And when they have wandered
abroad till that be spent, what can they then else do but
steal, and then justly pardy be hanged, or else go about
a-begging? And yet then also they be cast in prison as vagabonds,* because they go about and work not, whom no man will

set a-work, though they never so willingly proffer themselves thereto.

'"For one shepherd or herdman is enough to eat up that ground with cattle, to the occupying whereof about husbandry many hands were requisite. And this is also the cause why victuals be now in many places dearer. Yea, besides this the price of wool is so risen, that poor folks, which were wont to work it and make cloth thereof, be now able to buy none at all. And by this means very many be forced to forsake work and to give themselves to idleness. For after that so much ground was enclosed for pasture an infinite multitude of sheep died of the rot, such vengeance God took of their inordinate and insatiable covetousness, sending among the sheep that pestiferous murrain, which much more justly should have fallen on the sheepmasters' own heads. And though the number of sheep increase never so fast, yet the price falleth not one mite, because there be so few sellers. For they be almost all come into a few rich men's hands, whom no need forceth to sell before they lust, and they lust not before they may sell as dear as they lust.

'"Now the same cause bringeth in like dearth of the other kinds of cattle, yea, and that so much the more because that after farms plucked down and husbandry decayed there is no man that passeth for the breeding of young store.* For these rich men bring not up the young ones of great cattle as they do lambs. But first they buy them abroad very cheap, and afterward, when they be fatted in their pastures, they sell them again exceeding dear. And therefore (as I suppose) the whole incommodity hereof is not yet felt. For yet they make dearth only in those places where they sell. But when they shall fetch them away from thence where they be bred faster than they can be brought up,* then shall there also be felt great dearth, store beginning there to fail where the ware is bought. Thus the unreasonable covetousness of a few hath turned that thing to the utter undoing of your island, in the which thing the chief felicity of your realm did consist. For this great dearth of victuals causeth men to keep as little houses and as small hospitality as they possibly may, and to put away their servants;

The cause of dearth of victuals.

What inconvenience cometh of dearth of wool.

The cause of dearth of wool.

Dearth of cattle with the cause thereof.

Dearth of victuals is the decay of housekeeping, whereof ensueth beggary and theft.

whither, I pray you, but a-begging, or else (which these gentle bloods and stout stomachs will sooner set their minds unto) a-stealing?

'"Now to amend the matter, to this wretched beggary and miserable poverty is joined great wantonness, importunate superfluity, and excessive riot. For not only gentlemen's servants, but also handicraftsmen, yea, and almost the ploughmen of the country, with all other sorts of people, use much strange and proud newfangledness in their apparel, and too much prodigal riot and sumptuous fare at their table. Now bawds, queans, whores, harlots, strumpets, brothel-houses, stews; and yet another stews, wine-taverns, ale-houses, and tippling houses, with so many naughty, lewd, and unlawful games,* as dice, cards, tables, tennis, bowls, quoits, do not all these send the haunters of them straight a-stealing, when their money is gone? Cast out these pernicious abominations; make a law that they which plucked down farms and towns of husbandry shall re-edify them, or else yield and uprender the possession thereof to such as will go to the cost of building them anew. Suffer not these rich men to buy up all, to engross and forestall,* and with their monopoly to keep the market alone as please them. Let not so many be brought up in idleness; let husbandry and tillage be restored; let clothworking be renewed, that there may be honest labours for this idle sort to pass their time in profitably, which hitherto either poverty hath caused to be thieves, or else now be either vagabonds or idle serving men, and shortly will be thieves.

'"Doubtless, unless you find a remedy for these enormities, you shall in vain advance yourselves of executing justice upon felons.* For this justice is more beautiful in appearance, and more flourishing to the show than either just or profitable. For by suffering your youth wantonly and viciously to be brought up, and to be infected, even from their tender age, by little and little with vice, then, a God's name, to be punished when they commit the same faults after being come to man's state, which from their youth they were ever like to do; in this point, I pray you, what other thing do you than make thieves and then punish them?"

Excess in apparel and diet a maintainer of beggary and theft.

Bawds, whores, wine taverns, alehouses, and unlawful games be the very mother of thieves.

Rich men engrossers and forestallers.

The corrupt education of youth a mother of thievery.

'Now as I was thus speaking, the lawyer began to make himself ready to answer, and was determined with himself to use the common fashion and trade of disputers, which be more diligent in rehearsing than answering, as thinking the memory worthy of the chief praise. "Indeed, sir," quoth he, "you have said well, being but a stranger and one that might rather hear something of these matters, than have any exact or perfect knowledge of the same, as I will incontinent by open proof make manifest and plain. For first I will rehearse in order all that you have said; then I will declare wherein you be deceived through lack of knowledge in all our fashions, manners, and customs; and last of all I will answer your arguments, and confute them every one. First therefore I will begin where I promised. Four things you seemed to me—"

'"Hold your peace," quoth the Cardinal,* "for it appeareth that you will make no short answer, which make such a beginning. Wherefore at this time you shall not take the pains to make your answer, but keep it to your next meeting, which I would be right glad that it might be even to-morrow next, unless either you or Master Raphael have any earnest let. But now, Master Raphael, I would very gladly hear of you, why you think theft not worthy to be punished with death, or what other punishment you can devise more expedient to the weal-public. For I am sure you are not of that mind, that you would have theft escape unpunished. For if now the extreme punishment of death cannot cause them to leave stealing, then, if ruffians and robbers should be sure of their lives, what violence, what fear, were able to hold their hands from robbing which would take the mitigation of the punishment as a very provocation to the mischief?"*

He is worthily put to silence that is too full of words.

'"Surely, my lord," quoth I, "I think it not right nor justice that the loss of money should cause the loss of man's life. For mine opinion is, that all the goods in the world are not able to countervail man's life. But if they would thus say, that the breaking of justice and the transgression of the laws is recompensed with this punishment, and not the loss of the money, then why may not this extreme and rigorous justice well be called plain injury? For so cruel governance, so strait rules and

That theft ought not to be punished by death.

25

Strait laws not allowable.

unmerciful laws be not allowable, that if a small offence be committed, by and by the sword should be drawn. Nor so Stoical ordinances are to be borne withal, as to count all offenses of such equality, that the killing of a man or the taking of his money from him were both a matter, and the one no more heinous offence than the other: between the which two, if we have any respect to equity, no similitude or equality consisteth. God commandeth us that we shall not kill. And be we

That man's law ought not to be prejudicial to God's law.

then so hasty to kill a man for taking a little money? And if any man would understand killing by this commandment of God to be forbidden after no larger wise than man's constitutions define killing to be lawful,* then why may it not likewise by man's constitutions be determined after what sort* whoredom, fornication, and perjury may be lawful? For whereas, by the permission of God, no man hath power to kill neither himself nor yet any other man, then, if a law made by the consent of men concerning slaughter of men ought to be of such strength, force, and virtue, that they which contrary to the commandment of God have killed those whom this constitution of man commanded to be killed, be clean quit and exempt out of the bonds and danger of God's commandment, shall it not then, by this reason follow that the power of God's commandment shall extend no further than man's law doth define and permit? And so shall it come to pass, that in like manner man's constitutions in all things shall determine how far the observation of all God's commandments shall extend. To be

Theft in the old law not punished by death.

short, Moses's law, though it were ungentle and sharp (as a law that was given to bondmen, yea, and them very obstinate, stubborn, and stiff-necked), yet it punished theft by the purse, and not with death. And let us not think that God in the new law of clemency and mercy,* under the which he ruleth us with fatherly gentleness, as his dear children, hath given us greater scope and licence to the execution of cruelty one upon another.

'"Now ye have heard the reasons whereby I am persuaded that this punishment is unlawful. Furthermore, I think there is nobody that knoweth not how unreasonable, yea, how pernicious a thing it is to the weal-public that a thief and an

homicide or murderer should suffer equal and like punishment. For the thief seeing that man that is condemned for
theft in no less jeopardy nor judged to no less punishment than
him that is convict of manslaughter, through this cogitation
only he is strongly and forcibly provoked, and in a manner
constrained to kill him, whom else he would have but robbed.
For the murder being once done, he is in less fear and in more
hope that the deed shall not be bewrayed or known, seeing the
party is now dead and rid out of the way, which only might
have uttered and disclosed it. But if he chance to be taken and
descried, yet he is in no more danger and jeopardy than if he
had committed but single felony. Therefore while we go about
with such cruelty to make thieves afraid, we provoke them to
kill good men.

*What
inconvenience
ensueth of
punishing
theft with
death.*

*Punishment
of theft by
death causeth
the thief to be
a murderer.*

'"Now as touching this question, what punishment were
more commodious and better, that truly in my judgement is
easier to be found than what punishment might be worse. For
why should we doubt that to be a good and a profitable way for
the punishment of offenders, which we know did in times past
so long please the Romans,* men in the administration of a
weal-public most expert, politic, and cunning? Such as among
them were convict of great and heinous trespasses, them they
condemned into stone quarries, and into mines to dig metal,
there to be kept in chains all the days of their life. But as
concerning this matter, I allow the ordinance of no nation so
well as that which I saw, while I travelled abroad about the
world, used in Persia among the people that commonly be
called the Polylerites.* Whose land is both large and ample and
also well and wittily governed, and the people in all conditions
free and ruled by their own laws, saving that they pay a yearly
tribute to the great king of Persia. But because they be far from
the sea, compassed and enclosed almost round about with high
mountains, and do content themselves with the fruits of their
own land, which is of itself very fertile and fruitful, for this
cause neither they go to other countries, nor other come to
them. And according to the old custom of the land they desire
not to enlarge the bounds of their dominions; and those that
they have by reason of the high hills be easily defended, and

*What lawful
punishment
may be
devised for
theft.*

*How the
Romans
punished
theft.*

*A worthy and
commendable
punishment of
thieves in the
weal-public
of the
Polylerites in
Persia.*

the tribute which they pay to their chief lord and king setteth them quit and free from warfare. Thus their life is commodious rather than gallant, and may better be called happy or wealthy than notable or famous. For they be not known as much as by name, I suppose, saving only to their next neighbours and borderers.

'"They that in this land be attainted and convict of felony, make restitution of that which they stole to the right owner, and not (as they do in other lands) to the king, whom they think to have no more right to the thief-stolen thing than the thief himself hath. But if the thing be lost or made away, then the value of it is paid of the goods of such offenders, which else remaineth all whole to their wives and children.* And they themselves be condemned to be common labourers; and, unless the theft be very heinous, they be neither locked in prison nor fettered in gyves, but be untied and go at large, labouring in the common works. They that refuse labour, or go slowly and slackly to their work, be not only tied in chains, but also pricked forward with stripes.* But being diligent about their work they live without check or rebuke. Every night they be called in by name, and be locked in their chambers. Beside their daily labour, their life is nothing hard or incommodious. Their fare is indifferent good, borne at the charges of the weal-public, because they be common servants to the commonwealth. But their charges in all places of the land is not borne alike. For in some parts that which is bestowed upon them is gathered of alms. And though that way be uncertain, yet the people be so full of mercy and pity, that none is found more profitable or plentiful. In some places certain lands be appointed hereunto, of the revenues whereof they be maintained. And in some places every man giveth a certain tribute for the same use and purpose. Again, in some parts of the land these serving men (for so be these damned persons called) do no common work, but as every private man needeth labourers, so he cometh into the market-place and there hireth some of them for meat and drink and a certain limited wages by the day, somewhat cheaper than he should hire a free man. It is also lawful for them to chastise the sloth of these serving men with stripes.

A privy nip for them that be otherwise.

Thieves condemned to become labourers.

Serving men.

28

' "By this means they never lack work, and besides the gaining of their meat and drink, every one of them bringeth daily something into the common treasury. All and every one of them be apparelled in one colour. Their heads be not polled or shaven, but rounded a little above the ears. And the tip of the one ear is cut off. Every one of them may take meat and drink of their friends, and also a coat of their own colour;* but to receive money is death, as well to the giver as to the receiver. And no less jeopardy it is for a free man to receive money of a serving man for any manner of cause, and likewise for serving men to touch weapons. The serving men of every several shire be distinct and known from other by their several and distinct badges which to cast away is death, as it is also to be seen out of the precinct of their own shire, or to talk with a serving man of another shire. And it is no less danger to them for to intend to run away than to do it indeed. Yea, and to conceal such an enterprise in a serving man it is death, in a free man servitude. Of the contrary part, to him that openeth and uttereth such counsels, be decreed large gifts:* to a free man a great sum of money; to a serving man freedom; and to them both forgiveness and pardon of that they were of counsel in that pretence. So that it can never be so good for them to go forward in their evil purpose as, by repentance, to turn back.

An evil intent esteemed as the deed.

' "This is the law and order in this behalf, as I have showed you. Wherein what humanity is used, how far it is from cruelty, and how commodious it is, you do plainly perceive, forasmuch as the end of their wrath and punishment intendeth nothing else but the destruction of vices and saving of men, with so using and ordering them that they cannot choose but be good, and what harm soever they did before, in the residue of their life to make amends for the same.* Moreover it is so little feared that they should turn again to their vicious conditions, that wayfaring men will for their safeguard choose them to their guides before any other, in every shire changing and taking new. For if they would commit robbery, they have nothing about them meet for that purpose. They may touch no weapons; money found about them should betray the robbery. They should be no sooner taken with the manner,* but

The right end and intent of punishment.

forthwith they should be punished. Neither they can have any hope at all to scape away by fleeing. For how should a man that in no part of his apparel is like other men fly privily and unknown, unless he would run away naked? Howbeit, so also fleeing he should be descried by the rounding of his head and his ear mark. But it is a thing to be doubted that they will lay their heads together and conspire against the weal-public. No, no, I warrant you. For the serving men of one shire alone could never hope to bring to pass such an enterprise without soliciting, enticing, and alluring the serving men of many other shires to take their parts. Which thing is to them so impossible, that they may not as much as speak or talk together or salute one another. No, it is not to be thought that they would make their own countrymen and companions of their counsel in such a matter, which they know well should be jeopardy to the concealer thereof and great commodity and goodness to the opener and detector of the same. Whereas, on the other part, there is none of them all hopeless or in despair to recover again his former state of freedom, by humble obedience, by patient suffering, and by giving good tokens and likelihood of himself, that he will ever after that live like a true and an honest man.* For every year divers of them be restored to their freedom through the commendation of their patience."

'When I had thus spoken, saying moreover that I could see no cause why this order might not be had in England with much more profit than the justice which the lawyer so highly praised: "Nay," quoth the lawyer, "this could never be so stablished in England but that it must needs bring the weal-public into great jeopardy and hazard." And, as he was thus saying, he shaked his head and made a wry mouth, and so he held his peace. And all that were there present with one assent agreed to his saying.

' "Well," quoth the Cardinal, "yet it were hard to judge without a proof whether this order would do well here or no. But when the sentence of death is given, if then the king should command execution to be deferred and spared, and would prove this order and fashion, taking away the privileges of all sanctuaries,* if then the proof should declare the thing to

be good and profitable, then it were well done that it were
stablished; else the condemned and reprieved persons may as
well and as justly be put to death after this proof as when they
were first cast. Neither any jeopardy can in the mean space
grow hereof. Yea, and methinketh that these vagabonds may *Vagabonds.*
very well be ordered after the same fashion, against whom we
have hitherto made so many laws and so little prevailed."
When the Cardinal had thus said, then every man gave great
praise to my sayings, which a little before they had disallowed.
But most of all was esteemed that which was spoken of *The wavering*
vagabonds, because it was the Cardinal's own addition. *judgement of*
flatterers.

'I cannot tell whether it were best to rehearse the communication that followed, for it was not very sad. But yet you shall
hear it, for there was no evil in it, and partly it pertained to the
matter before said. There chanced to stand by a certain jesting
parasite or scoffer, which would seem to resemble and counterfeit the fool.* But he did in such wise counterfeit, that he was
almost the very same indeed that he laboured to represent: he
so studied with words and sayings brought forth so out of time
and place to make sport and move laughter, that he himself was
oftener laughed at than his jests were. Yet the foolish fellow
brought out now and then such indifferent and reasonable
stuff, that he made the proverb true, which saith, "he that
shooteth oft, at the last shall hit the mark".* So that when one
of the company said that through my communication a good
order was found for thieves, and that the Cardinal also had well
provided for vagabonds, so that only remained some good provision to be made for them that through sickness and age were *Sick, aged,*
fallen into poverty and were become so impotent and unwieldy *and impotent*
that they were not able to work for their living: "Tush," quoth *persons and*
he, "let me alone with them; you shall see me do well enough *beggars.*
with them. For I had rather than any good* that this kind of
people were driven somewhere out of my sight, they have so
sore troubled me many times and oft, when they have with
their lamentable tears begged money of me: and yet they could
never to my mind so tune their song that thereby they ever got
of me one farthing. For evermore the one of these two
chanced: either that I would not, or else that I could not

31

because I had it not. Therefore now they be waxed wise; for when they see me go by, because they will not lose their labour, they let me pass and say not one word to me. So they look for nothing of me, no, in good sooth, no more than if I were a priest or a monk. But I will make a law, that all these beggars shall be distributed and bestowed into houses of religion.* The men shall be made lay brethren,* as they call them, and the women nuns."

A common proverb among beggars.

'Hereat the Cardinal smiled, and allowed it in jest, yea, and all the residue in good earnest. But a certain friar, graduate in divinity, took such pleasure and delight in this jest of priests and monks, that he also being else a man of grisly and stern gravity, began merrily and wantonly to jest and taunt. "Nay," quoth he, "you shall not so be rid and dispatched of beggars unless you make some provision also for us friars."* "Why," quoth the jester, "that is done already, for my lord himself set a very good order for you when he decreed that vagabonds should be kept strait, and set to work; for you be the greatest and veriest vagabonds that be."

A merry talk between a friar and a fool.

'This jest also, when they saw the Cardinal not disprove it, every man took it gladly, saving only the friar. For he (and that no marvel) being thus touched on the quick, and hit on the gall, so fret, so fumed, and chafed at it, and was in such a rage, that he could not refrain himself from chiding, scolding, railing, and reviling. He called the fellow ribald, villain, javel, backbiter, slanderer, and the child of perdition, citing therewith terrible threatenings out of holy scripture. Then the jesting scoffer began to play the scoffer indeed, and verily he was good at that, for he could play a part in that play, no man better. "Patient yourself, good master friar," quoth he, "and be not angry, for scripture saith: 'In your patience you shall save your souls.'"* Then the friar (for I will rehearse his own very words): "No, gallows wretch, I am not angry," quoth he, "or at the least wise I do not sin; for the Psalmist saith, 'Be you angry, and sin not'."*

Talk qualified according to the person that speaketh.

'Then the Cardinal spake gently to the friar, and desired him to quiet himself. "No, my lord," quoth he, "I speak not but of a good zeal as I ought, for holy men had a good zeal.

Wherefore it is said: 'The zeal of thy house hath eaten me.'* And it is sung in the church, 'The scorners of Elisha, while he went up into the house of God, felt the zeal of the bald',* as peradventure this scorning villain ribald shall feel." "You do it", quoth the Cardinal, "perchance of a good mind and affection; but methinketh you should do, I cannot tell whether more holily, certes more wisely, if you would not set your wit to a fool's wit, and with a fool take in hand a foolish contention." "No, forsooth, my lord," quoth he, "I should not do more wisely. For Solomon the wise saith, 'answer a fool according to his folly', like as I do now, and do show him the pit that he shall fall into if he take not heed. For if many scorners of Elisha, which was but one bald man, felt the zeal of the bald, how much more shall one scorner of many friars feel, among whom be many bald men?* And we have also the Pope's bulls, whereby all that mock and scorn us be excommunicate, suspended, and accursed." The Cardinal, seeing that none end would be made, sent away the jester by a privy beck, and turned the communication to another matter. Shortly after, when he was risen from the table, he went to hear his suitors,* and so dismissed us.

'Look, Master More, with how long and tedious a tale I have kept you, which surely I would have been ashamed to have done, but that you so earnestly desired me, and did after such a sort give ear unto it as though you would not that any parcel of that communication should be left out. Which though I have done somewhat briefly, yet could I not choose but rehearse it for the judgement of them which, when they had disproved and disallowed my sayings, yet incontinent, hearing the Cardinal allow them, did themselves also approve the same, so impudently flattering him, that they were nothing ashamed to admit, yea, almost in good earnest, his jester's foolish inventions, because that he himself by smiling at them did seem not to disprove them. So that hereby you may right well perceive how little the courtiers would regard and esteem me and my sayings.'

'I ensure you, Master Raphael,' quoth I, 'I took great delectation in hearing you; all things that you said were spoken so wittily and so pleasantly. And methought myself to be in the meantime not only at home in my country, but also through the pleasant remembrance of the Cardinal, in whose house I was brought up of a child, to wax a child again. And, friend Raphael, though I did bear very great love towards you before, yet seeing you do so earnestly favour this man, you will not believe how much my love towards you is now increased. But yet, all this notwithstanding, I can by no means change my mind, but that I must needs believe that you, if you be disposed and can find in your heart to follow some prince's court, shall with your good counsels greatly help and further the commonwealth. Wherefore there is nothing more appertaining to your duty, that is to say to the duty of a good man. For whereas your Plato judgeth that weal-publics shall by this means attain perfect felicity, either if philosophers be kings, or else if kings give themselves to the study of philosophy,* how far, I pray you, shall commonwealths then be from this felicity, if philosophers will vouchsafe to instruct kings with their good counsel?'

'They be not so unkind,' quoth he, 'but they would gladly do it, yea, many have done it already in books that they have put forth, if kings and princes would be willing and ready to follow good counsel. But Plato doubtless did well foresee, unless kings themselves would apply their minds to the study of philosophy, that else they would never thoroughly allow the counsel of philosophers, being themselves before, even from their tender age, infected and corrupt with perverse and evil opinions. Which thing Plato himself proved true in King Dionysius.* If I should propose to any king wholesome decrees, doing my endeavour to pluck out of his mind the pernicious original causes of vice and naughtiness, think you not that I should forthwith either be driven away or else made a laughing-stock? Well, suppose I were with the French king,* and there sitting in his council while in that most secret consultation, the king himself there being present in his own person, they beat their brains, and search the very bottoms of their wits to discuss by what craft and means the king may still keep Milan and draw to him again fugitive Naples; and then how to conquer the Venetians, and how to bring under his jurisdiction all Italy; then how to win the dominion of

The French men privily be counselled from the desire of Italy.

34

Flanders, Brabant, and of all Burgundy, with divers other
lands whose kingdoms he hath long ago in mind and purpose
invaded. Here while one counselleth to conclude a league of
peace with the Venetians, so long to endure as shall be thought
meet and expedient for their purpose, and to make them also
of their counsel, yea, and besides that to give them part of the
prey which afterward, when they have brought their purpose
about after their own minds, they may require and claim again,
another thinketh best to hire the Germans. Another would   *Lance knights.**
have the favour of the Switzers won with money. Another's
advice is to appease the puissant power of the Emperor's majesty with gold as with a most pleasant and acceptable sacrifice.
While another giveth counsel to make peace with the King of
Aragon, and to restore unto him his own kingdom of Navarre
as a full assurance of peace. Another cometh in with his five
eggs,* and adviseth to hook in the King of Castile with some
hope of affinity or alliance,* and to bring to their part certain
peers of his court for great pensions. While they all stay at the
chiefest doubt of all, what to do in the mean time with England; and yet agree all in this to make peace with the Englishmen, and with most sure and strong bonds to bind that weak
and feeble friendship, so that they must be called friends, and
had in suspicion as enemies. And that therefore the Scots must
be had in a readiness,* as it were in a standing, ready at all
occasions, in aunters the Englishmen should stir never so little,
incontinent to set upon them. And moreover privily and
secretly (for openly it may not be done by the truce that is
taken), privily, therefore, I say, to make much of some peer of
England that is banished his country,* which must claim title
to the crown of the realm, and affirm himself just inheritor
thereof, that by this subtle means they may hold to them the
king, in whom else they have but small trust and affiance.
Here, I say, where so great and high matters be in consultation,
where so many noble and wise men counsel their king only to
war, here if I, silly man, should rise up and will them to turn
over the leaf, and learn a new lesson, saying that my counsel is
not to meddle with Italy, but to tarry still at home, and that the
kingdom of France alone is almost greater than that it may well

be governed of one man, so that the king should not need to study how to get more; and then should propose unto them the decrees of the people that be called the Achorians,* which be situate over against the island of Utopia on the south-east side.

A notable example, and worthy to be followed.

'These Achorians once made war in their king's quarrel for to get him another kingdom which he laid claim unto and advanced himself right inheritor to the crown thereof by the title of an old alliance. At the last, when they had got it, and saw that they had even as much vexation and trouble in keeping it as they had in getting it, and that either their new conquered subjects by sundry occasions were making daily insurrections to rebel against them, or else that other countries were continually with divers inroads and foragings invading them, so that they were ever fighting either for them or against them, and never could break up their camps: seeing themselves in the mean season pilled and impoverished, their money carried out of the realm, their own men killed to maintain the glory of another nation; when they had no war, peace nothing better than war, by reason that their people in war had so inured themselves to corrupt and wicked manners, that they had taken a delight and pleasure in robbing and stealing; that through manslaughter they had gathered boldness to mischief; that their laws were had in contempt, and nothing set by or regarded; that their king, being troubled with the charge and governance of two kingdoms, could not nor was not able perfectly to discharge his office towards them both: seeing again, that all these evils and troubles were endless, at the last laid their heads together, and like faithful and loving subjects gave to their king free choice and liberty to keep still the one of these two kingdoms, whether he would, alleging that he was not able to keep both, and that they were more than might well be governed of half a king, forasmuch as no man would be content to take him for his muleteer that keepeth another man's mules besides his. So this good prince was constrained to be content with his old kingdom and to give over the new to one of his friends. Who shortly after was violently driven out.

'Furthermore if I should declare unto them that all this busy preparance to war, whereby so many nations for his sake should be brought into a troublesome hurly-burly, when all his coffers were emptied, his treasures wasted, and his people destroyed, should at the length through some mischance be in vain and to none effect, and that therefore it were best for him to content himself with his own kingdom of France, as his forefathers and predecessors did before him: to make much of it, to enrich it, and to make it as flourishing as he could, to endeavour himself to love his subjects, and again to be beloved of them, willingly to live with them, peaceably to govern them, and with other kingdoms not to meddle, seeing that which he hath already is even enough for him, yea, and more than he can well turn him to: this mine advice, Master More, how think you it would be heard and taken?'

'So God help me, not very thankfully,' quoth I.

'Well, let us proceed then,' quoth he. 'Suppose that some king and his council were together whetting their wits and devising what subtle craft they might invent to enrich the king with great treasures of money. First one counselleth to raise and enhance the valuation of money when the king must pay any; and again to call down the value of coin to less than it is worth, when he must receive or gather any.* For thus great sums shall be paid with a little money, and where little is due much shall be received. Another counselleth to feign war,* that when under this colour and pretence the king hath gathered great abundance of money, he may, when it shall please him, make peace with great solemnity and holy ceremonies, to blind the eyes of the poor community as taking pity and compassion forsooth upon man's blood, like a loving and a merciful prince. Another putteth the king in remembrance of certain old and moth-eaten laws* that of long time have not been put in execution, which because no man can remember that they were made, every man hath transgressed. The fines of these laws he counselleth the king to require, for there is no way so profitable, nor more honourable as the which hath a show and colour of justice. Another adviseth him to forbid many things under great penalties and fines, specially such things as is for the people's profit not be used, and afterward to dispense for money with them, which by this prohibition sustain loss and

Enhancing and imbasing of coins.

Counterfeit wars.

The renewing of old laws.

Distraints.

damage.* For by this means the favour of the people is won, and profit riseth two ways. First by taking forfeits of them whom covetousness of gains hath brought in danger of this statute, and also by selling privileges and licences,* which the better that the prince is forsooth, the dearer he selleth them, as one that is loath to grant to any private person anything that is against the profit of his people. And therefore may sell none but at an exceeding dear price. Another giveth the king counsel to endanger unto his grace the judges of the realm, that he may have them ever on his side,* and that they may in every matter dispute and reason for the king's right. Yea, and further to call them into his palace and to require them there to argue and discuss his matters in his own presence. So there shall be no matter of his so openly wrong and unjust wherein one or other of them, either because he will have something to allege and object, or that he is ashamed to say that which is said already, or else to pick a thank with his prince, will not find some hole open to set a snare in, wherewith to take the contrary part in a trip.* Thus while the judges cannot agree amongst themselves, reasoning and arguing of that which is plain enough and bringing the manifest truth in doubt, in the mean season the king may take a fit occasion to understand the law as shall most make for his advantage, whereunto all other, for shame or for fear, will agree. Then the judges may be bold to pronounce on the king's side. For he that giveth sentence for the king cannot be without a good excuse. For it shall be sufficient for him to have equity on his part, or the bare words of the law, or a writhen and wrested understanding of the same, or else (which with good and just judges is of greater force than all laws be) the king's indisputable prerogative.*

'To conclude, all the counsellors agree and consent together with the rich Crassus,* that no abundance of gold can be sufficient for a prince which must keep and maintain an army. Furthermore that a king, though he would, can do nothing unjustly; for all that all men have, yea, also the men themselves, be all his. And that every man hath so much of his own as the king's gentleness hath not taken from him. And that it shall be most for the king's advantage that his subjects have

Selling of licences.

The saying of rich Crassus.

very little or nothing in their possession, as whose safeguard doth herein consist, that his people do not wax wanton and wealthy through riches and liberty, because where these things be, there men be not wont patiently to obey hard, unjust, and unlawful commandments. Whereas, on the other part, need and poverty doth hold down and keep under stout courages, and maketh them patient perforce, taking from them bold and rebelling stomachs.

'Here again, if I should rise up and boldly affirm that all these counsels be to the king dishonour and reproach, whose honour and safety is more and rather supported and upholden by the wealth and riches of his people than by his own treasures; and if I should declare that the commonalty chooseth their king for their own sake, and not for his sake, to the intent that through his labour and study they might all live wealthily safe from wrongs and injuries; and that therefore the king ought to take more care for the wealth of his people than for his own wealth, even as the office and duty of a shepherd is in that he is a shepherd: to feed his sheep rather than himself.*

'For as touching this, that they think the defence and maintenance of peace to consist in the poverty of the people, the thing itself showeth that they be far out of the way. For where shall a man find more wrangling, quarrelling, brawling, and chiding than among beggars? Who be more desirous of new mutations and alterations, than they that be not content with the present state of their life? Or, finally, who be bolder stomached to bring all in a hurlyburly (thereby trusting to get some windfall) than they that have now nothing to lose? And if any king were so smally regarded and so lightly esteemed, yea, so behated of his subjects, that other ways he could not keep them in awe, but only by open wrongs, by polling and shaving and by bringing them to beggary, surely it were better for him to forsake his kingdom than to hold it by this means, whereby though the name of a king be kept, yet the majesty is lost. For it is against the dignity of a king to have rule over beggars, but rather over rich and wealthy men. Of this mind was the hardy and courageous Fabricius* when he said that he had rather be a ruler of rich men than be rich himself. And, verily, one man to

Poverty the mother of debate and decay of realms.

A worthy saying of Fabricius.

live in pleasure and wealth while all others weep and smart for it, that is the part, not of a king, but of a jailer. To be short, as he is a foolish physician that cannot cure his patient's disease unless he cast him in another sickness, so he that cannot amend the lives of his subjects but by taking from them the wealth and commodity of life, he must needs grant that he knoweth not the feat how to govern men. But let him rather amend his own life, renounce unhonest pleasures, and forsake pride. For these be the chief vices that cause him to run in the contempt or hatred of his people. Let him live of his own, hurting no man. Let him do cost not above his power.* Let him restrain wickedness. Let him prevent vices, and take away the occasions of offences by well ordering his subjects, and not by suffering wickedness to increase, afterwards to be punished. Let him not be too hasty in calling again laws which a custom hath abrogated, specially such as have been long forgotten and never lacked nor needed. And let him never, under the cloak and pretence of transgression, take such fines and forfeits as no judge will suffer a private person to take as unjust and full of guile.

'Here if I should bring forth before them the law of the Macarians,* (which be not far distant from Utopia), whose king the day of his coronation is bound by a solemn oath that he shall never at any time have in his treasury above a thousand pound of gold or silver. They say a very good king, which took more care for the wealth and commodity of his country than for the enriching of himself, made this law to be a stop and a bar to kings from heaping and hoarding up so much money as might impoverish their people. For he foresaw that this sum of treasure would suffice to support the king in battle against his own people if they should chance to rebel, and also to maintain his wars against the invasions of his foreign enemies. Again, he perceived the same stock of money to be too little and insufficient to encourage and enable him wrongfully to take away other men's goods, which was the chief cause why the law was made. Another cause was this: he thought that by this provision his people should not lack money wherewith to maintain their daily occupying and chaffare. And seeing the king could

A strange and notable law of the Macarians.

not choose but lay out and bestow all that came in above the prescript sum of his stock, he thought he would seek no occasions to do his subjects injury. Such a king shall be feared of evil men and loved of good men. These, and such other informations, if I should use among men wholly inclined and given to the contrary part, how deaf hearers think you should I have?'

'Deaf hearers doubtless,' quoth I, 'and in good faith no marvel. And to be plain with you, truly I cannot allow that such communication shall be used, or such counsel given, as you be sure shall never be regarded nor received. For how can so strange information be profitable, or how can they be beaten into their heads, whose minds be already prevented with clean contrary persuasions? This school philosophy* is not unpleasant among friends in familiar communication, but in the councils of kings, where great matters be debated and reasoned with great authority, these things have no place.'

School philosophy in the consultations of princes hath no place.

'That is it which I meant,' quoth he, 'when I said philosophy had no place among kings.'

'Indeed,' quoth I, 'this school philosophy hath not, which thinketh all things meet for every place. But there is another philosophy more civil, which knoweth, as ye would say, her own stage, and thereafter, ordering and behaving herself in the play that she hath in hand, playeth her part accordingly with comeliness, uttering nothing out of due order and fashion. And this is the philosophy that you must use. Or else whiles a comedy of Plautus is playing, and the vile bondmen scoffing and trifling among themselves, if you should suddenly come upon the stage in a philosopher's apparel, and rehearse out of *Octavia* the place wherein Seneca disputeth with Nero,* had it not been better for you to have played the dumb person,* than, by rehearsing that which served neither for the time nor place, to have made such a tragical comedy or gallimaufry? For by bringing in other stuff that nothing appertaineth to the present matter, you must needs mar and pervert the play that is in hand, though the stuff that you bring be much better. What part soever you have taken upon you, play that as well as you can and make the best of it. And do not therefore disturb and

A fine and a fit similitude.

A dumb player.

bring out of order the whole matter because that another which is merrier and better cometh to your remembrance. So the case standeth in a commonwealth, and so it is in the consultations of kings and princes. If evil opinions and naughty persuasions cannot be utterly and quite plucked out of their hearts, if you cannot even as you would remedy vices which use and custom hath confirmed, yet for this cause you must not leave and forsake the commonwealth. You must not forsake the ship in a tempest because you cannot rule and keep down the winds. No, nor you must not labour to drive into their heads new and strange information which you know well shall be nothing regarded with them that be of clean contrary minds. But you must with a crafty wile and a subtle train study and endeavour yourself, as much as in you lieth, to handle the matter wittily and handsomely for the purpose; and that which you cannot turn to good, so to order it that it be not very bad. For it is not possible for all things to be well unless all men were good. Which I think will not be yet this good many years.'

'By this means,' quoth he, 'nothing else will be brought to pass, but whiles that I go about to remedy the madness of others I should be even as mad as they. For if I would speak such things that be true I must needs speak such things; but as for to speak false things, whether that be a philosopher's part or no I cannot tell, truly it is not my part. Howbeit, this communication of mine, though peradventure it may seem unpleasant to them, yet can I not see why it should seem strange or foolishly newfangled. If so be that I should speak *The Utopian* those things that Plato feigneth in his weal-public,* or that the *weal-public.* Utopians do in theirs, these things, though they were (as they be indeed) better, yet they might seem spoken out of place. Forasmuch as here amongst us, every man hath his possessions several to himself, and there all things be common. But what was in my communication contained that might not, and ought not, in any place to be spoken? Saving that to them which have thoroughly decreed and determined with themselves to run headlong the contrary way it cannot be acceptable and pleasant, because it calleth them back and showeth them the jeopardies.

'Verily, if all things that evil and vicious manners have caused to seem inconvenient and nought should be refused as things unmeet and reproachful, then we must among Christian people wink at the most part of all those things which Christ taught us and so straitly forbade them to be winked at, that those things also which he whispered in the ears of his disciples he commanded to be proclaimed in open houses.* And yet the most part of them is more dissident from the manners of the world nowadays than my communication was. But preachers, sly and wily men, following your counsel (as I suppose) because they saw men evil willing to frame their manners to Christ's rule, they have wrested and wried his doctrine, and like a rule of lead* have applied it to men's manners, that by some means, at the least way, they might agree together. Whereby I cannot see what good they have done, but that men may more securely be evil.

'And I truly should prevail even as little in kings' councils. For either I must say otherways than they say, and then I were as good to say nothing; or else I must say the same that they say, and (as Mitio saith in Terence),* help to further their madness. For that crafty wile and subtle train of yours, I cannot perceive to what purpose it serveth, wherewith you would have me to study and endeavour myself, if all things cannot be made good, yet to handle them wittily and handsomely for the purpose, that as far forth as is possible they may not be very evil. For there is no place to dissemble in nor to wink in. Naughty counsels must be openly allowed and very pestilent decrees must be approved. He shall be counted worse than a spy, yea, almost as evil as a traitor, that with a faint heart doth praise evil and noisome decrees. Moreover, a man can have no occasion to do good, chancing into the company of them which will sooner pervert a good man than be made good themselves, through whose evil company he shall be marred, or else, if he remain good and innocent, yet the wickedness and folly of others shall be imputed to him and laid in his neck. So that it is impossible with that crafty wile and subtle train to turn anything to better. Wherefore Plato by a goodly similitude declareth why wise men refrain to meddle in the commonwealth.* For when they

see the people swarm into the streets, and daily wet to the skin
with rain, and yet cannot persuade them to go out of the rain
and to take their houses, knowing well that if they should go
out to them they should nothing prevail nor win aught by it
but with them be wet also in the rain, they do keep themselves
within their houses, being content that they be safe themselves,
seeing they cannot remedy the folly of the people.

'Howbeit, doubtless, Master More (to speak truly as my
mind giveth me), where possessions be private, where money
beareth all the stroke, it is hard and almost impossible that
there the weal-public may justly be governed and prosperously
flourish. Unless you think thus: that justice is there executed
where all things come into the hands of evil men, or that
prosperity there flourisheth where all is divided among a few:
which few, nevertheless, do not lead their lives very wealthily,
and the residue live miserably, wretchedly, and beggarly.
Wherefore when I consider with myself and weigh in my mind
the wise and godly ordinances of the Utopians, among whom
with very few laws all things be so well and wealthily ordered
that virtue is had in price and estimation, and yet, all things
being there common, every man hath abundance of everything. Again, on the other part, when I compare with them so
many nations ever making new laws, yet none of them all well
and sufficiently furnished with laws, where every man calleth
that he hath gotten his own proper and private goods, where so
many new laws daily made be not sufficient for every man to
enjoy, defend, and know from another man's that which he
calleth his own; which thing the infinite controversies in the
law, daily rising, never to be ended, plainly declare to be true:
these things (I say) when I consider with myself, I hold well
with Plato, and do nothing marvel that he would make no laws
for them that refused those laws whereby all men should have
and enjoy equal portions of wealths and commodities.*

*Plato willed
all things in a
common-
wealth to be
common.*

'For the wise man did easily foresee this to be the one and
only way to the wealth of a commonalty, if equality of all
things should be brought in and stablished. Which, I think, is
not possible to be observed where every man's goods be proper
and peculiar to himself. For where every man under certain

titles and pretences draweth and plucketh to himself as much as he can, so that a few divide among themselves all the whole riches, be there never so much abundance and store, there to the residue is left lack and poverty. And for the most part it chanceth that this latter sort is more worthy to enjoy that state of wealth than the other be, because the rich men be covetous, crafty, and unprofitable. On the other part the poor be lowly, simple, and by their daily labour more profitable to the commonwealth than to themselves. Thus I do fully persuade myself that no equal and just distribution of things can be made, nor that perfect wealth shall ever be among men, unless this propriety be exiled and banished. But so long as it shall continue, so long shall remain among the most and best part of men the heavy and inevitable burden of poverty and wretchedness. Which, as I grant that it may be somewhat eased, so I utterly deny that it can wholly be taken away. For if there were a statute made that no man should possess above a certain measure of ground, and that no man should have in his stock above a prescript and appointed sum of money,* if it were by certain laws decreed that neither the king should be of too great power, neither the people too haut and wealthy, and that offices should not be obtained by inordinate suit, or by bribes and gifts, that they should neither be bought nor sold, nor that it should be needful for the officers to be at any cost or charge in their offices* (for so occasion is given to them by fraud and ravin to gather up their money again, and by reason of gifts and bribes the offices be given to rich men, which should rather have been executed of wise men): by such laws, I say, like as sick bodies that be desperate and past cure be wont with continual good cherishing to be kept and botched up for a time, so these evils also might be lightened and mitigated. But that they may be perfectly cured, and brought to a good and upright state, it is not to be hoped for, whiles every man is master of his own to himself. Yea, and whiles you go about to do your cure of one part you shall make bigger the sore of another part, so the help of one causeth another's harm, forasmuch as nothing can be given to any one unless it be taken from another.'

'But I am of a contrary opinion,' quoth I, 'for methinketh that men shall never there live wealthily, where all things be common. For how can there be abundance of goods or of anything where every man withdraweth his hand from labour? Whom the regard of his own gains driveth not to work, but the hope that he hath in other men's travails maketh him slothful. Then when they be pricked with poverty, and yet no man can by any law or right defend that for his own which he hath gotten with the labour of his own hands, shall not there of necessity be continual sedition and bloodshed? Specially the authority and reverence of magistrates being taken away, which, what place it may have with such men among whom is no difference, I cannot devise.'

'I marvel not', quoth he, 'that you be of this opinion. For you conceive in your mind either none at all, or else a very false image and similitude of this thing. But if you had been with me in Utopia and had presently seen their fashions and laws, as I did which lived there five years and more, and would never have come thence but only to make that new land known here, then doubtless you would grant that you never saw people well ordered but only there.'

'Surely,' quoth Master Peter, 'it shall be hard for you to make me believe that there is better order in that new land than is here in these countries that we know. For good wits be as well here as there, and I think our commonwealths be ancienter than theirs. Wherein long use and experience hath found out many things commodious for man's life, besides that many things here among us have been found by chance which no wit could ever have devised.'

'As touching the ancientness', quoth he, 'of common-wealths, then you might better judge, if you had read the histories and chronicles of that land, which if we may believe, cities were there before men were here. Now what thing soever hitherto by wit hath been devised or found by chance, that might be as well there as here. But I think verily, though it were so that we did pass them in wit, yet in study, in travail, and in laboursome endeavour they far pass us. For (as their chronicles testify) before our arrival there they never heard anything of us whom they call the ultra-equinoctials; saving that once about 1,200 years ago, a certain ship was lost by the isle of Utopia which was driven thither by tempest. Certain Romans and Egyptians were cast on land, which after that never went thence. Mark now what profit they took of this one occasion through diligence and earnest travail. There was no craft nor science within the empire of Rome whereof any profit could rise, but they either learned it of these strangers, or else of them taking occasion to search for it, found it out. So great profit was it to them that ever any went thither from hence. But if any like chance before this hath brought any man from thence hither, that is as quite out of remembrance as this also perchance in time to come shall be forgotten, that ever I was there. And like as they quickly, almost at the first meeting, made their own whatsoever is among us wealthily devised, so I suppose it would be long before we would receive anything that among them is better instituted than among us. And this, I suppose, is the chief cause why their commonwealths be wiselier governed and do flourish in more wealth than ours, though we neither in wit nor riches be their inferiors.'

'Therefore, gentle Master Raphael,' quoth I, 'I pray you and beseech you describe unto us the island. And study not to be short, but declare largely in order their grounds, their rivers, their cities, their people, their manners, their ordinances, their laws, and, to be short, all things that you shall think us desirous to know. And you shall think us desirous to know whatsoever we know not yet.'

'There is nothing', quoth he, 'that I will do gladlier. For all these things I have fresh in mind. But the matter requireth leisure.'

'Let us go in, therefore,' quoth I, 'to dinner; afterward we will bestow the time at our pleasure.'

'Content', quoth he, 'be it.'

So we went in and dined. When dinner was done, we came into the same place again, and sat us down upon the same bench, commanding our servants that no man should trouble us. Then I and Master Peter Giles desired Master Raphael to perform his promise. He, therefore, seeing us desirous and willing to hearken to him, when he had sit still and paused a little while musing and bethinking himself, thus he began to speak.

The End of the First Book

The Second Book of the Communication of
Raphael Hythloday, Concerning the Best State of
a Commonwealth: containing the description
of Utopia, with a large declaration of the
politic government and of all the good laws and
orders of the same island

The island of Utopia containeth in breadth in the middle part *The site and* of it (for there it is broadest) 200 miles. Which breadth con- *fashion of the* tinueth through the most part of the land. Saving that by little *new island* and little it cometh in and waxeth narrower towards both the *Utopia.* ends. Which fetching about a circuit or compass of 500 miles, do fashion the whole island like to the new moon. Between these two corners the sea runneth in, dividing them asunder by the distance of eleven miles or thereabouts, and there surmounteth into a large and wide sea, which by reason that the land on every side compasseth it about and sheltereth it from the winds, is not rough nor mounteth not with great waves, but almost floweth quietly, not much unlike a great standing pool, and maketh wellnigh all the space within the belly of the land in manner of a haven, and, to the great commodity of the inhabitants, receiveth in ships towards every part of the land.* The forefronts or frontiers of the two corners, what with fords and shelves and what with rocks, be very jeopardous and dangerous. In the middle distance between them both standeth up above the water a great rock, which therefore is nothing perilous because it is in sight. Upon the top of this rock is a fair and a strong tower builded, which they hold with a garrison of *A place* men. Other rocks there be lying hid under the water, which *naturally* therefore be dangerous. The channels be known only to them- *needeth but* selves. And therefore it seldom chanceth that any stranger *one garrison.* unless be he guided by an Utopian, can come into this haven. Insomuch that they themselves could scarcely enter without jeopardy, but that their way is directed and ruled by certain *A politic* landmarks standing on the shore. By turning, translating, and *device in the* changing of removing these marks into other places they may destroy their *land marks.*

enemies' navies, be they never so many. The outside or utter circuit of the land is also full of havens, but the landing is so surely fenced, what by nature and what by workmanship of man's hand, that a few defenders may drive back many armies.

Howbeit, as they say and as the fashion of the place itself doth partly show, it was not ever compassed about with the sea.

The island of Utopia named of King Utopus.

But King Utopus,* whose name as conqueror the island beareth (for before his time it was called Abraxa*), which also brought the rude and wild people to that excellent perfection in all good fashions, humanity, and civil gentleness, wherein they now go beyond all the people of the world, even at his first arriving and entering upon the land, forthwith obtaining the victory, caused fifteen miles space of uplandish ground, where the sea had no passage, to be cut and digged up. And so brought the sea round about the land. He set to this work not only the inhabitants of the island (because they should not think it done in contumely and despite) but also all his own

Many hands make light work.

soldiers. Thus the work, being divided into so great a number of workmen, was with exceeding marvellous speed dispatched. Insomuch that the borderers, which at the first began to mock and to jest at this vain enterprise, then turned their derision to marvel at the success and to fear.

Cities in Utopia.

There be in the island fifty-four large and fair cities, or shire towns, agreeing all together in one tongue, in like manners,

Similitude causeth concord.

institutions, and laws. They be all set and situate alike, and in all points fashioned alike, as far forth as the place or plot suffereth. Of these cities they that be nighest together be twenty-

A mean distance between city and city.

four miles asunder. Again, there is none of them distant from the next above one day's journey afoot. There come yearly to Amaurote* out of every city three old men, wise and well experienced, there to entreat and debate of the common matters of the land. For this city (because it standeth just in the midst of the island, and is therefore most meet for the ambassadors of all parts of the realm) is taken for the chief and head city. The precincts and bounds of the shires be so commodi-

The distribution of lands.

ously appointed out and set forth for the cities, that none of them all hath of any side less than twenty miles of ground, and of some side also much more, as of that part where the cities be

of farther distance asunder. None of the cities desire to enlarge
the bounds and limits of their shires, for they count themselves
rather the good husbands than the owners of their lands.

They have in the country, in all parts of the shire, houses or
farms builded, well appointed and furnished with all sorts of
instruments and tools belonging to husbandry. These houses
be inhabited of the citizens which come thither to dwell by
course. No household or farm in the country hath fewer than
forty persons, men and women, besides two bondmen which
be all under the rule and order of the good man and the good
wife of the house, being both very sage, discreet, and ancient
persons. And every thirty farms or families have one head
ruler which is called a Philarch,* being as it were a head bailiff.
Out of every one of these families or farms cometh every year
into the city twenty persons which have continued two years
before in the country. In their place so many fresh be sent
thither out of the city, who, of them that have been there a year
already, and be therefore expert and cunning in husbandry,
shall be instructed and taught. And they the next year shall
teach other. This order is used for fear that either scarceness of
victuals or some other like incommodity should chance,
through lack of knowledge, if they should be altogether new
and fresh and unexpert in husbandry. This manner and fashion of yearly changing and renewing the occupiers of husbandry, though it be solemn and customably used, to the intent
that no man shall be constrained against his will to continue
long in that hard and sharp kind of life, yet many of them have
such a pleasure and delight in husbandry that they obtain a
longer space of years. These husbandmen plough and till the
ground, and bryde up cattle, and provide and make ready
wood, which they carry to the city either by land or by water as
they may most conveniently.

They bring up a great multitude of pullen, and that by a
marvellous policy. For the hens do not sit upon the eggs, but
by keeping them in a certain equal heat they bring life into
them and hatch them. The chickens, as soon as they be come
out of the shell, follow men and women instead of the hens.
They bring up very few horses, nor none but very fierce ones;

*But this
nowadays is
the ground
of all
mischief.*

*Husbandry
and tillage
chiefly and
principally
regarded and
advanced.*

*The duties of
men of
husbandry.*

*A strange
fashion in the
hatching and
bringing up of
pullen.*

*The use of
horses.*

The use of oxen.

and that for none other use or purpose, but only to exercise their youth in riding and feats of arms. For oxen be put to all the labour of ploughing and drawing. Which they grant to be not so good as horses at a sudden brunt and (as we say) at a dead lift, but yet they hold opinion that oxen will abide and suffer much more labour, pain, and hardness than horses will. And they think that oxen be not in danger and subject unto so many diseases, and that they be kept and maintained with much less cost and charge, and finally that they be good for meat when they be past labour.

Bread and drink.

They sow corn only for bread, for their drink is either wine made of grapes or else of apples or pears, or else it is clear water. And many times mead made of honey or liquorice sodden in water, for thereof they have great store. And though they know certainly (for they know it perfectly indeed) how much victuals the city with the whole country or shire round about it doth spend, yet they sow much more corn and breed up much more cattle than serveth for their own use, parting the overplus among their borderers. Whatsoever necessary things be lacking in the country, all such stuff they fetch out of the city where without any exchange they easily obtain it of the magistrates of the city. For every month many of them go into the city on the holy day. When their harvest day draweth near and is at hand, then the Philarchs, which be the head officers and bailiffs of husbandry, send word to the magistrates of the city what number of harvest men is needful to be sent to them out of the city. The which company of harvest men being ready at the day appointed, almost in one fair day dispatcheth all the harvest work.

A great discretion in sowing of corn.

Mutual help quickly dispatcheth.

OF THE CITIES AND NAMELY OF AMAUROTE

As for their cities, whoso knoweth one of them knoweth them all, they be all so like one to another as far forth as the nature of the place permitteth. I will describe, therefore, to you one or other of them, for it skilleth not greatly which, but which rather than Amaurote? Of them all this is the worthiest and of most dignity. For the residue knowledge it for the head city because there is the council house. Nor to me any of them all is better beloved, as wherein I lived five whole years together.

The city of Amaurote standeth upon the side of a low hill, in fashion almost four-square. For the breadth of it beginneth a little beneath the top of the hill, and still continueth by the space of two miles until it come to the river of Anyder.* The length of it, which lieth by the river's side, is somewhat more. The river of Anyder riseth four and twenty miles above Amaurote out of a little spring. But being increased by other small rivers and brooks that run into it, and among other two somewhat big ones, before the city it is half a mile broad, and farther broader. And forty miles beyond the city it falleth into the ocean sea. By all that space that lieth between the sea and the city, and certain miles also above the city, the water ebbeth and floweth six hours together with a swift tide. When the sea floweth in, for the length of thirty miles it filleth all the Anyder with salt water, and driveth back the fresh water of the river. And somewhat farther it changeth the sweetness of the fresh water with saltness. But a little beyond that the river waxeth sweet, and runneth forby the city fresh and pleasant. And when the sea ebbeth and goeth back again, the fresh water followeth it almost even to the very fall into the sea. There goeth a bridge over the river, made not of piles or of timber, but of stonework with gorgeous and substantial arches at that part of the city that is farthest from the sea, to the intent that ships may pass along forby all the side of the city without let. They have also another river which indeed is not very great. But it runneth gently and pleasantly. For it riseth even out of the same hill that the city standeth upon, and runneth down a slope through the midst of the city into Anyder. And because it riseth a little without the city, the Amaurotians have enclosed the head spring of it, with strong fences and bulwarks, and so have joined it to the city. This is done to the intent that the water should not be stopped nor turned away or poisoned if their enemies should chance to come upon them. From thence the water is derived and conveyed down in channels of brick divers ways into the lower parts of the city. Where that cannot

The description of Amaurote, the chief city in Utopia.

The description of the river of Anyder.

The very like in England in the river of Thames.

Herein also doeth London agree with Amaurote.

The use of fresh water.

be done, by reason that the place will not suffer it, there they gather the rain water in great cisterns, which doeth them as good service. The city is compassed about with a high and thick stone wall full of turrets and bulwarks. A dry ditch, but deep and broad and overgrown with bushes, briars, and thorns, goeth about three sides or quarters of the city. To the fourth side the river itself serveth for a ditch.

The defence of town walls.

The streets be appointed and set forth very commodious and handsome, both for carriage and also against the winds. The houses be of fair and gorgeous building, and on the street side they stand joined together in a long row through the whole street without any partition or separation. The streets be twenty foot broad. On the back side of the houses, through the whole length of the street, lie large gardens enclosed round about with the back part of the streets. Every house hath two doors, one into the street, and a postern door on the back side into the garden. These doors be made with two leaves never locked nor bolted, so easy to be opened, that they will follow the least drawing of a finger, and shut again alone. Whoso will may go in,* for there is nothing within the houses that is private or any man's own. And every tenth year they change their houses by lot.

Streets.

Buildings and houses.

To every dwelling house a garden plot adjoining.

This gear smelleth at Plato his community.

They set great store by their gardens. In them they have vineyards, all manner of fruit, herbs, and flowers, so pleasant, so well furnished, and so finely kept, that I never saw thing more fruitful nor better trimmed in any place. Their study and diligence herein cometh not only of pleasure, but also of a certain strife and contention that is between street and street concerning the trimming, husbanding, and furnishing of their gardens, every man for his own part. And verily you shall not lightly find in all the city anything that is more commodious, either for the profit of the citizens or for pleasure. And therefore it may seem that the first founder of the city minded nothing so much as these gardens.

The commodity of gardens is commended also of Virgil.

For they say that King Utopus himself, even at the first beginning, appointed and drew forth the platform of the city into this fashion and figure that it hath now, but the gallant garnishing and the beautiful setting forth of it, whereunto he saw that one man's age would not suffice, that he left to his posterity. For their chronicles, which they keep written with all diligent circumspection, containing the history of 1,760 years,* even from the first conquest of the island, record and witness that the houses in the beginning were very low and like homely cottages or poor shepherd houses, made, at all adventures, of every rude piece of timber that came first to hand, with mud walls and ridged roofs thatched over with straw. But now the houses be curiously builded after a gorgeous and gallant sort, with three storeys one over another. The outsides of the walls be made either of hard flint or of plaster, or else of brick, and the inner sides be well strengthened with timber work. The roofs be plain and flat, covered with a certain kind of plaster that is of no cost, and yet so tempered that no fire can hurt or perish it, and withstandeth the violence of the weather better than any lead. They keep the wind out of their windows with glass, for it is there much used, and somewhere also with fine linen cloth dipped in oil or amber,* and that for two commodities, for by this means more light cometh in, and the wind is better kept out.

Glassed or canvased windows.

OF THE MAGISTRATES

Every thirty families or farms choose them yearly an officer which in their old language is called the Syphogrant, and by a newer name the Philarch. Every ten Syphogrants, with all their thirty families, be under an officer which was once called the Tranibore, now the chief Philarch.* Moreover, as concerning the election of the prince,* all the Syphogrants, which be in number 200, first be sworn to choose him whom they think most meet and expedient. Then by a secret election they name prince one of those four whom the people before named unto them. For out of the four quarters of the city there be four chosen, out of every quarter one, to stand for the election, which be put up to the council. The prince's office continueth all his lifetime, unless he be deposed or put down for suspicion of tyranny. They choose the Tranibores yearly, but lightly they

A tranibore in the Utopian tongue signifieth a head or chief peer.

A marvellous strange fashion in choosing magistrates.

Tyranny in a well ordered weal-public utterly to be abhorred.

change them not. All the other officers be but for one year. The Tranibores every third day, and sometimes, if need be, oftener, come into the council house with the prince. Their counsel is concerning the commonwealth. If there be any controversies among the commoners, which be very few, they dispatch and end them by and by. They take ever two Syphogrants to them in council, and every day a new couple. And it is provided that nothing touching the commonwealth shall be confirmed and ratified unless it have been reasoned of and debated three days in the council before it be decreed. It is death to have any consultation for the commonwealth out of the council or the place of the common election. This statute, they say, was made to the intent that the prince and Tranibores might not easily conspire together to oppress the people by tyranny, and to change the state of the weal-public. Therefore matters of great weight and importance be brought to the election house of the Syphogrants, which open the matter to their families. And afterward, when they have consulted among themselves, they show their device to the council. Sometimes the matter is brought before the council of the whole Island. Furthermore, this custom also the council useth, to dispute or reason of no matter the same day that it is first proposed or put forth, but to defer it to the next sitting of the council. Because that no man, when he hath rashly there spoken that cometh to his tongue's end, shall then afterward rather study for reasons wherewith to defend and maintain his first foolish sentence, than for the commodity of the commonwealth, as one rather willing the harm or hindrance of the weal-public than any loss or diminution of his own existimation, and as one that would be ashamed (which is a very foolish shame) to be counted anything at the first overseen in the matter. Who at the first ought to have spoken rather wisely than hastily or rashly.

Suits and controversies between party and party forthwith to be ended which nowadays of a set purpose be unreasonably delayed.

Against hasty and rash decrees of statutes.

A custom worthy to be used these days in our counsels* and parliaments.

Husbandry or tillage practised of all estates, which nowadays is reject but in a few of the basest sort.

OF SCIENCES, CRAFTS, AND OCCUPATIONS

Husbandry is a science common to them all in general, both men and women, wherein they be all expert and cunning. In this they be all instructed even from their youth, partly in their schools with traditions and precepts, and partly in the country nigh the city, brought up, as it were in playing, not only beholding the use of it, but by occasion of exercising their bodies practising it also. Besides husbandry, which (as I said) is common to them all, every one of them learneth one or other several and particular science as his own proper craft. That is most commonly either clothworking in wool or flax, or masonry, or the smith's craft, or the carpenter's science. For there is none other occupation that any number to speak of doth use there. For their garments, which throughout all the island be of one fashion (saving that there is a difference between the man's garment and the woman's, between the married and the unmarried), and this one continueth for evermore unchanged, seemly and comely to the eye, no let to the moving and wielding of the body, also fit both for winter and summer: as for these garments (I say) every family maketh their own. But of the other foresaid crafts every man learneth one. And not only the men, but also the women. But the women, as the weaker sort, be put to the easier crafts, as to work wool and flax. The more laboursome sciences be committed to the men. For the most part every man is brought up, in his father's craft. For most commonly they be naturally thereto bent and inclined. But if a man's mind stand to any other, he is by adoption put into a family of that occupation which he doth most fantasy. Whom not only his father but also the magistrates do diligently look to that he be put to a discreet and an honest householder. Yea, and if any person when he hath learned one craft be desirous to learn also another, he is likewise suffered and permitted. When he hath learned both, he occupieth whether he will, unless the city have more need of the one than of the other.

The chief and almost the only office of the Syphogrants is to see and take heed that no man sit idle, but that every one apply his own craft with earnest diligence. And yet for all that, not to be wearied from early in the morning to late in the evening with continual work, like labouring and toiling beasts. For this is worse than the miserable and wretched condition of

Sciences or occupations should be learned for necessity's sake, and not for the maintenance of riotous excess and wanton pleasure.

Similitude in apparel.

No citizen without a science.

To what occupation everyone is naturally inclined, that let him learn.

Idle persons to be driven out of the weal-public.

A moderation in the labour and toil of artificers.

bondmen. Which nevertheless is almost everywhere the life of workmen and artificers, saving in Utopia.* For they, dividing the day and the night into twenty-four just hours, appoint and assign only six of those hours to work before noon, upon the which they go straight to dinner.* And after dinner, when they have rested two hours, then they work three hours, and upon that they go to supper. About eight of the clock in the evening (counting one of the clock at the first hour after noon) they go to bed; eight hours they give to sleep. All the void time that is between the hours of work, sleep, and meat, that they be suffered to bestow, every man as he liketh best himself. Not to the intent that they should misspend this time in riot or slothfulness, but being then licensed from the labour of their own occupations, to bestow the time well and thriftily upon some other science as shall please them. For it is a solemn custom

The study of good literature.

there, to have lectures daily early in the morning, where to be present they only be constrained that be namely chosen and appointed to learning. Howbeit, a great multitude of every sort of people, both men and women, go to hear lectures, some one and some another, as every man's nature is inclined. Yet, this notwithstanding, if any man had rather bestow this time upon his own occupation (as it chanceth in many, whose minds rise not in the contemplation of any science liberal), he is not letted nor prohibited, but is also praised and commended as profit-

Playing after supper.

able to the commonwealth. After supper they bestow one hour in play, in summer in their gardens, in winter in their common halls where they dine and sup. There they exercise themselves in music, or else in honest and wholesome communication.

But nowadays dice play is the pastime of princes.

Dice-play and such other foolish and pernicious games they know not. But they use two games not much unlike the chess. The one is the battle of numbers, wherein one number stealeth away another. The other is wherein vices fight with virtues, as

Plays or games also profitable.

it were in battle array or a set field.* In the which game is very properly showed both the strife and discord that vices have among themselves, and again their unity and concord against virtues. And also what vices be repugnant to what virtues; with what power and strength they assail them openly; by what wiles and subtlety they assault them secretly; with what help and aid the virtues resist and overcome the puissance of the vices; by what craft they frustrate their purposes; and, finally, by what sleight or means the one getteth the victory.

But here lest you be deceived, one thing you must look more narrowly upon. For seeing they bestow but six hours in work, perchance you may think that the lack of some necessary things hereof may ensue. But this is nothing so. For that small time is not only enough but also too much for the store and abundance of all things that be requisite, either for the necessity or commodity of life. The which thing you also shall perceive if you weigh and consider with yourselves how great a part of the people in other countries liveth idle. First, almost all women, which be the half of the whole number, or else, if the women be somewhere occupied, there most commonly in their stead the men be idle. Besides this, how great and how idle a company is there of priests and religious men, as they call them! Put thereto all rich men, specially all landed men, which commonly be called gentlemen and noblemen. Take into this number also their servants: I mean all that flock of stout bragging rush-bucklers. Join to them also sturdy and valiant beggars, cloaking their idle life under the colour of some disease or sickness. And truly you shall find them much fewer than you thought, by whose labour all these things are wrought that in men's affairs are now daily used and frequented. Now consider with yourself of these few that do work, how few be occupied in necessary works. For where money beareth all the swing,* there many vain and superfluous occupations must needs be used, to serve only for riotous superfluity and unhonest pleasure. For the same multitude that now is occupied in work, if they were divided into so few occupations as the necessary use of nature requireth, in so great plenty of things as then of necessity would ensue doubtless the prices would be too little for the artificers to maintain their livings. But if all these that be now busied about unprofitable occupations, with all the whole flock of them that live idly and slothfully, which consume and waste every one of them more of these things that come by other men's labour than two of the workmen themselves do, if all these (I say) were set to

The kinds and sorts of idle people.

Women.

Priests and religious men.

Rich men and landed men.

Serving men.

Sturdy and valiant beggars.

Wonderful wittily spoke.

profitable occupations, you easily perceive how little time would be enough, yea, and too much, to store us with all things that may be requisite either for necessity or for commodity, yea, or for pleasure, so that the same pleasure be true and natural.

And this in Utopia the thing itself maketh manifest and plain. For there, in all the city with the whole country or shire adjoining to it, scarcely 500 persons of all the whole number of men and women that be neither too old nor too weak to work be licensed and discharged from labour. Among them be the Syphogrants, who, though they be by the laws exempt and privileged from labour, yet they exempt not themselves, to the intent that they may the rather by their example provoke others to work. The same vacation from labour do they also enjoy, to whom the people, persuaded by the commendation of the priests and secret election of the Syphogrants, have given a perpetual licence from labour to learning. But if any one of them prove not according to the expectation and hope of him conceived, he is forthwith plucked back to the company of artificers. And contrariwise, often it chanceth that a handi-craftsman doth so earnestly bestow his vacant and spare hours in learning, and through diligence so profiteth therein, that he is taken from his handy occupation and promoted to the company of the learned.

Not as much as the magistrates live idly.

Only learned men called to offices.

Out of this order of the learned be chosen ambassadors, priests, Tranibores, and finally the prince himself. Whom they in their old tongue call Barzanes and, by a newer name, Adamus.* The residue of the people being neither idle nor yet occupied about unprofitable exercises, it may be easily judged in how few hours how much good work by them may be done and dispatched towards those things that I have spoken of. This commodity they have also above other, that in the most part of necessary occupations they need not so much work as other nations do. For, first of all, the building or repairing of houses asketh everywhere so many men's continual labour, because that the unthrifty here suffereth the houses that his father built in continuance of time to fall in decay. So that which he might have upholden with little cost, his successor is

How to avoid excessive cost in building.

constrained to build it again anew, to his great charge. Yea, many times also the house that stood one man in much money,* another is of so nice and so delicate a mind, that he setteth nothing by it. And, it being neglected, and therefore shortly falling into ruin, be buildeth up another in another place with no less cost and charge. But among the Utopians, where all things be set in a good order and the commonwealth in a good stay, it very seldom chanceth that they choose a new plot to build an house upon. And they do not only find speedy and quick remedies for present faults, but also prevent them that be like to fall. And by this means their houses continue and last very long with little labour and small reparations; insomuch that this kind of workmen sometimes have almost nothing to do, but that they be commanded to hew timber at home, and to square and trim up stones, to the intent that if any work chance it may the speedlier rise.

Now, sir, in their apparel mark (I pray you) how few workmen they need. First of all, whiles they be at work they be covered homely with leather or skins that will last seven years. When they go forth abroad they cast upon them a cloak which hideth the other homely apparel. These cloaks throughout the whole island be all of one colour, and that is the natural colour of the wool. They therefore do not only spend much less woollen cloth than is spent in other countries, but also the same standeth them in much less cost. But linen cloth is made with less labour, and is therefore had more in use. But in linen cloth only whiteness, in woollen only cleanliness, is regarded. As for the smallness or fineness of the thread, that is nothing passed for. And this is the cause wherefore in other places four or five cloth gowns of divers colours and as many silk coats be not enough for one man. Yea, and if he be of the delicate and nice sort ten be too few, whereas there one garment will serve a man most commonly two years. For why should he desire more, seeing if he had them he should not be the better hapt or covered from cold, neither in his apparel any whit the comelier? Wherefore, seeing they be all exercised in profitable occupations, and that few artificers in the same crafts be sufficient, this is the cause that, plenty of all things being among

How to lessen the charge in apparel.

them, they do sometimes bring forth an innumerable company of people to amend the highways if any be broken. Many times also, when they have no such work to be occupied about, an open proclamation is made that they shall bestow fewer hours in work. For the magistrates do not exercise their citizens against their wills in unneedful labours. For why, in the institution of that weal-public this end is only and chiefly pretended and minded, that what time may possibly be spared from the necessary occupations and affairs of the commonwealth, all that, the citizens should withdraw from the bodily service to the free liberty of the mind and garnishing of the same. For herein they suppose the felicity of this life to consist.

OF THEIR LIVING AND MUTUAL
CONVERSATION TOGETHER

But now will I declare how the citizens use themselves one towards another, what familiar occupying and entertainment there is among the people, and what fashion they use in the distribution of everything. First, the city consisteth of families; the families most commonly be made of kindreds. For the women, when they be married at a lawful age, they go into their husbands' houses. But the male children, with all the whole male offspring, continue still in their own family and be governed of the eldest and ancientest father, unless he dote for age, for then the next to him in age is placed in his room. But *The number* to the intent the prescript number of the citizens should nei- *of citizens.* ther decrease nor above measure increase, it is ordained that no family (which in every city be six thousand in the whole besides them of the country,) shall at once have fewer children of the age of fourteen years or thereabout than ten, or more than sixteen, for of children under this age no number can be prescribed or appointed. This measure or number is easily observed and kept by putting them that in fuller families be above the number into families of smaller increase. But if chance be that in the whole city the store increase above the just number, therewith they fill up the lack of other cities. But if so be that the multitude throughout the whole island pass and exceed the due number, then they choose out of every city certain citizens, and build up a town under their own laws in the next land where the inhabitants have much waste and unoccupied ground, receiving also of the same country people to them, if they will join and dwell with them. They thus joining and dwelling together do easily agree in one fashion of living, and that to the great wealth of both the peoples. For they so bring the matter about by their laws, that the ground which before was neither good nor profitable for the one nor for the other is now sufficient and fruitful enough for them both. But if the inhabitants of that land will not dwell with them to be ordered by their laws, then they drive them out of those bounds which they have limited and appointed out for themselves. And if they resist and rebel, then they make war against them. For they count this the most just cause of war, when any people holdeth a piece of ground void and vacant to no good nor profitable use, keeping others from the use and possession of it which notwithstanding by the law of nature ought thereof to be nourished and relieved. If any chance do so much diminish the number of any of their cities that it cannot be filled up again without the diminishing of the just number of the other cities (which they say chanced but twice since the beginning of the land through a great pestilent plague), then they fulfil and make up the number with citizens fetched out of their own foreign towns; for they had rather suffer their foreign towns to decay and perish than any city of their own island to be diminished.

But now again to the conversation of the citizens among themselves. The eldest (as I said) ruleth the family. The wives be ministers to their husbands, the children to their parents, and, to be short, the younger to their elders. Every city is divided into four equal parts or quarters. In the midst of every quarter there is a market-place of all manner of things. Thither the works of every family be brought into certain houses. And every kind of thing is laid up several in barns or storehouses. From hence the father of every family or every householder fetcheth whatsoever he and his have need of, and carrieth it

So might we well be discharged and eased of the whole company of serving men.

away with him without money, without exchange, without any gage, pawn, or pledge. For why should anything be denied unto him, seeing there is abundance of all things, and that it is not to be feared lest any man will ask more than he needeth? For why should it be thought that that man would ask more than enough which is sure never to lack? Certainly in all kinds of living creatures either fear of lack doth cause covetousness and ravin, or in man only pride, which counteth it a glorious thing to pass and excel other in the superfluous and vain ostentation of things. The which kind of vice among the Utopians can have no place.

The cause of covetous and extortion.

Next to the market-places that I spake of stand meat markets,* whither be brought not only all sorts of herbs and the fruits of trees, with bread, but also fish, and all manner of four-footed beasts and wild fowl that be man's meat. But first the filthiness and ordure thereof is clean washed away in the running river without the city in places appointed meet for the same purpose. From thence the beasts be brought in, killed, and clean washed by the hands of their bondmen. For they permit not their free citizens to accustom themselves to the killing of beasts, through the use whereof they think clemency, the gentlest affection of our nature, by little and little to decay and perish. Neither they suffer anything that is filthy, loathsome, or uncleanly to be brought into the city, lest the air, by the stench thereof infected and corrupt, should cause pestilent diseases. Moreover, every street hath certain great large halls set in equal distance one from another, every one known by a several name. In these halls dwell the Syphogrants. And to every one of the same halls be appointed thirty families, on either side fifteen. The stewards of every hall at a certain hour come in to the meat markets, where they receive meat according to the number of their halls.*

Of the slaughter of beasts we have learned manslaughter.

Filth and ordure bring the infection of pestilence into cities.

But first and chiefly of all, respect is had to the sick, that be cured in the hospitals.* For in the circuit of the city, a little without the walls, they have four hospitals, so big, so wide, so ample, and so large, that they may seem four little towns, which were devised of that bigness partly to the intent the sick, be they never so many in number, should not lie too throng

Care, diligence, and attendance about the sick.

or strait, and therefore uneasily and incommodiously; and partly that they which were taken and holden with contagious diseases, such as be wont by infection to creep from one to another, might be laid apart far from the company of the residue. These hospitals be so well appointed, and with all things necessary to health so furnished, and, moreover, so diligent attendance through the continual presence of cunning physicians is given, that though no man be sent thither against his will, yet notwithstanding there is no sick person in all the city that had not rather lie there than at home in his own house.

When the steward of the sick hath received such meat as the physicians have prescribed, then the best is equally divided among the halls, according to the company of every one, saving that there is had a respect to the prince, the bishop, the Tranibores, and to ambassadors and all strangers, if there be any, which be very few and seldom. But they also, when they be there, have certain several houses appointed and prepared for them. To these halls at the set hours of dinner and supper cometh all the whole Syphogranty or ward, warned by the noise of a brazen trumpet, except such as be sick in the hospitals, or else in their own houses. Howbeit, no man is prohibited or forbid, after the halls be served, to fetch home meat out of the market to his own house. For they know that no man will do it without a cause reasonable. For though no man be prohibited to dine at home, yet no man doth it willingly because it is counted a point of small honesty. And also it were a folly to take the pain to dress a bad dinner at home, when they may be welcome to good and fine fare so nigh hand at the hall. *Every man is at his liberty, so that nothing is done by compulsion.*

In this hall all vile service, all slavery and drudgery, with all laboursome toil and base business, is done by bondmen. But the women of every family, by course, have the office and charge of cookery for seething and dressing the meat and ordering all things thereto belonging. They sit at three tables or more, according to the number of their company. The men sit upon the bench next the wall, and the women against them on the other side of the table, that if any sudden evil should chance to them, as many times happeneth to women with *Women both dress and serve the meat.*

child, they may rise without trouble or disturbance of anybody, and go thence into the nursery. The nurses sit several alone with their young sucklings in a certain parlour appointed and deputed to the same purpose, never without fire and clean water, nor yet without cradles, that when they will they may lay down the young infants, and at their pleasure take them out of their swathing clothes, and hold them to the fire, and refresh them with play. Every mother is nurse to her own child unless either death or sickness be the let. When that chanceth, the wives of the Syphogrants quickly provide a nurse. And that is not hard to be done. For they that can do it proffer themselves to no service so gladly as to that, because that there this kind of pity is much praised, and the child that is nourished ever after taketh his nurse for his own natural mother. Also among the nurses sit all the children that be under the age of five years. All the other children of both kinds as well boys as girls, that be under the age of marriage, do either serve at the tables or else, if they be too young thereto, yet they stand by with marvellous silence. That which is given to them from the table they eat, and other several dinner time they have none.

The Syphogrant and his wife sit in the midst of the high table, forasmuch as that is counted the honourablest place, and because from thence all the whole company is in their sight. For that table standeth overthwart the over end of the hall. To them be joined two of the ancientest and eldest, for at every table they sit four at a mess. But if there be a church standing in that Syphogranty or ward, then the priest and his wife sitteth with the Syphogrant, as chief in the company. On both sides of them sit young men, and next unto them again old men. And thus throughout all the house equal of age be set together, and yet be mixed and matched with unequal ages. This, they say, was ordained to the intent that the sage gravity and reverence of the elders should keep the youngers from wanton licence of words and behaviour. Forasmuch as nothing can be so secretly spoken or done at the table, but either they that sit on the one side or on the other must needs perceive it. The dishes be not set down in order from the first place, but all the old men (whose places be marked with some special token

Nurses.

Nothing sooner provoketh men to well doing than praise and commendation.

The education of young children.

The young mixed with their elders.

Old men regarded and reverenced.

66

to be known) be first served of their meat, and then the residue equally. The old men divide their dainties as they think best to the younger on each side of them. Thus the elders be not defrauded of their due honour, and nevertheless equal commodity cometh to every one.

They begin every dinner and supper of reading something that pertaineth to good manners and virtue.* But it is short, because no man shall be grieved therewith. Hereof the elders take occasion of honest communication, but neither sad nor unpleasant. Howbeit, they do not spend all the whole dinner time themselves with long and tedious talks, but they gladly hear also the young men, yea, and purposely provoke them to talk, to the intent that they may have a proof of every man's wit and towardness or disposition to virtue, which commonly in the liberty of feasting doth show and utter itself. Their dinners be very short, but their suppers be somewhat longer, because that after dinner followeth labour, after supper sleep and natural rest, which they think to be of more strength and efficacy to wholesome and healthful digestion. No supper is passed without music. Nor their banquets lack no conceits nor junkets. They burn sweet gums and spices or perfumes and pleasant smells, and sprinkle about sweet ointments and waters, yea, they leave nothing undone that maketh for the cheering of the company. For they be much inclined to this opinion: to think no kind of pleasure forbidden whereof cometh no harm.

This nowadays is observed in our universities.

Talk at the table.

This is repugnant to the opinion of our physicians.

Music at the table.

Pleasure without harm not discommendable.

Thus, therefore, and after this sort they live together in the city; but in the country they that dwell alone far from any neighbours do dine and sup at home in their own houses. For no family there lacketh any kind of victuals, as from whom cometh all that the citizens eat and live by.

OF THEIR JOURNEYING OR TRAVELLING ABROAD, WITH DIVERS OTHER MATTERS CUNNINGLY REASONED AND WITTILY DISCUSSED

But if any be desirous to visit either their friends dwelling in another city, or to see the place itself, they easily obtain licence of their Syphogrants and Tranibores, unless there be some profitable let. No man goeth out alone, but a company is sent forth together with their prince's letters, which do testify that they have licence to go that journey, and prescribeth also the day of their return. They have a wagon given them with a common bondman which driveth the oxen and taketh charge of them. But unless they have women in their company, they send home the wagon again as an impediment and a let. And though they carry nothing forth with them, yet in all their journey they lack nothing, for wheresoever they come they be at home. If they tarry in a place longer than one day, then there every one of them falleth to his own occupation, and be very gently entertained of the workmen and companies of the same crafts. If any man, of his own head and without leave, walk out of his precinct and bounds, taken without the prince's letters he is brought again for a fugitive or a runaway with great shame and rebuke, and is sharply punished. If he be taken in that fault again, he is punished with bondage. If any be desirous to walk abroad into the fields or into the country that belongeth to the same city that he dwelleth in, obtaining the goodwill of his father and the consent of his wife, he is not prohibited. But into what part of the country soever he cometh he hath no meat given him until he have wrought out his forenoon's task or dispatched so much work as there is wont to be wrought before supper. Observing this law and condition, he may go whither he will within the bounds of his own city. For he shall be no less profitable to the city than if he were within it.

Now you see how little liberty they have to loiter, how they can have no cloak or pretence to idleness. There be neither wine-taverns, nor ale-houses, nor stews, nor any occasion of vice or wickedness, no lurking corners, no places of wicked councils or unlawful assemblies. But they be in the present sight and under the eyes of every man. So that of necessity they must either apply their accustomed labours, or else recreate themselves with honest and laudable pastimes. This fashion and trade of life being used among the people, it cannot be chosen but that they must of necessity have store and plenty of

O holy common-wealth, and of Christians to be followed.

all things. And seeing they be all thereof partners equally, therefore can no man there be poor or needy.

In the council of Amaurote, whither, as I said, every city sendeth three men apiece yearly, as soon as it is perfectly known of what things there is in every place plenty, and again what things be scant in any place, incontinent the lack of the one is performed and filled up with the abundance of the other.* And this they do freely without any benefit, taking nothing again of them to whom the things is given, but those cities that have given of their store to any other city that lacketh, requiring nothing again of the same city, do take such things as they lack of another city, to the which they gave nothing. So the whole island is as it were one family or household. But when they have made sufficient provision of store for themselves (which they think not done until they have provided for two years following, because of the uncertainty of the next year's proof), then of those things whereof they have abundance they carry forth into other countries great plenty: as grain, honey, wool, flax, wood, madder, purple-dyed fells, wax, tallow, leather, and living beasts. And the seventh part of all these things they give frankly and freely to the poor of that country. The residue they sell at a reasonable and mean price.

By this trade of traffic or merchandise they bring into their own country not only great plenty of gold and silver, but also all such things as they lack at home, which is almost nothing but iron. And by reason they have long used this trade, now they have more abundance of these things than any men will believe. Now, therefore, they care not whether they sell for ready money, or else upon trust to be paid at a day* and to have the most part in debts. But in so doing they never follow the credence of private men,* but the assurance or warranties of the whole city by instruments and writings made in that behalf accordingly. When the day of payment is come and expired, the city gathereth up the debt of the private debtors and putteth it into the common box, and so long hath the use and profit of it until the Utopians, their creditors, demand it. The most part of it they never ask. For that thing which is to them no profit to take it from other to whom it is profitable, they

Equality is the cause that every man has enough.

A commonwealth is nothing else but a great household.

The traffic and merchandise of the Utopians.

In all things and above all things to their continuity they have an eye.

By what policy money may be in less estimation.

It is better either with money or by policy to avoid war than with much loss of man's blood to fight.

O fine wit.

think it no right nor conscience. But if the case so stand that they must lend part of that money to another people, then they require their debt, or when they have war. For the which purpose only they keep at home all the treasure which they have, to be helpen and succoured by it either in extreme jeopardies, or in sudden dangers. But especially and chiefly to hire therewith, and that for unreasonable great wages, strange soldiers. For they had rather put strangers in jeopardy than their own countrymen, knowing that for money enough their enemies themselves many times may be bought or sold, or else through treason be set together by the ears among themselves.* For this cause they keep an inestimable treasure. But yet not as a treasure, but so they have it and use it, as in good faith I am ashamed to show, fearing that my words shall not be believed. And this I have more cause to fear, for that I know how difficult and hardly I myself would have believed another man telling the same, if I had not presently seen it with mine own eyes. For it must needs be that how far a thing is dissonant and disagreeing from the guise and trade of the hearers, so far shall it be out of their belief. Howbeit, a wise and indifferent esteemer of things will not greatly marvel perchance, seeing all their other laws and customs do so much differ from ours, if the use also of gold and silver among them be applied rather to their own fashions than to ours. I mean, in that they occupy not money themselves, but keep it for that chance which, as it may happen, so it may be that it shall never come to pass.

In the meantime gold and silver, whereof money is made, they do so use as none of them doth more esteem it than the very nature of the thing deserveth. And then who doth not plainly see how far it is under iron, as without the which men can no better live than without fire and water? Whereas to gold and silver nature hath given no use that we may not well lack if that the folly of men had not set it in higher estimation for the rareness's sake. But of the contrary part, nature, as a most tender and loving mother, hath placed the best and most necessary things open abroad, as the air, the water, and the earth itself. And hath removed and hid farthest from us vain and unprofitable things. Therefore if these metals among them

Gold worse than iron as touching the necessary use thereof.

should be fast locked up in some tower, it might be suspected that the prince and the council (as the people is ever foolishly imagining) intended by some subtlety to deceive the commons and to take some profit of it to themselves. Furthermore, if they should make thereof plate and such other finely and cunningly wrought stuff, if at any time they should have occasion to break it and melt it again, therewith to pay their soldiers' wages, they see and perceive very well that men would be loath to part from those things, that they once began to have pleasure and delight in.

To remedy all this they have found out a means which, as it is agreeable to all their other laws and customs, so it is from ours (where gold is so much set by and so diligently kept) very far discrepant and repugnant, and therefore incredible, but only to them that be wise. For whereas they eat and drink in earthen and glass vessels which, indeed, be curiously and properly made and yet be of very small value, of gold and silver they make commonly chamber-pots and other vessels that serve for most vile uses not only in their common halls but in every man's private house. Furthermore, of the same metals they make great chains, fetters, and gyves wherein they tie their bondmen. Finally whosoever for any offence be infamed, by their ears hang rings of gold, upon their fingers they wear rings of gold, and about their necks chains of gold, and, in conclusion, their heads be tied about with gold. Thus by all means possible they procure to have gold and silver among them in reproach and infamy. And these metals, which other nations do as grievously and sorrowfully forgo, as in a manner their own lives, if they should altogether at once be taken from the Utopians, no man there would think that he had lost the worth of one farthing.

They gather also pearls by the seaside, and diamonds and carbuncles upon certain rocks; and yet they seek not for them, but by chance finding them, they cut and polish them. And therewith they deck their young infants. Which, like as in the first years of their childhood they make much and be fond and proud of such ornaments, so when they be a little more grown in years and discretion, perceiving that none but children do

O wonderful contumely of gold.

Gold the reproachful badge of infamed persons.

Gems and precious stones toys for young children to play withal.

wear such toys and trifles, they lay them away even of their own shamefastness, without any bidding of their parents, even as our children, when they wax big, do cast away nuts,* brooches, and puppets. Therefore these laws and customs, which be so far different from all other nations, how divers fantasies also and minds they do cause, did I never so plainly perceive as in the ambassadors of the Anemolians.*

A very pleasant tale.
These ambassadors came to Amaurote while I was there. And because they came to entreat of great and weighty matters, those three citizens apiece out of every city* were come thither before them. But all the ambassadors of the next countries, which had been there before and knew the fashions and manners of the Utopians, among whom they perceived no honour given to sumptuous apparel, silks to be condemned, gold also to be infamed and reproachful, were wont to come thither in very homely and simple array. But the Anemolians, because they dwell far thence and had very little acquaintance with them, hearing that they were all apparelled alike, and that very rudely and homely, thinking them not to have the things which they did not wear, being therefore more proud than wise, determined in the gorgeousness of their apparel to represent very gods, and with the bright shining and glistering of their gay clothing to dazzle the eyes of the silly poor Utopians. So there came in three ambassadors with an hundred servants all apparelled in changeable colours,* the most of them in silks, the ambassadors themselves (for at home in their own country they were noblemen) in cloth of gold, with great chains of gold, with gold hanging at their ears, with gold rings upon their fingers, with brooches and aglets of gold upon their caps which glistered full of pearls and precious stones, to be short, trimmed and adorned with all those things which among the Utopians were either the punishment of bondmen or the reproach of infamed persons or else trifles for young children to play withal.

Therefore it would have done a man good at his heart to have seen how proudly they displayed their peacock's feathers, how much they made of their painted sheaths, and how loftily they set forth and advanced themselves when they compared their gallant apparel with the poor raiment of the Utopians. For all the people were swarmed forth into the streets. And on the other side it was no less pleasure to consider how much they were deceived and how far they missed of their purpose, being contrariwise taken than they thought they should have been. For to the eyes of all the Utopians, except very few which had been in other countries for some reasonable cause, all that gorgeousness of apparel seemed shameful and reproachful. Insomuch that they most reverently saluted the vilest and most abject of them for lords, passing over the ambassadors themselves without any honour, judging them by their wearing of golden chains to be bondmen. Yea, you should have seen children also that had cast away their pearls and precious stones, when they saw the like sticking upon the ambassadors' caps, dig and push their mothers under the sides, saying thus to them: 'look, mother, how great a lubber doth yet wear pearls and precious stones, as though he were a little child still.' But the mother, yea and that also in good earnest, 'peace, son,' saith she, 'I think he be some of the ambassadors' fools'. *O witty head.* Some found fault at their golden chains as to no use nor purpose, being so small and weak that a bondman might easily break them, and again so wide and large, that when it pleased him he might cast them off and run away at liberty whither he would.

But when the ambassadors had been there a day or two and saw so great abundance of gold so lightly esteemed, yea, in no less reproach than it was with them in honour, and, besides that, more gold in the chains and gyves of one fugitive bondman than all the costly ornaments of them three was worth, they began to abate their courage, and for very shame laid away all that gorgeous array whereof they were so proud. And specially when they had talked familiarly with the Utopians, and had learned all their fashions and opinions. For they marvel that any men be so foolish as to have delight and pleasure in the doubtful glistering of a little trifling stone, which may behold any of the stars, or else the sun itself. Or that any man is so mad as to count himself the nobler for the smaller or finer thread of wool, which self-same wool (be it now in never so *Doubtful he calleth it, either in consideration and respect of counterfeit stones, or else he calleth doubtful very little worth.**

fine a spun thread) a sheep did once wear, and yet was she all that time no other thing than a sheep.* They marvel also that gold, which of its own nature is a thing so unprofitable, is now among all people in so high estimation, that man himself, by whom, yea, and for the use of whom, it is so much set by, is in much less estimation than the gold itself. Insomuch that a lumpish blockheaded churl, and which hath no more wit than an ass, yea, and as full of naughtiness as of folly, shall have nevertheless many wise and good men in subjection and bondage only for this, because he hath a great heap of gold. Which if it should be taken from him by any fortune, or by some subtle wile and cautel of the law (which no less than fortune doth both raise up the low and pluck down the high) and be given to the most vile slave and abject drivel of all his household, then shortly after he shall go into the service of his servant, as an augmentation or overplus beside his money.* But they much more marvel at and detest the madness of them which to those rich men, in whose debt and danger they be not, do give almost divine honours for none other consideration but because they be rich, and yet knowing them to be such niggish pennyfathers, that they be sure as long as they live not the worth of one farthing of that heap of gold shall come to them.

These and suchlike opinions have they conceived, partly by education, being brought up in that commonwealth whose laws and customs be far different from these kinds of folly, and partly by good literature and learning. For though there be not many in every city which be exempt and discharged of all other labours and appointed only to learning (that is to say, such in whom, even from their very childhood, they have perceived a singular towardness, a fine wit, and a mind apt to good learning), yet all in their childhood be instruct in learning. And the better part of the people, both men and women, throughout all their whole life do bestow in learning those spare hours which we said they have vacant from bodily labours. They be taught learning in their own native tongue. For it is both copious in words and also pleasant to the ear, and for the utterance of a man's mind very perfect and sure. The

A true saying and a witty.

How much more wit is in the heads of the Utopians than of the common sort of Christians.

The studies and literature among the Utopians.

most part of all that side of the world useth the same language, saving that among the Utopians it is finest and purest, and according to the diversity of the countries it is diversely altered.

Of all these philosophers whose names be here famous in this part of the world to us known, before our coming thither not as much as the fame of any of them was common among them. And yet in music, logic, arithmetic, and geometry they have found out in a manner all that our ancient philosophers have taught. But as they in all things be almost equal to our old ancient clerks, so our new logicians in subtle inventions have far passed and gone beyond them. For they have not devised one of all those rules of restrictions, amplifications, and suppositions, very wittily invented in the *Small Logicals* which here our children in every place do learn. Furthermore, they were never yet able to find out the Second Intentions, insomuch that none of them all could ever see man himself in common, as they call him, though he be (as you know) bigger than ever was any giant, yea, and pointed to of us* even with our finger.*

Music, logic, arithmetic, geometry.

In this place seemeth to be a nipping taunt.

But they be in the course of the stars and the movings of the heavenly spheres* very expert and cunning. They have also wittily excogitated and devised instruments of divers fashions, wherein is exactly comprehended and contained the movings and situations of the sun, the moon, and of all the other stars which appear in their horizon. But as for the amities and dissensions of the planets, and all that deceitful divination by the stars,* they never as much as dreamed thereof. Rains, winds, and other courses of tempest they know before by certain tokens which they have learned by long use and observation. But of the causes of all these things and of the ebbing, flowing, and saltness of the sea, and finally of the original beginning and nature of heaven and of the world, they hold partly the same opinions that our old philosophers hold, and partly, as our philosophers vary among themselves, so they also, while they bring new reasons of things, do disagree from all them, and yet among themselves in all points they do not accord.

Astronomy.

Yet among Christians this gear is highly esteemed these days.

Natural philosophy is a knowledge most uncertain.

In that part of philosophy which entreateth of manners and virtue their reasons and opinions agree with ours. They

Moral philosophy.

The order of good things.

The end of good things.

The Utopians hold opinion that felicity consisteth in honest pleasure.

The principles of philosophy grounded upon religion.

The theology of the Utopians.

The immortality of the soul, whereof these days certain Christians be in doubt.

As every pleasure ought not to be embraced, so grief is not to be pursued, but for virtue's sake.

dispute of the good qualities of the soul, of the body, and of fortune.* And whether the name of goodness may be applied to all these or only to the endowments and gifts of the soul. They reason of virtue and pleasure. But the chief and principal question is in what thing, be it one or more, the felicity of man consisteth. But in this point they seem almost too much given and inclined to the opinion of them which defend pleasure, wherein they determine either all or the chiefest part of man's felicity to rest.* And (which is more to be marvelled at) the defence of this so dainty and delicate an opinion they fetch even from their grave, sharp, bitter, and rigorous religion. For they never dispute of felicity or blessedness but they join unto the reasons of philosophy certain principles taken out of religion, without the which to the investigation of true felicity they think reason of itself weak and unperfect. Those principles be these and suchlike: that the soul is immortal, and by the bountiful goodness of God ordained to felicity. That to our virtues and good deeds rewards be appointed after this life, and to our evil deeds punishments. Though these be pertaining to religion, yet they think it meet that they should be believed and granted by proofs of reason. But if these principles were condemned and disannulled, then without any delay they pronounce no man to be so foolish which would not do all his diligence and endeavour to obtain pleasure by right or wrong, only avoiding this inconvenience, that the less pleasure should not be a let or hindrance to the bigger; that he laboured not for that pleasure which would bring after it displeasure, grief, and sorrow. For they judge it extreme madness to follow sharp and painful virtue, and not only to banish the pleasure of life, but also willingly to suffer grief, without any hope of profit thereof ensuing. For what profit can there be if a man, when he hath passed over all his life unpleasantly, that is to say, miserably, shall have no reward after his death? But now, sir, they think not felicity to rest in all pleasure, but only in that pleasure that is good and honest, and that hereto as to perfect blessedness our nature is allured and drawn even of virtue, whereto only they that be of the contrary opinion do attribute felicity.

For they define virtue to be life ordered according to nature, and that we be hereunto ordained of God. And that he doth follow the course of nature, which in desiring and refusing things is ruled by reason. Furthermore, that reason doth chiefly and principally kindle in men the love and veneration of the divine majesty. Of whose goodness it is that we be, and that we be in possibility to attain felicity. And that secondarily it both stirreth and provoketh us to lead our life out of care in joy and mirth, and also moveth us to help and further all other in respect of the society of nature to obtain and enjoy the same. For there was never man so earnest and painful a follower of virtue and hater of pleasure, that would so enjoin you labours, watchings, and fastings, but he would also exhort you to ease, lighten, and relieve, to your power, the lack and misery of others, praising the same as a deed of humanity and pity. Then, if it be a point of humanity for man to bring health and comfort to man, and specially (which is a virtue most peculiarly belonging to man) to mitigate and assuage the grief of others, and by taking from them the sorrow and heaviness of life to restore them to joy, that is to say, to pleasure, why may it not then be said that nature doth provoke every man to do the same to himself? For a joyful life, that is to say, a pleasant life, is either evil; and if it be so, then thou shouldest not only help no man thereto, but rather, as much as in thee lieth, withdraw all men from it as noisome and hurtful; or else if thou not only mayst, but also of duty art bound, to procure it to other, why not chiefly to thyself? To whom thou art bound to show as much favour and gentleness as to other. For when nature biddeth thee to be good and gentle to other she commandeth thee not to be cruel and ungentle to thyself. Therefore even very nature (say they) prescribeth to us a joyful life, that is to say, pleasure, as the end of all our operations. And they define virtue to be life ordered according to the prescript of nature.

But in that that nature doth allure and provoke men one to help another to live merrily (which surely she doth not without a good cause, for no man is so far above the lot of man's state or condition, that nature doth cark and care for him only which equally favoureth all that be comprehended under the communion of one shape, form, and fashion), verily she

In this definition of virtue they agree with the Stoics.

The work and effect of reason in man.

But nowadays some there be that willingly procure unto themselves painful griefs, as though therein rested some high point of religion, whereas rather the religiously disposed person, if they happen to be either by chance or else by natural necessity, ought patiently to receive and suffer them.

commandeth thee to use diligent circumspection, that thou do
not so seek for thine own commodities that thou procure
others' incommodities. Wherefore their opinion is, that not
*Bargains and
laws.* only covenants and bargains made among private men ought
to be well and faithfully fulfilled, observed, and kept, but
also common laws, which either a good prince hath justly
published, or else the people, neither oppressed with tyranny,
neither deceived by fraud and guile, hath by their common
consent constituted and ratified concerning the partition of
the commodities of life, that is to say, the matter of pleasure.
These laws not offended, it is wisdom that thou look to thine
own wealth. And to do the same for the common wealth is no
less than thy duty, if thou bearest any reverent love, or any
natural zeal and affection to thy native country. But to go about
to let another man of his pleasure whiles thou procurest thine
own, that is open wrong. Contrariwise, to withdraw something
from thyself to give others, that is a point of humanity and
gentleness, which never taketh away so much commodity as it
*The mutual
recourse of
kindness.* bringeth again. For it is recompensed with the return of benefits; and the conscience of the good deed, with the remembrance of the thankful love and benevolence of them to whom
thou hast done it, doth bring more pleasure to thy mind than
that which thou hast withholden from thyself could have
brought to thy body. Finally (which to a godly-disposed and a
religious mind is easy to be persuaded), God recompenseth the
gift of a short and small pleasure with great and everlasting joy.
Therefore, the matter diligently weighed and considered, thus
they think, that all our actions, and in them the virtues themselves, be referred at the last to pleasure as their end and felicity.
*The definition
of pleasure.* Pleasure they call every motion and state of the body or
mind wherein man hath naturally delectation. Appetite they
join to nature, and that not without a good cause. For like as
not only the senses, but also right reason, coveteth whatsoever
is naturally pleasant, so that it may be gotten without wrong or
injury, not letting or debarring a greater pleasure, nor causing
painful labour, even so those things that men by vain imagina-
*False and
counterfeit
pleasures.* tion do feign against nature to be pleasant (as though it lay in
their power to change the things, as they do the names of

78

things), all such pleasures they believe to be of so small help and furtherance to felicity, that they count them a great let and hindrance. Because that in whom they have once taken place, all his mind they possess with a false opinion of pleasure. So that there is no place left for true and natural delectations. For there be many things which of their own nature contain no pleasantness, yea, the most part of them much grief and sorrow. And yet, through the perverse and malicious flickering enticements of lewd and unhonest desires, be taken not only for special and sovereign pleasures, but also be counted among the chief causes of life.

In this counterfeit kind of pleasure they put them that I spake of before, which the better gowns they have on, the better men they think themselves. In the which thing they do twice err. For they be no less deceived in that they think their gown the better, than they be in that they think themselves the better. For if you consider the profitable use of the garment, why should wool of a finer-spun thread be thought better than the wool of a coarse-spun thread? Yet they, as though the one did pass the other by nature and not by their mistaking, advance themselves, and think the price of their own persons thereby greatly increased. And therefore the honour which in a coarse gown they durst not have looked for, they require, as it were of duty, for their finer gown's sake. And if they be passed by without reverence, they take it displeasantly and disdainfully. And again, is it not like madness to take a pride in vain and unprofitable honours? For what natural or true pleasure dost thou take of another man's bare head or bowed knees? Will this ease the pain of thy knees or remedy the frenzy of thy head? In this image of counterfeit pleasure they be of a marvellous madness, which for the opinion of nobility rejoice much in their own conceit,* because it was their fortune to come of such ancestors whose stock of long time hath been counted rich (for now nobility is nothing else), specially rich in lands. And though their ancestors left them not one foot of land, or else they themselves have pissed it against the walls, yet they think themselves not the less noble therefore of one hair.

In this number also they count them that take pleasure and

The error of them that esteem themselves the more for apparel's sake.

Foolish honours.

Vain nobility.

*Pleasure in
precious
stones most
foolish.*

*The opinion
and fashion
of people doth
augment and
diminish the
price and
estimation of
precious
stones.*

*Beholders of
treasure, not
occupying the
same.*

*Hiders of
treasure.*

*A pretty
fiction and a
witty.*

Dice play.

*Hunting and
hawking.*

delight (as I said) in gems and precious stones, and think themselves almost gods if they chance to get an excellent one, specially of that kind which in that time of their own countrymen is had in highest estimation. For one kind of stone keepeth not his price still in all countries and at all times. Nor they buy them not, but taken out of the gold and bare;* no nor so neither, until they have made the seller to swear that he will warrant and assure it to be a true stone and no counterfeit gem. Such care they take lest a counterfeit stone should deceive their eyes instead of a right stone. But why shouldest thou not take even as much pleasure in beholding a counterfeit stone, which thine eye cannot discern from a right stone? They should both be of like value to thee, even as to the blind man. What shall I say of them that keep superfluous riches, to take delectation only in the beholding and not in the use or occupying thereof? Do they take true pleasure, or else be they deceived with false pleasure? Or of them that be in a contrary vice, hiding the gold which they shall never occupy, nor peradventure never see more? And whiles they take care lest they shall lose it, do lose it indeed. For what is it else when they hide it in the ground, taking it both from their own use and perchance from all other men's also? And yet thou, when thou hast hid thy treasure, as one out of all care hoppest for joy. The which treasure, if it should chance to be stolen, and thou ignorant of the theft shouldst die ten years after, all that ten years' space that thou livest after thy money was stolen, what matter was it to thee whether it had been taken away or else safe as thou leftest it? Truly both ways like profit came to thee.

To these so foolish pleasures they join dicers, whose madness they know by hearsay and not by use. Hunters also, and hawkers. For what pleasure is there (say they) in casting the dice upon a table, which thou hast done so often, that if there were any pleasure in it, yet the oft use might make thee weary thereof? Or what delight can there be, and not rather displeasure, in hearing the barking and howling of dogs? Or what greater pleasure is there to be felt when a dog followeth an hare than when a dog followeth a dog? For one thing is done in both, that is to say, running, if thou hast pleasure therein. But if the hope of slaughter and the expectation of tearing in pieces the beast doth please thee, thou shouldest rather be moved with pity to see a silly innocent hare murdered of a dog: the weak of the stronger, the fearful of the fierce, the innocent of the cruel and unmerciful. Therefore all this exercise of hunting, as a thing unworthy to be used of free men, the Utopians have rejected to their butchers, to the which craft (as we said before) they appoint their bondmen. For they count hunting the lowest, the vilest, and most abject part of butchery, and the other parts of it more profitable and more honest, as bringing much more commodity, in that they kill beasts only for necessity. Whereas the hunter seeketh nothing but pleasure of the silly and woeful beast's slaughter and murder. The which pleasure in beholding death they think doth rise in the very beasts, either of a cruel affection of mind, or else to be changed in continuance of time into cruelty by long use of so cruel a pleasure.

Hunting the basest part of butchery among the Utopians and yet this is now the exercise of most noble men.

These, therefore, and all suchlike, which be innumerable, though the common sort of people doth take them for pleasures, yet they, seeing there is no natural pleasantness in them, do plainly determine them to have no affinity with true and right pleasure. For as touching that they do commonly move the sense with delectation (which seemeth to be a work of pleasure), this doth nothing diminish their opinion. For not the nature of the thing, but their perverse and lewd custom is the cause hereof. Which causeth them to accept bitter or sour things for sweet things even as women with child in their vitiate and corrupt taste think pitch and tallow sweeter than any honey. Howbeit, no man's judgement depraved and corrupt, either by sickness or by custom, can change the nature of pleasure more than it can do the nature of other things.

They make divers kinds of true pleasures. For some they attribute to the soul and some to the body. To the soul they give intelligence and that delectation that cometh of the contemplation of truth. Hereunto is joined the pleasant remembrance of the good life past. The pleasure of the body they divide into two parts. The first is when delectation is sensibly felt and perceived. Which many times chanceth by the

The kinds of true pleasure.

The pleasures of the body.

renewing and refreshing of those parts which our natural heat drieth up. This cometh by meat and drink. And sometimes whiles those things be expulsed and voided, whereof is in the body over-great abundance. This pleasure is felt when we do our natural easement, or when we be doing the act of generation, or when the itching of any part is eased with rubbing or scratching. Sometimes pleasure riseth exhibiting to any member nothing that it desireth, nor taking from it any pain that it feeleth, which nevertheless tickleth and moveth our senses with a certain secret efficacy, but with a manifest motion turneth them to it; as is that which cometh of music. The second part of bodily pleasure, they say, is that which consisteth and resteth in the quiet and upright state of the body. And that truly is every man's own proper health, intermingled and disturbed with no grief. For this, if it be not letted, nor assaulted with no grief, is delectable of itself, though it be moved with no external or outward pleasure. For though it be not so plain and manifest to the sense as the greedy lust of eating and drinking, yet, nevertheless, many take it for the chiefest pleasure. All the Utopians grant it to be a right sovereign pleasure and, as you would say, the foundation and ground of all pleasures, as which even alone is able to make the state and condition of life delectable and pleasant; and it being once taken away, there is no place left for any pleasure.

Bodily health.

For to be without grief not having health, that they call insensibility and not pleasure: the Utopians have long ago rejected and condemned the opinion of them which said that steadfast and quiet health (for this question also hath been diligently debated among them) ought not therefore to be counted a pleasure,* because, they say, it cannot be presently and sensibly perceived and felt by some outward motion. But of the contrary part now they agree almost all in this, that health is a most sovereign pleasure. For seeing that in sickness (say they) is grief, which is a mortal enemy to pleasure, even as sickness is to health, why should not then pleasure be in the quietness of health? For they say it maketh nothing to this matter, whether you say that sickness is a grief, or that in sickness is grief, for all cometh to one purpose. For whether

health be a pleasure itself, or a necessary cause of pleasure, as
fire is of heat, truly both ways it followeth that they cannot be
without pleasure that be in perfect health. Furthermore,
whiles we eat (say they), then health, which began to be
appaired, fighteth by the help of food against hunger. In the
which fight, whiles health by little and little getteth the upper
hand, that same proceeding and, (as ye would say), that
onwardness to the wont strength ministreth that pleasure
whereby we be so refreshed.* Health, therefore, which in the
conflict is joyful, shall it not be merry when it hath gotten the
victory? But as soon as it hath recovered the pristinate
strength, which thing only in all the fight it coveted, shall it
incontinent be astonied? Nor shall it not know nor embrace the
own wealth and goodness?* For where it is said health cannot be
felt, this, they think, is nothing true. For what man waking, say
they, feeleth not himself in health, but he that is not?* Is there
any man so possessed with stonish insensibility or with leth-
argy, that is to say, the sleeping sickness, that he will not grant
health to be acceptable to him, and delectable? But what other *Delectation.*
thing is delectation than that which by another name is called
pleasure?

They embrace chiefly the pleasures of the mind, for them *The pleasures*
they count the chiefest and most principal of all. The chief *of the mind.*
part of them they think doth come of the exercise of virtue and
conscience of good life.* Of these pleasures that the body ministreth, they give the pre-eminence to health. For the delight of
eating and drinking, and whatsoever hath any like pleasantness, they determine to be pleasures much to be desired, but
no other ways than for health's sake. For such things of their
own proper nature be not so pleasant, but in that they resist
sickness privily stealing on. Therefore, like as it is a wise man's
part rather to avoid sickness than to wish for medicines, and
rather to drive away and put to flight careful griefs than to call
for comfort, so it is much better not to need this kind of
pleasure than thereby to be eased of the contrary grief. The
which kind of pleasure if any man take for his felicity, that man
must needs grant that then he shall be in most felicity, if he
live that life which is led in continual hunger, thirst, itching,

eating, drinking, scratching, and rubbing.* The which life how not only foul and unhonest, but also how miserable and wretched it is, who perceiveth not? These doubtless be the basest pleasures of all, as unpure and unperfect. For they never come, but accompanied with their contrary griefs, as with the pleasure of eating is joined hunger, and that after no very equal sort. For of these two the grief is both the more vehement and also of longer continuance. For it beginneth before the pleasure, and endeth not until the pleasure die with it.

Wherefore such pleasures they think not greatly to be set by, but in that they be necessary. Howbeit, they have delight also in these, and thankfully knowledge the tender love of mother nature, which with most pleasant delectation allureth her children to that, to the necessary use whereof they must from time to time continually be forced and driven. For how wretched and miserable should our life be, if these daily griefs of hunger and thirst could not be driven away but with bitter potions and sour medicines, as the other diseases be wherewith we be *The gifts of* seldomer troubled? But beauty, strength, nimbleness: these as *nature.* peculiar and pleasant gifts of nature they make much of. But those pleasures that be received by the ears, the eyes, and the nose, which nature willeth to be proper and peculiar to man (for no other living creature doth behold the fairness and the beauty of the world or is moved with any respect of savours, but only for the diversity of meats, neither perceiveth the concordant and discordant distances of sounds and tunes), these pleasures, I say, they accept and allow as certain pleasant rejoicings of life. But in all things this cautel they use, that a less pleasure hinder not a bigger, and that the pleasure be no cause of displeasure, which they think to follow of necessity if the pleasure be unhonest. But yet to despise the comeliness of beauty, to waste the bodily strength, to turn nimbleness into sluggishness, to consume and make feeble the body with fasting, to do injury to health, and to reject the pleasant motions of nature (unless a man neglect these commodities whiles he doth with a fervent zeal procure the wealth of others or the common profit, for the which pleasure forborne he is in hope of a greater pleasure at God's hand), else for a vain shadow of

virtue for the wealth and profit of no man, to punish himself,
or to the intent he may be able courageously to suffer adversity
(which perchance shall never come to him), this to do they
think it a point of extreme madness, and a token of a man
cruelly minded towards himself and unkind towards nature, as
one so disdaining to be in her danger, that he renounceth and
refuseth all her benefits. This is their sentence and opinion of
virtue and pleasure. And they believe that by man's reason
none can be found truer than this, unless any godlier be
inspired into man from heaven. Wherein whether they believe *Mark this*
well or no, neither the time doth suffer us to discuss, neither it *well.*
is now necessary. For we have taken upon us to show and
declare their laws and ordinances, and not to defend them.

But this thing I believe verily: howsoever these decrees be,
that there is in no place of the world neither a more excellent
people, neither a more flourishing commonwealth. They be *The wealth*
light and quick of body, full of activity and nimbleness, and of *and*
more strength than a man would judge them by their stature, *description of*
the Utopians.
which for all that is not too low. And though their soil be not
very fruitful, nor their air very wholesome, yet against the air
they so defend them with temperate diet, and so order and
husband their ground with diligent travail, that in no country
is greater increase and plenty of corn and cattle, nor men's
bodies of longer life and subject or apt to fewer diseases.
There, therefore, a man may see well and diligently exploited
and furnished, not only those things which husbandmen do
commonly in other countries, as by craft and cunning to
remedy the barrenness of the ground, but also a whole wood by
the hands of the people plucked up by the roots in one place,
and set again in another place. Wherein was had regard and
consideration, not of plenty, but of commodious carriage, that
wood and timber might be nigher to the sea or the rivers or the
cities. For it is less labour and business to carry grain far
by land than wood. The people be gentle, merry, quick, and
fine witted, delighting in quietness and, when need requireth,
able to abide and suffer much bodily labour. Else they be not
greatly desirous and fond of it; but in the exercise and study of
the mind they be never weary.

The utility of the Greek tongue.

When they had heard me speak of the Greek literature or learning (for in Latin there was nothing that I thought they would greatly allow, besides historians and poets)* they made wonderful earnest and importunate suit unto me that I would teach and instruct them in that tongue and learning. I began, therefore, to read unto them, at the first, truly, more because I would not seem to refuse the labour than that I hoped that they would anything profit therein. But when I had gone forward a little, I perceived incontinent by their diligence that my labour

A wonderful openness to learning in the Utopians.

But now most blockheaded asses be set to learning, and most pregnant wits corrupt with pleasures.

should not be bestowed in vain. For they began so easily to fashion their letters, so plainly to pronounce the words, so quickly to learn by heart, and so surely to rehearse the same, that I marvelled at it, saving that the most part of them were fine and chosen wits, and of ripe age, picked out of the company of the learned men which not only of their own free and voluntary will, but also by the commandment of the council, undertook to learn this language. Therefore in less than three years' space there was nothing in the Greek tongue that they lacked. They were able to read good authors without any stay, if the book were not false.* This kind of learning, as I suppose, they took so much the sooner because it is somewhat alliant to them. For I think that this nation took their beginning of the Greeks, because their speech, which in all other points is not much unlike the Persian tongue, keepeth divers signs and tokens of the Greek language in the names of their cities and of their magistrates.

They have of me (for when I was determined to enter into my fourth voyage, I cast into the ship in the stead of merchandise a pretty fardel of books, because I intended to come again rather never than shortly), they have, I say, of me the most part of Plato's works, more of Aristotle's, also Theophrastus* of plants, but in divers places (which I am sorry for) unperfect. For whiles we were a-shipboard a marmoset chanced upon the book as it was negligently laid by, which wantonly playing therewith plucked out certain leaves and tore them in pieces. Of them that have written the grammar, they have only Lascaris, for Theodorus I carried not with me, nor never a dictionary but Hesychius and Dioscorides. They set great store by Plutarch's books, and they be delighted with Lucian's merry conceits and jests. Of the poets they have Aristophanes, Homer, Euripides, and Sophocles in Aldus's small print. Of the historians they have Thucydides, Herodotus, and Herodian. Also, my companion Tricius Apinatus carried with him physic books, certain small works of Hippocrates, and Galen's *Microtechne*.* The which book they have in great estimation.

For though there be almost no nation under heaven that hath less need of physic than they, yet this notwithstanding, physic is nowhere in greater honour. Because they count the *Physic highly regarded.* knowledge of it among the goodliest and most profitable parts of philosophy. For whiles they by the help of this philosophy search out the secret mysteries of nature, they think themselves to receive thereby not only wonderful great pleasure, but also to obtain great thanks and favour of the author and maker thereof. Whom they think, according to the fashion of other artificers, to have set forth the marvellous and gorgeous *The contemplation of nature.* frame of the world for man with great affection intentively to behold. Whom only he hath made of wit and capacity to consider and understand the excellency of so great a work. And therefore he beareth (say they) more goodwill and love to the curious and diligent beholder and viewer of his work and marveller at the same than he doth to him which, like a very brute beast without wit and reason, or as one without sense or moving, hath no regard to so great and so wonderful a spectacle.

The wits, therefore, of the Utopians, inured and exercised in learning, be marvellous quick in the invention of feats helping anything to the advantage and wealth of life. Howbeit, two feats they may thank us for, that is, the science of imprinting and the craft of making paper. And yet not only us, but chiefly and principally themselves. For when we showed to them Aldus his print in books of paper, and told them of the stuff whereof paper is made, and of the feat of graving letters, speaking somewhat more than we could plainly declare (for there was none of us that knew perfectly either the one or the other), they forthwith very wittily conjectured the thing. And whereas before they wrote only in skins, in barks of trees, and in reeds, now they have attempted to make paper and to imprint letters. And though at the first it proved not all of the best, yet by often assaying the same they shortly got the feat of both. And have so brought the matter about that if they had copies of Greek authors they could lack no books. But now they have no more than I rehearsed before, saving that by printing of books they have multiplied and increased the same into many thousands of copies.

Whosoever cometh thither to see the land, being excellent in any gift of wit, or through much and long journeying well experienced and seen in the knowledge of many countries (for the which cause we were very welcome to them), him they receive and entertain wondrous gently and lovingly. For they have delight to hear what is done in every land, howbeit very few merchant-men come thither. For what should they bring thither, unless it were iron, or else gold and silver, which they had rather carry home again? Also such things as are to be carried out of their land, they think it more wisdom to carry that gear forth themselves, than that other should come thither to fetch it, to the intent they may the better know the outlands on every side of them, and keep in use the feat and knowledge of sailing.

OF BONDMEN, SICK PERSONS, WEDLOCK, AND DIVERS OTHER MATTERS

A marvellous equity of this nation.

They neither make bondmen of prisoners taken in battle, unless it be in battle that they fought themselves, nor of bondmen's children, nor, to be short, of any such as they can get out of foreign countries,* though he were there a bondman. But either such as among themselves for heinous offenses be punished with bondage, or else such as in the cities of other lands for great trespasses be condemned to death. And of this sort of bondmen they have most store. For many of them they bring home, sometimes paying very little for them, yea, most commonly getting them for gramercy. These sorts of bondmen they keep not only in continual work and labour, but also in bonds. But their own men they handle hardest, whom they judge more desperate, and to have deserved greater punishment, because they being so godly brought up to virtue in so excellent a commonwealth, could not for all that be refrained from misdoing. Another kind of bondmen they have, when a vile drudge being a poor labourer in another country doth choose of his own free will to be a bondman among them. These they entreat and order honestly, and entertain almost as gently as their own free citizens, saving that they put them to a little more labour, as thereto accustomed. If any such be disposed to depart thence (which seldom is seen) they neither hold him against his will, neither send him away with empty hands.

The sick (as I said) they see to with great affection, and let nothing at all pass concerning either physic or good diet, whereby they may be restored again to their health. Such as be sick of incurable diseases they comfort with sitting by them, with talking with them, and, to be short, with all manner of helps that may be. But if the disease be not only incurable, but also full of continual pain and anguish, then the priests and the magistrates exhort the man (seeing he is not able to do any duty of life, and by overliving his own death is noisome and irksome to other and grievous to himself), that he will determine with himself no longer to cherish that pestilent and painful disease. And, seeing his life is to him but a torment, that he will not be unwilling to die, but rather take a good hope to him, and either dispatch himself out of that painful life, as out of a prison or a rack of torment, or else suffer himself willingly to be rid out of it by other. And in so doing they tell him he shall do wisely, seeing by his death he shall lose no commodity, but end his pain. And because in that act he shall follow the counsel of the priests, that is to say, of the interpreters of God's will and pleasure, they show him that he shall do like a godly and a virtuous man. They that be thus persuaded finish their lives willingly, either with hunger, or else die in their sleep without any feeling of death. But they cause none such to die against his will, nor they use no less diligence and attendance about him, believing this to be an honourable death. Else he that killeth himself before that the priests and the council have

Of them that be sick.

Voluntary death.

allowed the cause of his death, him as unworthy either to be buried or with fire to be consumed, they cast unburied into some stinking marsh.

Of wedlock. The woman is not married before she be eighteen years old. The man is four years older before he marry. If either the man or the woman be proved to have actually* offended before their marriage, with another, the party that so hath trespassed is sharply punished. And both the offenders be forbidden ever after in all their life to marry, unless the fault be forgiven by the prince's pardon. But both the good man and the good wife of the house where that offence was committed, as being slack and negligent in looking to their charge, be in danger of great reproach and infamy. That offence is so sharply punished because they perceive that unless they be diligently kept from the liberty of this vice, few will join together in the love of marriage, wherein all the life must be led with one, and also all the griefs and displeasures coming therewith patiently be taken and borne.

Furthermore, in choosing wives and husbands they observe earnestly and straitly a custom which seemed to us very fond *Though not* and foolish.* For a sad and an honest matron showeth the *very honestly,* woman, be she maid or widow, naked to the wooer. And like-*yet not* wise a sage and discreet man exhibiteth the wooer naked to the *unwisely.* woman. At this custom we laughed, and disallowed it as foolish. But they, on the other part, do greatly wonder at the folly of all other nations which, in buying a colt,* whereas a little money is in hazard, be so chary and circumspect, that though he be almost all bare, yet they will not buy him unless the saddle and all the harness be taken off, lest under those coverings be hid some gall or sore. And yet in choosing a wife, which shall be either pleasure or displeasure to them all their life after, they be so reckless, that all the residue of the woman's body being covered with clothes, they esteem her scarcely by one handbreadth (for they can see no more but her face), and so to join her to them not without great jeopardy of evil agreeing together, if anything in her body afterward should chance to offend and mislike them. For all men be not so wise as to have respect to the virtuous conditions of the party. And the

endowments of the body cause the virtues of the mind more to
be esteemed and regarded, yea, even in the marriages of wise
men. Verily so foul deformity may be hid under those coverings, that it may quite alienate and take away the man's mind
from his wife, when it shall not be lawful for their bodies to be
separate again. If such deformity happen by any chance after
the marriage is consummate and finished, well, there is no
remedy but patience. Every man must take his fortune well a
worth. But it were well done that a law were made whereby all
such deceits might be eschewed and avoided beforehand.

And this were they constrained more earnestly to look
upon, because they only of the nations in that part of the world
be content every man with one wife apiece. And matrimony is
there never broken but by death, except adultery break the
bond, or else the intolerable wayward manners of either party. *Divorcement.*
For if either of them find themself for any such cause grieved,
they may by the licence of the council change and take
another.* But the other party liveth ever after in infamy and out
of wedlock. Howbeit, the husband to put away his wife for no
other fault but for that some mishap is fallen to her body, this
by no means they will suffer. For they judge it a great point of
cruelty that anybody in their most need of help and comfort
should be cast off and forsaken, and that old age, which both
bringeth sickness with it and is a sickness itself,* should
unkindly and unfaithfully be dealt withal. But now and then it
chanceth whereas the man and the woman cannot well agree
between themselves, both of them finding other, with whom
they hope to live more quietly and merrily, that they by the full
consent of them both be divorced asunder and married again
to other. But that not without the authority of the council.
Which agreeth to no divorces before they and their wives have
diligently tried and examined the matter. Yea, and then also
they be loath to consent to it, because they know this to be the
next way to break love between man and wife, to be in easy
hope of a new marriage. Breakers of wedlock be punished with
most grievous bondage; and if both the offenders were married, then the parties which in that behalf have suffered wrong,
being divorced from the avoutrers, be married together, if they

will, or else to whom they lust. But if either of them both do still continue in love toward so unkind a bedfellow, the use of wedlock is not to them forbidden, if the party faultless be disposed to follow in toiling and drudgery the person which for that offence is condemned to bondage. And very oft it chanceth that the repentance of the one and the earnest diligence of the other doth so move the prince with pity and compassion, that he restoreth the bond person from servitude to liberty and freedom again. But if the same party be taken eftsoons in that fault, there is no other way but death.

To other trespasses no prescript punishment is appointed by any law. But according to the heinousness of the offence, or contrary, so the punishment is moderated by the discretion of the council. The husbands chastise their wives, and the parents their children, unless they have done any so horrible an offence, that the open punishment thereof maketh much for the advancement of honest manners.* But most commonly the most heinous faults be punished with the incommodity of bondage. For that they suppose to be to the offenders no less grief, and to the commonwealth more profit, than if they should hastily put them to death, and so make them quite out of the way. For there cometh more profit of their labour than of their death, and by their example they fear other the longer from like offenses. But if they, being thus used, do rebel and kick again, then forsooth they be slain as desperate and wild beasts, whom neither prison nor chain could restrain and keep under. But they which take their bondage patiently be not left all hopeless. For after they have been broken and tamed with long miseries, if then they show such repentance as thereby it may be perceived that they be sorrier for their offence than for their punishment, sometimes by the prince's prerogative, and sometimes by the voice and consent of the people, their bondage either is mitigated or else clean released and forgiven. He that moveth to advoutry is in no less danger and jeopardy than if he had committed advoutry in deed. For in all offenses they count the intent and pretenced purpose as evil as the act or deed itself, thinking that no let ought to excuse him that did his best to have no let.

They have singular delight and pleasure in fools.* And as it is a great reproach to do any of them hurt or injury, so they prohibit not to take pleasure of foolishness. For that, they think, doth much good to the fools. And if any man be so sad and stern that he cannot laugh neither at their words nor at their deeds, none of them be committed to his tuition, for fear lest he would not entreat them gently and favourably enough: to whom they should bring no delectation (for other goodness in them is none), much less any profit should they yield him. To mock a man for his deformity or for that he lacketh any part or limb of his body is counted great dishonesty and reproach, not to him that is mocked, but to him that mocketh. Which unwisely doth embraid any man of that as a vice that was not in his power to eschew.

Also, as they count and reckon very little wit to be in him that regardeth not natural beauty and comeliness, so to help the same with paintings* is taken for a vain and a wanton pride, not without great infamy. For they know, even by very experience, that no comeliness of beauty doth so highly commend and advance the wives in the conceit of their husbands as honest conditions and lowliness.* For as love is oftentimes won with beauty, so it is not kept, preserved and continued but by virtue and obedience. They do not only fear their people from doing evil by punishments, but also allure them to virtue with rewards of honour. Therefore they set up in the market-place the images of notable men and of such as have been great and bountiful benefactors to the commonwealth, for the perpetual memory of their good acts, and also that the glory and renown of the ancestors may stir and provoke their posterity to virtue. He that inordinately and ambitiously desireth promotions is left all hopeless for ever attaining any promotion as long as he liveth.

They live together lovingly. For no magistrate is either haughty or fearful. Fathers they be called, and like fathers they use themselves. The citizens (as it is their duty) willingly exhibit unto them due honour without any compulsion. Nor the prince himself is not known from the other by princely apparel or a robe of state, nor by a crown or diadem royal or

cap of maintenance,* but by a little sheaf of corn carried before
him. And so a taper of wax is borne before the bishop, whereby
only he is known. They have but few laws. For to people so
instruct and institute very few do suffice. Yea, this thing they
chiefly reprove among other nations, that innumerable books
of laws and expositions upon the same be not sufficient. But
they think it against all right and justice that men should be
bound to those laws which either be in number more than be
able to be read. Or else blinder and darker than that any man
can well understand them. Furthermore, they utterly exclude
and banish all attorneys, proctors, and sergeants at the law,*
which craftily handle matters, and subtly dispute of the laws.
For they think it most meet that every man should plead his
own matter, and tell the same tale before the judge that he
would tell to his man of law. So shall there be less circumstance
of words, and the truth shall sooner come to light, whiles the
judge with a discreet judgement doth weigh the words of him
whom no lawyer hath instruct with deceit, and whiles he
helpeth and beareth out simple wits against the false and
malicious circumventions of crafty children.

    This is hard to be observed in other countries, in so infinite
a number of blind and intricate laws. But in Utopia every man
is a cunning lawyer. For (as I said) they have very few laws, and
the plainer and grosser that any interpretation is, that they
allow as most just. For all laws (say they) be made and published only to the intent that by them every man should be put
in remembrance of his duty. But the crafty and subtle interpretation of them (forasmuch as few can attain thereto) can put
very few in that remembrance, whereas the simple, the plain,
and gross meaning of the laws is open to every man. Else as
touching the vulgar sort of the people, which be both most in
number and have most need to know their duties, were it not as
good for them that no law were made at all, as, when it is made,
to bring so blind an interpretation upon it, that without great
wit and long arguing no man can discuss it? To the finding out
whereof neither the gross judgement of the people can attain,
neither the whole life of them that be occupied in working for
their livings can suffice thereto.

Few laws.

The multitude of lawyers superfluous.

The intent of laws.

These virtues of the Utopians have caused their next neighbours and borderers, which live free and under no subjection (for the Utopians long ago have delivered many of them from tyranny), to take magistrates of them, some for a year and some for five years' space. Which, when the time of their office is expired, they bring home again with honour and praise, and take new again with them into their country.* These nations have undoubtedly very well and wholesomely provided for their commonwealths. For seeing that both the making and marring of the weal-public doth depend and hang upon the manners of the rulers and magistrates, what officers could they more wisely have chosen than those which cannot be led from honesty by bribes (for to them that shortly after shall depart thence into their own country money should be unprofitable) nor yet be moved either with favour or malice towards any man, as being strangers and unacquainted with the people? The which two vices of affection and avarice, where they take place in judgements, incontinent they break justice,* the strongest and surest bond of a commonwealth. These peoples which fetch their officers and rulers from them, the Utopians call their fellows. And others to whom they have been beneficial, they call their friends.

As touching leagues, which in other places between country *Of leagues.* and country be so oft concluded, broken, and renewed, they never make none with any nation. For to what purpose serve leagues, say they? As though nature had not set sufficient love between man and man. And who so regardeth not nature, think you that he will pass for words? They be brought into this opinion chiefly because that in those parts of the world leagues between princes be wont to be kept and observed very slenderly. For here in Europe, and especially in these parts where the faith and religion of Christ reigneth, the majesty of leagues is everywhere esteemed holy and inviolable, partly through the justice and goodness of princes, and partly at the reverence and motion of the head bishops.* Which, like as they make no promise themselves but they do very religiously perform the same, so they exhort all princes in any wise to abide by their promises, and them that refuse or deny so to do, by

Thomas More

their pontifical power and authority they compel thereto. And
surely they think well that it might seem a very reproachful
thing if, in the leagues of them which by a peculiar name be
called faithful, faith should have no place. But in that new-
found part of the world, which is scarcely so far from us
beyond the line equinoctial as our life and manners be dissident from theirs, no trust nor confidence is in leagues. But the
more and holier ceremonies the league is knit up with, the
sooner it is broken by some cavillation found in the words,
which many times of purpose be so craftily put in and placed,
that the bands can never be so sure nor so strong but they will
find some hole open to creep out at, and to break both league
and truth. The which crafty dealing, yea, the which fraud and
deceit, if they should know it to be practised among private
men in their bargains and contracts, they would incontinent
cry out at it with an open mouth and a sour countenance, as an
offence most detestable, and worthy to be punished with a
shameful death; yea, even very they that advance themselves
authors of like counsel given to princes. Wherefore it may well
be thought, either that all justice is but a base and a low virtue
and which avaleth itself far under the high dignity of kings, or,
at the least wise, that there be two justices: the one meet for the
inferior sort of the people, going afoot and creeping low by the
ground, and bound down on every side with many bands
because it shall not run at rovers;* the other a princely virtue,
which like as it is of much higher majesty than the other poor
justice, so also it is of much more liberty, as to the which
nothing is unlawful that it lusteth after.

These manners of princes (as I said) which be there so evil
keepers of leagues, cause the Utopians, as I suppose, to make
no leagues at all, which perchance would change their mind
if they lived here. Howbeit, they think that though leagues
be never so faithfully observed and kept, yet the custom of
making leagues was very evil begun. For this causeth men (as
though nations which be separate asunder by the space of a
little hill or a river were coupled together by no society or bond
of nature) to think themselves born adversaries and enemies
one to another, and that it were lawful for the one to seek the

death and destruction of the other if leagues were not; yea, and that after the leagues be accorded, friendship doth not grow and increase, but the licence of robbing and stealing doth still remain, as far forth as, for lack of foresight and advisement in writing the words of the league, any sentence or clause to the contrary is not therein sufficiently comprehended. But they be of a contrary opinion. That is, that no man ought to be counted an enemy which hath done no injury. And that the fellowship of nature is a strong league, and that men be better and more surely knit together by love and benevolence than by covenants of leagues; by hearty affection of mind than by words.

OF WARFARE

War or battle as a thing very beastly, and yet to no kind of beasts in so much use as to man, they do detest and abhor. And contrary to the custom almost of all other nations they count nothing so much against glory as glory gotten in war. And therefore, though they do daily practise and exercise themselves in the discipline of war, and not only the men, but also the women upon certain appointed days, lest they should be to seek in the feat of arms if need should require,* yet they never go to battle but either in the defence of their own country or to drive out of their friends' land the enemies that have invaded it, or by their power to deliver from the yoke and bondage of tyranny some people that be therewith oppressed. Which thing they do of mere pity and compassion. Howbeit, they send help to their friends, not ever in their defence, but sometimes also to requite and revenge injuries before to them done. But this they do not unless their counsel and advice in the matter be asked, whiles it is yet new and fresh. For if they find the cause probable, and if the contrary part* will not restore again such things as be of them justly demanded, then they be the chief authors and makers of the war. Which they do not only as oft as, by inroads and invasions of soldiers, preys and booties be driven away, but then also much more mortally when their friends' merchants in any land, either under the pretence of unjust laws or else by the wresting and wrong understanding of good laws, do sustain an unjust accusation under the colour of justice.* Neither the battle which the Utopians fought for the Nephelogetes against the Alaopolitans* a little before our time was made for any other cause, but that the Nephelogete merchant men, as the Utopians thought, suffered wrong of the Alaopolitans under the pretence of right. But whether it were right or wrong, it was with so cruel and mortal war revenged, the countries round about joining their help and power to the puissance and malice of both parties, that most flourishing and wealthy peoples being some of them shrewdly shaken, and some of them sharply beaten, the mischiefs were not finished nor ended until the Alaopolitans at the last were yielded up as bondmen into the jurisdiction of the Nephelogetes. For the Utopians fought not this war for themselves. And yet the Nephelogetes before the war, when the Alaopolitans flourished in wealth, were nothing to be compared with them.

So eagerly the Utopians prosecute the injuries done to their friends: yea, in money matters, and not their own likewise. For if they by covin or guile be wiped beside their goods, so that no violence be done to their bodies, they wreak their anger by abstaining from occupying with that nation until they have made satisfaction. Not for because they set less store by their own citizens than by their friends, but that they take the loss of their friends' money more heavily than the loss of their own. Because that their friends' merchant-men,* forasmuch as that they lose is their own private goods, sustain great damage by the loss. But their own citizens lose nothing but of the common goods, and of that which was at home plentiful and almost superfluous, else had it not been sent forth. Therefore no man feeleth the loss. And for this cause they think it too cruel an act to revenge that loss with the death of many, the incommodity of the which loss no man feeleth neither in his life nor yet in his living. But if it chance that any of their men in any other country be maimed or killed, whether it be done by a common or a private counsel, knowing and trying out the truth of the matter by their ambassadors, unless the offenders be rendered unto them in recompense of the injury, they will not be appeased, but incontinent they proclaim war against them. The offenders yielded, they punish either with death or with bondage.

They be not only sorry, but also ashamed to achieve the victory with bloodshed, counting it great folly to buy precious wares too dear. They rejoice and avaunt themselves, if they vanquish and oppress their enemies by craft and deceit. And for that act they make a general triumph, and as if the matter were manfully handled, they set up a pillar of stone in the place where they so vanquished their enemies, in token of the victory. For then they glory, then they boast, and crack that they have played the men indeed when they have so overcome, as no other living creature but only man could: that is to say, by the might and puissance of wit. For with bodily strength (say they) bears, lions, boars, wolves, dogs, and other wild beasts do fight. And as the most part of them do pass us in strength and fierce courage, so in wit and reason we be much stronger than they all.

Victory bought dear.

Their chief and principal purpose in war is to obtain that thing, which if they had before obtained, they would not have moved battle. But if that be not possible, they take so cruel vengeance of them which be in the fault, that ever after they be afeard to do the like. This is their chief and principal intent, which they immediately and first of all prosecute and set forward. But yet so that they be more circumspect in avoiding and eschewing jeopardies than they be desirous of praise and renown. Therefore immediately after that war is once solemnly denounced, they procure many proclamations signed with their own common seal to be set up privily at one time in their enemy's land in places most frequented. In these proclamations they promise great rewards to him that will kill their enemy's prince, and somewhat less gifts, but them very great also, for every head of them whose names be in the said proclamations contained. They be those whom they count their chief adversaries, next unto the prince. Whatsoever is prescribed unto him that killeth any of the proclaimed persons, that is doubled to him that bringeth any of the same to them alive; yea, and to the proclaimed persons themselves, if they will change their minds and come in to them, taking their parts, they proffer the same great rewards with pardon and surety of their lives. Therefore it quickly cometh to pass that their enemies have all other men in suspicion, and be unfaithful and mistrusting among themselves one to another, living in great fear and in no less jeopardy. For it is well known, that divers times the most part of them (and specially the prince himself) hath been betrayed of them in whom they put their most hope and trust. So that there is no manner of act nor deed that gifts and rewards do not enforce men unto. And in rewards they keep no measure. But, remembering and considering into how great hazard and jeopardy they call them, endeavour themselves to recompense the greatness of the danger with like great benefits. And therefore they promise not only wonderful great abundance of gold, but also lands of great revenues lying in most safe places among their friends. And their promises they perform faithfully without any fraud or covin.

This custom of buying and selling adversaries among other people is disallowed as a cruel act of a base and a cowardly mind. But they in this behalf think themselves much praiseworthy, as who like wise men by this means dispatch great wars without any battle or skirmish. Yea, they count it also a deed of pity and mercy, because that by the death of a few offenders the lives of a great number of innocents, as well of their own men as also of their enemies, be ransomed and saved, which in fighting should have been slain. For they do no less pity the base and common sort of their enemies' people, than they do their own, knowing that they be driven and enforced to war against their wills by the furious madness of their princes and heads. If by none of these means the matter go forward as they would have it, then they procure occasions of debate, and dissension to be spread among their enemies, as by bringing the prince's brother or some of the noblemen in hope to obtain the kingdom. If this way prevail not, then they raise up the people that be next neighbours and borderers to their enemies,

and them they set in their necks* under the colour of some old
title of right, such as kings do never lack. To them they promise their help and aid in their war. And as for money, they give
them abundance. But of their own citizens they send to them
few or none. Whom they make so much of and love so entirely,
that they would not be willing to change any of them for their
adversaries' prince. But their gold and silver, because they
keep it all for this only purpose, they lay it out frankly and
freely, as who should live even as wealthily if they had
bestowed it every penny. Yea, and besides their riches which
they keep at home, they have also an infinite treasure abroad,
by reason that (as I said before) many nations be in their debt.

Therefore they hire soldiers out of all countries and send
them to battle, but chiefly of the Zapoletes.* This people is 500
miles from Utopia eastward. They be hideous, savage, and
fierce, dwelling in wild woods and high mountains where they
were bred and brought up. They be of an hard nature, able to
abide and sustain heat, cold, and labour, abhorring from all
delicate dainties, occupying no husbandry nor tillage of the
ground, homely and rude both in building of their houses and
in their apparel, given unto no goodness, but only to the breeding and bringing up of cattle. The most part of their living is
by hunting and stealing. They be born only to war, which they
diligently and earnestly seek for. And when they have gotten it
they be wondrous glad thereof. They go forth of their country
in great companies together, and whosoever lacketh soldiers,
there they proffer their service for small wages. This is only
the craft they have to get their living by. They maintain their
life by seeking their death. For them whomwith they be in
wages they fight hardly, fiercely, and faithfully. But they bind
themselves for no certain time. But upon this condition they
enter into bonds, that the next day they will take part with the
other side for greater wages, and the next day after that they
will be ready to come back again for a little more money. There
be few wars thereaway, wherein is not a great number of them
in both parties. Therefore it daily chanceth that nigh kinsfolk
which were hired together on one part, and there very friendly
and familiarly used themselves one with another, shortly after

being separate in contrary parts, run one against another enviously and fiercely, and, forgetting both kindred and friendship, thrust their swords one in another. And that for none other cause but that they be hired of contrary princes for a little money. Which they do so highly regard and esteem, that they will easily be provoked to change parts for a halfpenny more wages by the day, so quickly they have taken a smack in covetousness, which for all that is to them no profit. For that they get by fighting, immediately they spend unthriftily and wretchedly in riot. This people fighteth for the Utopians against all nations, because they give them greater wages than any other nation will. For the Utopians, like as they seek good men to use well, so they seek these evil and vicious men to abuse. Whom, when need requireth, with promises of great rewards they put forth into great jeopardies. From whence the most part of them never cometh again to ask their rewards. But to them that remain alive they pay that which they promised faithfully, that they may be the more willing to put themselves in like danger another time. Nor the Utopians pass not how many of them they bring to destruction, for they believe that they should do a very good deed for all mankind if they could rid out of the world all that foul stinking den of that most wicked and cursed people.

Next unto this they use the soldiers of them for whom they fight. And then the help of their other friends. And last of all they join to their own citizens, among whom they give to one of tried virtue and prowess the rule, governance, and conduction of the whole army. Under him they appoint two other which, whiles he is safe, be both private and out of office.* But if he be taken or slain, the one of the other two succeedeth him, as it were by inheritance. And if the second miscarry, then the third taketh his room, lest that (as the chance of battle is uncertain and doubtful) the jeopardy or death of the captain should bring the whole army in hazard. They choose soldiers out of every city those which put forth themselves willingly. For they thrust no man forth into war against his will, because they believe if any man be fearful and faint-hearted of nature he will not only do no manful and hardy act himself, but also be occasion of cowardness to his fellows. But if any battle be made against their own country, then they put these cowards (so that they be strong-bodied) in ships among other bold-hearted men. Or else they dispose them upon the walls, from whence they may not fly. Thus what for shame that their enemies be at hand, and what for because they be without hope of running away, they forget all fear. And many times extreme necessity turneth cowardness into prowess and manliness.

But as none of them is thrust forth of his country into war against his will, so women that be willing to accompany their husbands in times of war be not prohibited or letted. Yea, they provoke and exhort them to it with praises, and in set field* the wives do stand every one by their own husband's side. Also every man is compassed next about with his own children, kinsfolk, and alliance. That they whom nature chiefly moveth to mutual succour, thus standing together, may help one another. It is a great reproach and dishonesty for the husband to come home without his wife, or the wife without her husband, or the son without his father. And therefore if the other part stick so hard by it that the battle come to their hands, it is fought with great slaughter and bloodshed, even to the utter destruction of both parts. For as they make all the means and shifts that may be to keep themselves from the necessity of fighting or that they may dispatch the battle by their hired soldiers, so when there is no remedy, but that they must needs fight themselves, then they do as courageously fall to it, as before, whiles they might, they did wisely avoid and refuse it. Nor they be not most fierce at the first brunt. But in continuance by little and little their fierce courage increaseth with so stubborn and obstinate minds, that they will rather die than give back an inch. For that surety of living which every man hath at home being joined with no careful anxiety or remembrance how their posterity shall live after them (for this pensiveness oftentimes breaketh and abateth courageous stomachs) maketh them stout and hardy and disdainful to be conquered. Moreover, their knowledge in chivalry and feats of arms putteth them in a good hope. Finally the wholesome and virtuous opinions wherein they were brought up even from their childhood, partly through learning and partly through the good ordinances and laws of their weal-public, augment and increase their manful courage. By reason whereof they neither set so little store by their lives that they will rashly and unadvisedly cast them away, nor they be not so far in lewd and fond love therewith, that they will shamefully covet to keep them when honesty biddeth leave them.

When the battle is hottest and in all places most fierce and fervent, a band of chosen and picked young men, which be sworn to live and die together, take upon them to destroy their adversaries' captain, whom they invade, now with privy wiles, now by open strength. At him they strike both near and far off. He is assailed with a long and a continual assault, fresh men still coming in the wearied men's places. And seldom it chanceth (unless he save himself by flying) that he is not either slain, or else taken prisoner and yielded to his enemies alive. If they win the field they persecute not their enemies with the violent rage of slaughter. For they had rather take them alive than kill them. Neither they do so follow the chase and pursuit of their enemies, but they leave behind them one part of their host in battle array under their standards. Insomuch that if all their whole army be discomfited and overcome, saving the rearward, and that they therewith achieve the victory, then they had rather let all their enemies escape than to follow them out of array. For they remember it hath chanced unto themselves more than once, the whole power and strength of their host vanquished and put to flight, whiles their enemies rejoicing in the victory have persecuted them, flying some one way and some another, a small company of their men lying in an ambush, there ready at all occasions, have suddenly risen upon them thus dispersed and scattered out of array and through presumption of safety unadvisedly pursuing the chase, and have incontinent changed the fortune of the whole battle, and spite of their teeth* wresting out of their hands the sure and undoubted victory, being a little before conquered, have for their part conquered the conquerors. It is hard to say whether they be craftier in laying an ambush, or wittier in avoiding the same. You would think they intend to fly when

The captain is chiefly to be pursued to the intent that the battle may the sooner be ended.

they mean nothing less. And contrariwise, when they go about
that purpose you would believe it were the least part of their
thought. For if they perceive themselves either overmatched in
number or closed in too narrow a place, then they remove their
camp; either in the night season with silence or by some policy
they deceive their enemies, or in the daytime they retire back
so softly, that it is no less jeopardy to meddle with them when
they give back than when they press on. They fence and fortify
their camp surely with a deep and a broad trench. The earth
thereof is cast inward. Nor they do not set drudges and slaves
awork about it. It is done by the hands of the soldiers themselves. All the whole army worketh upon it, except them that
keep watch and ward in harness before the trench for sudden
adventures.* Therefore, by the labour of so many a large trench
closing in a great compass of ground is made in less time than
any man would believe.

Their armour or harness which they wear is sure and strong *Their armour.*
to receive strokes, and handsome for all movings and gestures
of the body, insomuch that it is not unwieldy to swim in. For in
the discipline of their warfare among other feats they learn to
swim in harness. Their weapons be arrows aloof, which they
shoot both strongly and surely, not only footmen, but also
horsemen. At hand strokes they use not swords but pole-axes,
which be mortal as well in sharpness as in weight, both for
foins and downstrokes. Engines for war they devise and invent
wondrous wittily. Which when they be made they keep very
secret, lest, if they should be known before need require, they
should be but laughed at and serve to no purpose. But in
making them, hereunto they have chief respect, that they be
both easy to be carried and handsome to be moved and turned
about. Truce taken with their enemies for a short time they do *Of truces.*
so firmly and faithfully keep, that they will not break it, no, not
though they be thereunto provoked. They do not waste nor
destroy their enemies' land with foragings, nor they burn not
up their corn. Yea, they save it as much as may be from being
overrun and trodden down either with men or horses, thinking
that it groweth for their own use and profit.

They hurt no man that is unarmed, unless he be an espial.

All cities that be yielded unto them they defend. And such as they win by force of assault they neither despoil nor sack, but them that withstood and dissuaded the yielding up of the same they put to death; the other soldiers they punish with bondage. All the weak multitude they leave untouched. If they know that any citizens counselled to yield and render up the city, to them they give part of the condemned men's goods. The residue they distribute and give freely among them whose help they had in the same war. For none of themselves taketh any portion of the prey. But when the battle is finished and ended, they put their friends to never a penny cost of all the charges that they were at, but lay it upon their necks that be conquered.* Them they burden with the whole charge of their expenses, which they demand of them partly in money to be kept for like use of battle, and partly in lands of great revenues to be paid unto them yearly for ever. Such revenues they have now in many countries. Which, by little and little rising of divers and sundry causes, be increased above seven hundred thousand ducats by the year. Thither they send forth some of their citizens as lieutenants, to live there sumptuously like men of honour and renown. And yet, this notwithstanding, much money is saved which cometh to the common treasury, unless it so chance that they had rather trust the country with the money. Which many times they do so long until they have need to occupy it. And it seldom happeneth that they demand all. Of these lands they assign part unto them which at their request and exhortation put themselves in such jeopardies as I spake of before. If any prince stir up war against them, intending to invade their land, they meet him incontinent out of their own borders with great power and strength. For they never lightly make war in their own country. Nor they be never brought into so extreme necessity as to take help out of foreign lands into their own island.

OF THE RELIGIONS IN UTOPIA

There be divers kinds of religion not only in sundry parts of

the island, but also in divers places of every city. Some worship
for God the sun, some the moon, some some other of the
planets. There be that give worship to a man that was once of
excellent virtue or of famous glory, not only as God, but also as
the chiefest and highest God. But the most and the wisest part
(rejecting all these,) believe that there is a certain Godly power
unknown, everlasting, incomprehensible, inexplicable, far
above the capacity and reach of man's wit, dispersed throughout all the world, not in bigness, but in virtue and power. Him
they call the father of all. To him alone they attribute the
beginnings, the increasings, the proceedings, the changes, and
the ends of all things. Neither they give any divine honours to
any other than to him. Yea, all the other also, though they be in
divers opinions, yet in this point they agree all together with
the wisest sort in believing that there is one chief and principal
God, the maker and ruler of the whole world, whom they all
commonly in their country language call Mithra.* But in this
they disagree, that among some he is counted one, and among
some another. For every one of them, whatsoever that is which
he taketh for the chief God, thinketh it to be the very same
nature to whose only divine might and majesty the sum and
sovereignty of all things by the consent of all people is attributed and given. Howbeit, they all begin by little and little to
forsake and fall from this variety of superstitions, and to agree
together in that religion which seemeth by reason to pass and
excel the residue. And it is not to be doubted but all the other
would long ago have been abolished, but that whatsoever un-
prosperous thing happened to any of them, as he was minded
to change his religion, the fearfulness of people did take it, not
as a thing coming by chance, but as sent from GOD out of
heaven, as though the God whose honour he was forsaking
would revenge that wicked purpose against him. But after they
heard us speak of the name of Christ, of his doctrine, laws,
miracles, and of the no less wonderful constancy of so many
martyrs, whose blood willingly shed brought a great number of
nations throughout all parts of the world into their sect, you
will not believe with how glad minds they agreed unto the
same, whether it were by the secret inspiration of GOD, or else

for that they thought it nighest unto that opinion which among them is counted the chiefest. Howbeit, I think this was no small help and furtherance in the matter, that they heard us say that Christ instituted among his all things common, and that the same community doth yet remain amongst the rightest Christian communities.* Verily, howsoever it came to pass, many of them consented together in our religion and were washed in the holy water of baptism. But because among us four (for no more of us was left alive, two of our company being dead) there was no priest, which I am right sorry for, they being entered and instructed in all other points of our religion, lack only those sacraments which here none but priests do minister. Howbeit, they understand and perceive them and be very desirous of the same. Yea, they reason and dispute the matter earnestly among themselves, whether, without the sending of a Christian bishop, one chosen out of their own people may receive the order of priesthood. And truly they were minded to choose one, but at my departure from them they had chosen none.

They also which do not agree to Christ's religion fear no man from it nor speak against any man that hath received it. Saving that one of our company* in my presence was sharply punished. He, as soon as he was baptized, began against our wills, with more earnest affection than wisdom, to reason of Christ's religion, and began to wax so hot in his matter, that he did not only prefer our religion before all other, but also did utterly despise and condemn all other, calling them profane, and the followers of them wicked and devilish and the children of everlasting damnation. When he had thus long reasoned the matter they laid hold on him, accused him, and condemned him into exile, not as a despiser of religion but as a seditious person and a raiser up of dissension among the people. For this is one of the ancientest laws among them, that no man shall be blamed for reasoning in the maintenance of his own religion. For King Utopus, even at the first beginning hearing that the inhabitants of the land were before his coming thither at continual dissension and strife among themselves for their religions, perceiving also that this common dissension (whiles

Religious houses.

every several sect took several parts in fighting for their country) was the only occasion of his conquest over them all, as soon as he had gotten the victory: first of all he made a decree that it should be lawful for every man to favour and follow what religion he would, and that he might do the best he could to bring other to his opinion, so that he did it peaceably, gently, quietly, and soberly, without hasty and contentious rebuking and inveighing against other. If he could not by fair and gentle speech induce them unto his opinion, yet he should use no kind of violence, and refrain from displeasant and seditious words. To him that would vehemently and fervently in this cause strive and contend was decreed banishment or bondage. *Seditious reasoners punished.*

This law did King Utopus make, not only for the maintenance of peace, which he saw through continual contention and mortal hatred utterly extinguished, but also because he thought this decree should make for the furtherance of religion. Whereof he durst define and determine nothing unadvisedly, as doubting whether God, desiring manifold and diverse sorts of honour, would inspire sundry men with sundry kinds of religion. And this surely he thought a very unmeet and foolish thing, and a point of arrogant presumption, to compel all other by violence and threatenings to agree to the same that thou believest to be true. Furthermore, though there be one religion which alone is true, and all other vain and superstitious, yet did he well foresee (so that the matter were handled with reason and sober modesty) that the truth of the own power would at the last issue out and come to light. But if contention and debate in that behalf should continually be used, as the worst men be most obstinate and stubborn and in their evil opinion most constant, he perceived that then the best and holiest religion would be trodden underfoot and destroyed by most vain superstitions, even as good corn is by thorns and weeds overgrown and choked.

Therefore all this matter he left undiscussed, and gave to every man free liberty and choice to believe what he would. *No vile* Saving that he earnestly and straitly charged them that no man *opinion to be* should conceive so vile and base an opinion of the dignity of *conceived of man's worthy* man's nature as to think that the souls do die and perish with *nature.*

the body, or that the world runneth at all adventures, governed by no divine providence. And therefore they believe that after this life vices be extremely punished and virtues bountifully rewarded. Him that is of a contrary opinion they count not in the number of men, as one that hath avaled the high nature of his soul to the vileness of brute beasts' bodies, much less in the number of their citizens whose laws and ordinances, if it were not for fear, he would nothing at all esteem. For you may be sure that he will study either with craft privily to mock, or else violently to break the common laws of his country, in whom remaineth no further fear than of the laws nor no further hope than of the body. Wherefore he that is thus minded is deprived of all honours, excluded from all offices, and reject from all common administrations in the weal-public. And thus he is of all sorts despised as of an unprofitable and of a base and vile nature. Howbeit, they put him to no punishment, because they be persuaded that it is in no man's power to believe what he list. No nor they constrain him not with threatenings to dissemble his mind and show countenance contrary to his thought; for deceit and falsehood and all manners of lies, as next unto fraud, they do marvellously detest and abhor. But they suffer him not to dispute in his opinion, and that only among the common people.* For else, apart among the priests and men of gravity they do not only suffer, but also exhort him to dispute and argue, hoping that at the last that madness will give place to reason.

There be also other, and of them no small number, which be not forbidden to speak their minds, as grounding their opinion upon some reason, being in their living neither evil nor vicious. Their heresy is much contrary to the other; for they believe that the souls of brute beasts be immortal and everlasting. But nothing to be compared with ours in dignity, neither ordained nor predestinate to like felicity. For all they believe certainly and surely that man's bliss shall be so great, that they do mourn and lament every man's sickness, but no man's death, unless it be one whom they see depart from his life carefully and against his will. For this they take for a very evil token, as though the soul, being in despair and vexed in conscience

Irreligious people secluded from all honours.

A very strange saying.

Deceit and falsehood detested.

A marvellous strange opinion touching the souls of brute beasts.

To die unwillingly an evil token.

through some privy and secret forefeeling of the punishment now at hand, were afeard to depart. And they think he shall not be welcome to God, which, when he is called, runneth not to him gladly but is drawn by force and sore against his will. They, therefore, that see this kind of death do abhor it, and them that so die they bury with sorrow and silence. And when they have prayed God to be merciful to the soul and mercifully to pardon the infirmities thereof, they cover the dead corpse with earth. Contrariwise, all that depart merrily and full of good hope, for them no man mourneth, but followeth the hearse with joyful singing, commending the souls to God with great affection. And at the last, not with mourning sorrow, but with a great reverence, they burn the bodies. And in the same place they set up a pillar of stone with the dead man's titles therein graved. When they be come home they rehearse his virtuous manners and his good deeds. But no part of his life is so oft or gladly talked of as his merry death. *A willing and a merry death not to be lamented.*

They think that this remembrance of the virtue and goodness of the dead doth vehemently provoke and enforce the living to virtue. And that nothing can be more pleasant and acceptable to the dead. Whom they suppose to be present among them when they talk of them, though to the dull and feeble eyesight of mortal men they be invisible. For it were an inconvenient thing that the blessed should not be at liberty to go whither they would. And it were a point of great unkindness in them to have utterly cast away the desire of visiting and seeing their friends to whom they were in their lifetime joined by mutual love and amity. Which in good men after their death they count to be rather increased than diminished. They believe, therefore, that the dead be presently conversant among the quick* as beholders and witnesses of all their words and deeds. Therefore they go more courageously to their business, as having a trust and affiance in such overseers. And this same belief of the present conversation of their forefathers and ancestors among them feareth them from all secret dishonesty.

They utterly despise and mock soothsayings and divinations of things to come by the flight or voices of birds, and all other divinations of vain superstition, which in other countries be in *Soothsayers not regarded nor credited.*

Miracles. great observation. But they highly esteem and worship miracles that come by no help of nature, as works and witnesses of the present power of God. And such they say do chance there very often. And sometimes in great and doubtful matters by common intercession and prayers they procure and obtain them with a sure hope and confidence and a steadfast belief.

The life contemplative. They think that the contemplation of nature, and the praise thereof coming,* is to God a very acceptable honour. Yet there be many so earnestly bent and affectioned to religion, that they pass nothing for learning, nor give their minds to any knowledge of things. But idleness they utterly forsake and eschew, thinking felicity after this life to be gotten and obtained by busy labours and good exercises. Some, therefore, of them *The life active.* attend upon the sick, some amend highways, cleanse ditches, repair bridges, dig turfs, gravel, and stones, fell and cleave wood, bring wood, corn, and other things into the cities in carts, and serve not only in common works, but also in private labours as servants, yea, more than bondmen. For whatsoever unpleasant, hard, and vile work is anywhere from the which labour, loathsomeness, and desperation doth fray other, all that they take upon them willingly and gladly, procuring quiet and rest to other, remaining in continual work and labour themselves, not embraiding others therewith.* They neither reprove other men's lives nor glory in their own.

These men, the more serviceable they behave themselves, the more they be honoured of all men. Yet they be divided into two sects. The one is of them that live single and chaste, abstaining not only from the company of women but also from eating of flesh, and some of them from all manner of beasts.* Which, utterly rejecting the pleasures of this present life as hurtful, be all wholly set upon the desire of the life to come by watching and sweating, hoping shortly to obtain it, being in the mean season merry and lusty. The other sect is no less desirous of labour; but they embrace matrimony, not despising the solace thereof, thinking that they cannot be discharged of their bounden duties towards nature without labour and toil, nor towards their native country without procreation of children. They abstain from no pleasure that doth nothing hinder them from labour. They love the flesh of four-footed beasts because they believe that by that meat they be made hardier and stronger to work. The Utopians count this sect the wiser, but the other the holier. Which in that they prefer single life before matrimony and that sharp life before an easier life, if herein they grounded upon reason they would mock them. But now forasmuch as they say they be led to it by religion, they honour and worship them. And these be they whom in their language by a peculiar name they call Buthrescas,,* the which word by interpretation signifieth to us men of religion or religious men.

It is not all one to be wise and good.

They have priests of exceeding holiness and therefore very few. For there be but thirteen in every city according to the number of their churches, saving when they go forth to battle. For then seven of them go forth with the army, in whose steads so many new be made at home. But the other at their return home again re-enter every one into his own place. They that be above the number, until such time as they succeed into the places of the other at their dying, be in the mean season continually in company with the bishop. For he is the chief head of them all. They be chosen of the people, as the other magistrates be, by secret voices* for the avoiding of strife. After their election they be consecrate of their own company.* They be overseers of all divine matters, orderers of religions, and, as it were, judges and masters of manners. And it is a great dishonesty and shame to be rebuked or spoken to by any of them for dissolute and incontinent living. But as it is their office to give good exhortations and counsel, so is it the duty of the prince and the other magistrates to correct and punish offenders, saving that the priests, whom they find exceeding vicious livers them they excommunicate from having any interest in divine matters.* And there is almost no punishment among them more feared. For they run in very great infamy and be inwardly tormented with a secret fear of religion, and shall not long scape free with their bodies. For unless they by quick repentance approve the amendment of their lives to the priests, they be taken and punished of the council as wicked and irreligious.

Priests.

Excommunication.

Both childhood and youth is instructed and taught of them.

113

Nor they be not more diligent to instruct them in learning than in virtue and good manners. For they use with very great endeavour and diligence to put into the heads of their children, whiles they be yet tender and pliant, good opinions and profitable for the conservation of their weal-public. Which, when they be once rooted in children, do remain with them all their life after and be wondrous profitable for the defence and maintenance of the state of the commonwealth. Which never decayeth but through vices rising of evil opinions.

Women priests.

The priests, unless they be women (for that kind is not excluded from priesthood, howbeit few be chosen, and none but widows and old women), the men priests, I say, take to their wives the chiefest women in all their country. For to no office among the Utopians is more honour and pre-eminence given. Insomuch that if they commit any offence they be under no common judgement, but be left only to God and themselves. For they think it not lawful to touch him with man's

The majesty and pre-eminence of priests.

hand, be he never so vicious, which after so singular a sort was dedicate and consecrate to God as a holy offering. This manner may they easily observe because they have so few priests, and do choose them with such circumspection. For it scarcely ever chanceth that the most virtuous among virtuous, which in respect only of his virtue is advanced to so high a dignity, can fall to vice and wickedness. And if it should chance indeed (as man's nature is mutable and frail), yet by reason they be so few and promoted to no might nor power, but only to honour, it were not to be feared that any great damage by them should happen and ensue to the commonwealth. They have so rare and few priests, lest if the honour were communicated to many, the dignity of the order, which among them now is so highly esteemed, should run in contempt. Specially because they think it hard to find many so good as to be meet for that dignity, to the execution and discharge whereof it is not sufficient to be endued with mean virtues.

Furthermore, these priests be not more esteemed of their own countrymen than they be of foreign and strange countries. Which thing may hereby plainly appear. And I think also that this is the cause of it. For whiles the armies be fighting

together in open field they a little beside, not far off, kneel
upon their knees in their hallowed vestments, holding up their
hands to heaven, praying first of all for peace, next for victory
of their own part, but to neither part a bloody victory. If their
host get the upper hand, they run into the main battle and
restrain their own men from slaying and cruelly pursuing their
vanquished enemies. Which enemies, if they do but see them
and speak to them, it is enough for the safeguard of their lives.
And the touching of their clothes defendeth and saveth all
their goods from ravin and spoil. This thing hath advanced
them to so great worship and true majesty among all nations,
that many times they have as well preserved their own citizens
from the cruel force of their enemies as they have their
enemies from the furious rage of their own men. For it is well
known that when their own army hath reculed, and in despair
turned back and run away, their enemies fiercely pursuing with
slaughter and spoil, then the priests coming between have
stayed the murder and parted both the hosts. So that peace
hath been made and concluded between both parts upon equal
and indifferent conditions. For there was never any nation so
fierce, so cruel, and rude but they had them in such reverence,
that they counted their bodies hallowed and sanctified, and
therefore not to be violently and unreverently touched.

They keep holy the first and the last day of every month and
year, dividing the year into months which they measure by the
course of the moon, as they do the year by the course of the
sun. The first days they call in their language Cynemernes,
and the last Trapemernes,* the which words may be interpreted
primifest and finifest, or else, in our speech, first feast and last
feast. Their churches be very gorgeous, and not only of fine
and curious workmanship, but also (which in the fewness of
them was necessary) very wide and large, and able to receive a
great company of people. But they be all somewhat dark.
Howbeit, that was not done through ignorance in building,
but, as they say, by the counsel of the priests, because they
thought that over much light doth disperse men's cogitations,
whereas in dim and doubtful light they be gathered together,
and more earnestly fixed upon religion and devotion. Which

*The
observation
of holy days
among the
Utopians.*

*Their
churches.*

*Church is of
dim light and
a reason why.*

because it is not there of one sort among all men, and yet all the kinds and fashions of it, though they be sundry and manifold, agree together in the honour of the divine nature, as going divers ways to one end, therefore nothing is seen nor heard in the churches, but that seemeth to agree indifferently with them all. If there be a distinct kind of sacrifice* peculiar to any several sect, that they execute at home in their own houses. The common sacrifices be so ordered that they be no derogation nor prejudice to any of the private sacrifices and religions. Therefore no image of any god is seen in the church, to the intent it may be free for every man to conceive God by their religion after what likeness and similitude they will. They call upon no peculiar name of god but only Mithra. In the which word they all agree together in one nature of the divine majesty whatsoever it be. No prayers be used but such as every man may boldly pronounce without the offending of any sect.

They come, therefore, to the church the last day of every month and year, in the evening yet fasting, there to give thanks to GOD for that they have prosperously passed over the year or month whereof that holy day is the last day. The next day they come to the church early in the morning to pray to GOD that they may have good fortune and success all the new year or month which they do begin of that same holy day. But in the holy days that be the last days of the months and years, before they come to the church the wives fall down prostrate before their husbands' feet at home, and the children before the feet of their parents, confessing and acknowledging themselves offenders either by some actual deed or by omission of their duty, and desire pardon for their offence. Thus if any cloud of privy displeasure was risen at home, by this satisfaction it is overblown, that they may be present at the sacrifices with pure and charitable minds. For they be afeard to come there with troubled consciences. Therefore if they know themselves to bear any hatred or grudge towards any man, they presume not to come to the sacrifices before they have reconciled themselves and purged their consciences, for fear of great vengeance and punishment for their offence. When they come thither the men go into the right side of the church and the

The confession of the Utopians.

An order for places in the church.

women into the left side. There they place themselves in such
order, that all they which be of the male kind in every household sit before the good man of the house, and they of the
female kind before the good wife. Thus it is foreseen that all
their gestures and behaviours be marked and observed abroad
of them by whose authority and discipline they be governed at
home. This also they diligently see unto, that the younger
evermore be coupled with his elder, lest, children being joined
together, they should pass over that time in childish wantonness, wherein they ought principally to conceive a religious
and devout fear towards God, which is the chief and almost the
only incitation to virtue.

They kill no living beast in sacrifice, nor they think not that *Ceremonies.*
the merciful clemency of God hath delight in blood and
slaughter, which hath given life to beasts to the intent they
should live. They burn frankincense and other sweet savours,
and light also a great number of wax candles and tapers, not
supposing this gear to be anything available to the divine
nature, as neither the prayers of men.* But this unhurtful and
harmless kind of worship pleaseth them. And by these sweet
savours and lights and other such ceremonies men feel themselves secretly lifted up and encouraged to devotion with more
willing and fervent hearts.

The people weareth in the church white apparel. The priest
is clothed in changeable colours.* Which in workmanship be
excellent, but in stuff not very precious. For their vestments be
neither embroidered with gold nor set with precious stones.
But they be wrought so finely and cunningly with divers feathers of fowls,* that the estimation of no costly stuff is able to
countervail the price of the work. Furthermore, in these birds'
feathers and in the due order of them which is observed in
their setting, they say, is contained certain divine mysteries.
The interpretation whereof known, which is diligently taught
by the priests, they be put in remembrance of the bountiful
benefits of God toward them, and of the love and honour
which of their behalf is due to God, and also of their duties
one toward another. When the priest first cometh out of the
vestry thus apparelled, they fall down incontinent every one

reverently to the ground, with so still silence on every part, that the very fashion of the thing striketh into them a certain fear of God, as though he were there personally present. When they have lain a little space on the ground, the priest giveth them a sign for to rise. Then they sing praises unto God, *Their church* which they intermix with instruments of music, for the most *music.* part of other fashions than these that we use in this part of the world. And like as some of ours be much sweeter than theirs, so some of theirs do far pass ours. But in one thing doubtless they go exceeding far beyond us. For all their music, both that they play upon instruments and that they sing with man's voice, doth so resemble and express natural affections, the sound and tune is so applied and made agreeable to the thing, that whether it be a prayer or else a ditty of gladness, of patience, of trouble, of mourning, or of anger, the fashion of the melody doth so represent the meaning of the thing, that it doth wonderfully move, stir, pierce, and inflame the hearers' minds.

Prayers. At the last the people and the priest together rehearse solemn prayers in words expressly pronounced, so made that every man may privately apply to himself that which is commonly spoken of all. In these prayers every man recognizeth and knowledgeth God to be his maker, his governor, and the principal cause of all other goodness, thanking him for so many benefits received at his hand. But namely that through the favour of God he hath chanced into that public weal which is most happy and wealthy, and hath chosen that religion which he hopeth to be most true. In the which thing if he do anything err, or if there be any other better than either of them is, being more acceptable to God, he desireth him that he will of his goodness let him have knowledge thereof, as one that is ready to follow what way soever he will lead him. But if this form and fashion of a commonwealth be best, and his own religion most true and perfect, then he desireth GOD to give him a constant steadfastness in the same, and to bring all other people to the same order of living and to the same opinion of God, unless there be anything that in this diversity of religions doth delight his unsearchable pleasure. To be short, he prayeth

him, that after his death he may come to him. But how soon or
late, that he dare not assign or determine. Howbeit, if it might
stand with his majesty's pleasure, he would be much gladder to
die a painful death and so to go to God, than by long living in
worldly prosperity to be away from him. When this prayer is
said they fall down to the ground again, and a little after they
rise up and go to dinner. And the residue of the day they pass
over in plays and exercise of chivalry.

Now I have declared and described unto you as truly as I
could the form and order of that commonwealth, which verily
in my judgement is not only the best, but also that which alone
of good right may claim and take upon it the name of a commonwealth or public weal. For in other places they speak still of
the commonwealth. But every man procureth his own private
gain. Here, where nothing is private, the common affairs be
earnestly looked upon. And truly on both parts they have good
cause so to do as they do. For in other countries who knoweth
not that he shall starve for hunger, unless he make some several
provision for himself, though the commonwealth flourish never
so much in riches? And therefore he is compelled even of very
necessity to have regard to himself rather than to the people,
that is to say, to other. Contrariwise, there where all things be
common to every man, it is not to be doubted that any man
shall lack any thing necessary for his private uses, so that the
common store, houses and barns, be sufficiently stored. For
there nothing is distributed after a niggish sort, neither there is
any poor man or beggar. And though no man have anything, yet
every man is rich. For what can be more rich than to live
joyfully and merrily, without all grief and pensiveness, not car-
ing for his own living, nor vexed or troubled with his wife's
importunate complaints, nor dreading poverty to his son, nor
sorrowing for his daughter's dowry? Yea, they take no care at all
for the living and wealth of themselves and all theirs, of their
wives, their children, their nephews, their children's children,
and all the succession that ever shall follow in their posterity.
And yet, besides this, there is no less provision for them that
were once labourers and be now weak and impotent, than for
them that do now labour and take pain.

Here now would I see if any man dare be so bold as to compare with this equity the justice of other nations. Among whom I forsake God, if I can find any sign or token of equity and justice. For what justice is this, that a rich goldsmith* or an usurer or, to be short, any of them which either do nothing at all, or else that which they do is such that it is not very necessary to the commonwealth, should have a pleasant and a wealthy living, either by idleness or by unnecessary business, when in the meantime poor labourers, carters, ironsmiths, carpenters, and ploughmen, by so great and continual toil, as drawing and bearing beasts be scant able to sustain, and again so necessary toil, that without it no commonwealth were able to continue and endure one year, should yet get so hard and poor a living and live so wretched and miserable a life, that the state and condition of the labouring beasts may seem much better and wealthier? For they be not put to so continual labour, nor their living is not much worse, yea, to them much pleasanter, taking no thought in the mean season for the time to come. But these silly poor wretches be presently tormented with barren and unfruitful labour, and the remembrance of their poor, indigent, and beggarly old age killeth them up.* For their daily wages is so little that it will not suffice for the same day, much less it yieldeth any overplus that may daily be laid up for the relief of old age. Is not this an unjust and an unkind public weal, which giveth great fees and rewards to gentlemen, as they call them, and to goldsmiths and to such other, which be either idle persons, or else only flatterers and devisers of vain pleasures? And of the contrary part maketh no gentle provision for poor ploughmen, colliers, labourers, carters, ironsmiths, and carpenters, without whom no commonwealth can continue? But after it hath abused the labours of their lusty and flowering age, at the last, when they be oppressed with old age and sickness, being needy, poor, and indigent of all things, then, forgetting their so many painful watchings, not remembering their so many and so great benefits, recompenseth and acquiteth them most unkindly with miserable death. And yet besides this the rich men, not only by private fraud but also by common laws,* do every day pluck and snatch away from the poor some part of their daily living. So whereas it seemed before unjust to recompense with unkindness their pains that have been beneficial to the public weal, now they have to this their wrong and unjust dealing (which is yet a much worse point) given the name of justice, yea, and that by force of a law.

Therefore, when I consider and weigh in my mind all these commonwealths which nowadays anywhere do flourish, so God help me, I can perceive nothing but a certain conspiracy of rich men procuring their own commodities under the name and title of the commonwealth. They invent and devise all means and crafts, first how to keep safely, without fear of losing, that they have unjustly gathered together, and next how to hire and abuse the work and labour of the poor for as little money as may be. These devices, when the rich men have decreed to be kept and observed under colour of the commonalty, that is to say, also of the poor people, then they be made laws. But these most wicked and vicious men, when they have by their unsatiable covetousness divided among themselves all those things which would have sufficed all men, yet how far be they from the wealth and felicity of the Utopian commonwealth! Out of the which, in that all the desire of money with the use thereof is utterly secluded and banished, how great a heap of cares is cut away? How great an occasion of wickedness and mischief is plucked up by the roots? For who knoweth not that fraud, theft, ravin, brawling, quarrelling, brabbling, strife, chiding, contention, murder, treason, poisoning, which by daily punishments are rather revenged than refrained, do die when money dieth? And also that fear, grief, care, labours, and watchings do perish even the very same moment that money perisheth?

Contempt of money.

Yea, poverty itself, which only seemed to lack money if money were gone, it also would decrease and vanish away. And that you may perceive this more plainly, consider with yourselves some barren and unfruitful year wherein many thousands of people have starved for hunger. I dare be bold to say that in the end of that penury so much corn or grain might have been found in the rich men's barns, if they had been searched, as, being divided among them whom famine and pestilence then consumed, no man at all should have felt that plague and penury. So easily might men get their living, if that same worthy princess Lady Money did not alone stop up the way between us and our living, which, a God's name, was very excellently devised and invented, that by her the way thereto should be opened.* I am sure the rich men perceive this, nor they be not ignorant how much better it were to lack no necessary thing than to abound with overmuch superfluity, to be rid out of innumerable cares and troubles, than to be besieged and encumbered with great riches. And I doubt not that either the

A marvellous saying.

respect of every man's private commodity, or else the authority of our saviour Christ (which for his great wisdom could not but know what were best, and for his inestimable goodness could not but counsel to that which he knew to be best) would have brought all the world long ago into the laws of this weal-public, if it were not that one only beast, the princess and

Pride.

mother of all mischief, Pride, doth withstand and let it. She measureth not wealth and prosperity by her own commodities, but by the misery and incommodities of other; she would not by her good will be made a goddess if there were no wretches left over whom she might like a scornful lady rule and triumph, over whose miseries her felicities might shine, whose poverty she might vex, torment, and increase by gorgeously setting forth her riches. This hell hound creepeth into men's hearts and plucketh them back from entering the right path of life, and is so deeply rooted in men's breasts, that she cannot be plucked out.

This form and fashion of a weal-public, which I would gladly wish unto all nations, I am glad yet that it hath chanced to the Utopians, which have followed those institutions of life whereby they have laid such foundations of their commonwealth as shall continue and last not only wealthily, but also, as far as man's wit may judge and conjecture, shall endure for ever. For, seeing the chief causes of ambition and sedition with other vices be plucked up by the roots and abandoned at home, there can be no jeopardy of domestical dissension,* which alone hath cast under foot and brought to naught the well fortified and strongly defenced wealth and riches of many cities. But forasmuch as perfect concord remaineth, and wholesome laws be executed at home, the envy of all foreign princes be not able to shake or move the empire, though they have many times long ago gone about to do it, being evermore driven back.

Thus when Raphael had made an end of his tale, though many things came to my mind which in the manners and laws of that people seemed to be instituted and founded of no good reason, not only in the fashion of their chivalry and in their sacrifices and religions and in other of their laws, but also, yea, and chiefly, in that which is the principal foundation of all their ordinances, that is to say, in the community of their life and living without any occupying of money (by the which thing only all nobility, magnificence, worship, honour, and majesty, the true ornaments and honours, as the common opinion is, of a commonwealth, utterly be overthrown and destroyed), yet because I knew that he was weary of talking, and was not sure whether he could abide that anything should be said against his mind (specially remembering that he had reprehended this fault in other, which be afeard lest they should seem not to be wise enough, unless they could find some fault in other men's inventions), therefore I, praising both their institutions and his communication, took him by the hand and led him in to supper, saying that we would choose another time to weigh and examine the same matters and to talk with him more at large therein. Which would God it might once come to pass. In the mean time, as I can not agree and consent to all things that he said, being else without doubt a man singularly well learned and also in all worldly matters exactly and profoundly experienced: so must I needs confess and grant that many things be in the Utopian weal-public which in our cities I may rather wish for than hope after.

Thus endeth the afternoon's talk
of Raphael Hythloday concerning the laws and institu-
tions of the Island
of Utopia.

To the Right Honourable Hierome Buslide
Provost of Arienn and Counsellor to the
Catholic King Charles, Peter Giles, Citizen of Antwerp,
Wisheth Health and Felicity*

Thomas More, the singular ornament of this our age, as you
yourself (right honourable Buslide) can witness, to whom he is
perfectly well known, sent unto me this other day the *Island of
Utopia*, to very few as yet known, but most worthy. Which, as
far excelling Plato's *Commonwealth*, all people should be willing to know: specially of a man most eloquent, so finely set
forth, so cunningly painted out, and so evidently subject to the
eye, that as oft as I read it, methinketh that I see somewhat
more than when I heard Raphael Hythloday himself (for I was
present at that talk as well as Master More) uttering and pro-
nouncing his own words. Yea, though the same man according
to his pure eloquence did so open and declare the matter, that
he might plainly enough appear to report not things which he
had learned of others only by hearsay, but which he had with
his own eyes presently seen and thoroughly viewed, and
wherein he had no small time been conversant and abiding: a
man, truly, in mine opinion, as touching the knowledge of
regions, peoples, and worldly experience, much passing, yea,
even the very famous and renowned traveller Ulysses; and
indeed such a one, as for the space of these 800 years past
I think nature into the world brought not forth his like, in
comparison of whom Vespucci may be thought to have seen
nothing. Moreover, whereas we be wont more effectually and
pithily to declare and express things that we have seen than
which we have but only heard, there was besides that in this
man a certain peculiar grace and singular dexterity to describe
and set forth a matter withal.

Yet the selfsame things as oft as I behold and consider them
drawn and painted out with Master More's pencil, I am therewith so moved, so delighted, so inflamed, and so rapt, that
sometime methink I am presently conversant, even in the

island of Utopia. And I promise you, I can scant believe that
Raphael himself, by all that five years' space that he was in
Utopia abiding, saw there so much as here in Master More's
description is to be seen and perceived. Which description
with so many wonders and miraculous things is replenished,
that I stand in great doubt whereat first and chiefly to muse
or marvel: whether at the excellency of his perfect and sure
memory, which could well-nigh word by word rehearse so
many things once only heard, or else at his singular prudence,
who so well and wittily marked and bare away all the original
causes and fountains (to the vulgar people commonly most
unknown) whereof both issueth and springeth the mortal
confusion and utter decay of a commonwealth and also the
advancement and wealthy state of the same may rise and
grow, or else at the efficacy and pith of his words which in
so fine a Latin style, with such force of eloquence, hath
couched together and comprised so many and divers matters,
specially being a man continually encumbered with so many
busy and troublesome cares, both public and private, as he
is. Howbeit, all these things cause you little to marvel (right
honourable Buslide) for that you are familiarly and thoroughly
acquainted with the notable, yea, almost divine wit of the
man.

But now to proceed to other matters, I surely know nothing
needful or requisite to be adjoined unto his writings. Only a
metre of four verses written in the Utopian tongue, which
after Master More's departure Hythloday by chance showed
me, that have I caused to be added thereto, with the alphabet of
the same nation, and have also garnished the margin of the
book with certain notes. For, as touching the situation of the
island, that is to say, in what part of the world Utopia standeth,
the ignorance and lack whereof not a little troubleth and grie-
veth Master More, indeed Raphael left not that unspoken of.
Howbeit, with very few words he lightly touched it, inciden-
tally by the way passing it over, as meaning of likelihood to
keep and reserve that to another place. And the same, I wot not
how, by a certain evil and unlucky chance escaped us both. For
when Raphael was speaking thereof, one of Master More's

servants came to him and whispered in his ear. Wherefore, I being then of purpose more earnestly addict to hear, one of the company, by reason of cold (taken, I think, a-shipboard,) coughed out so loud, that he took from my hearing certain of his words. But I will never stint nor rest until I have got the full and exact knowledge hereof, insomuch that I will be able perfectly to instruct you, not only in the longitude or true meridian of the island, but also in the just latitude thereof, that is to say, in the sublevation or height of the pole in that region, if our friend Hythloday be in safety and alive. For we hear very uncertain news of him. Some report that he died in his journey homeward. Some again affirm that he returned into his country; but partly for that he could not away with the fashions of his country folk, and partly for that his mind and affection was altogether set and fixed upon Utopia, they say that he hath taken his voyage thitherward again. Now as touching this, that the name of this island is nowhere found among the old and ancient cosmographers, this doubt Hythloday himself very well dissolved. 'For why, it is possible enough', quoth he, 'that the name which it had in old time was afterward changed, or else that they never had knowledge of this island, forasmuch as now in our time divers lands be found which to the old geographers were unknown.'

Howbeit, what needeth it in this behalf to fortify the matter with arguments, seeing Master More is author hereof sufficient? But whereas he doubteth of the edition or imprinting of the book, indeed herein I both commend and also knowledge the man's modesty. Howbeit, unto me it seemeth a work most unworthy to be long suppressed and most worthy to go abroad into the hands of men; yea, and under the title of your name to be published to the world, either because the singular endowments and qualities of Master More be to no man better known than to you, or else because no man is more fit and meet than you with good counsels to further and advance the commonwealth, wherein you have many years already continued and travailed with great glory and commendation, both of wisdom and knowledge, and also of integrity and uprightness. Thus, O liberal supporter of good learning, and flower of this our time, I bid you most heartily well to fare.

At Antwerp 1516, the first day of November

A Metre of Four Verses* in the Utopian Tongue, briefly touching as well the strange beginning, as also the happy and wealthy continuance, of the same commonwealth

Utopos ha Boccas peula chama polta chamaan.
Bargol he maglomi Baccan soma gymnosophaon.
Agrama gymnosophon labarem bacha bodamilomin.
Volvala barchin heman la lavolvala dramme pagloni.

Which verses the translator, according to his simple knowledge and mean understanding in the Utopian tongue, hath thus rudely Englished:

My king and conqueror Utopos by name,
A prince of much renown and immortal fame,
Hath made me an isle that erst no island was,
Full fraught with worldly wealth, with pleasure and solace.
I one of all other without philosophy
Have shaped for man a philosophical city.
As mine I am nothing dangerous to impart,
So better to receive I am ready with all my heart.

A short metre of Utopia,* written by Anemolius poet laureate and nephew to Hythloday by his sister

Me Utopie cleped Antiquity,
Void of haunt and herborough,
Now am I like to Plato's city,
Whose fame flieth the world through.
Yea, like, or rather more likely
Plato's plat to excel and pass.
For what Plato's pen hath platted briefly
In naked words, as in a glass,

The same have I performed fully,
With laws, with men, and treasure fitly.
Wherefore not Utopie, but rather rightly
My name is Eutopie:* a place of felicity.

Gerard Noviomage* of Utopia

Doth pleasure please? Then place thee here, and well thee rest;
Most pleasant pleasures thou shalt find here.
Doth profit ease? Then here arrive, this isle is best.
For passing profits do here appear.
Doth both thee tempt, and wouldst thou grip both gain and pleasure?
This isle is fraught with both bounteously.
To still thy greedy intent, reap here incomparable treasure
Both mind and tongue to garnish richly.
The hid wells and fountains both of vice and virtue
Thou hast them here subject unto thine eye.
Be thankful now, and thanks where thanks be due:
Give to Thomas More London's immortal glory.

Cornelius Graphey* to the Reader

Wilt thou know what wonders strange be in the land that late was found?
Wilt thou learn thy life to lead by divers ways that godly be?
Wilt thou of virtue and of vice understand the very ground?
Wilt thou see this wretched world, how full it is of vanity?
Then read and mark and bear in mind for thy behoof, as thou may best,
All things that in this present work, that worthy clerk Sir Thomas More,
With wit divine full learnedly unto the world hath plain expressed,
In whom London well glory may, for wisdom and for godly lore.

The Printer to the Reader*

The Utopian Alphabet, good Reader, which in the above written epistle is promised, hereunto I have not now adjoined, because I have not as yet the true characters or forms of the Utopian letters. And no marvel, seeing it is a tongue to us much stranger than the Indian, the Persian, the Syrian, the Arabic, the Egyptian, the Macedonian, the Sclavonian, the Cyprian, the Scythian, etc. Which tongues, though they be nothing so strange among us as the Utopian is, yet their characters we have not. But I trust, God willing, at the next impression hereof, to perform that which now I cannot: that is to say, to exhibit perfectly unto thee the Utopian Alphabet. In the meantime accept my goodwill. And so farewell.

Imprinted at London in Paul's
Church yard, at the sign of the
Lamb, by Abraham Veal

MDLVI

VTOPIAE INSVLAE FIGVRA

Woodcut from the first edition of *Utopia* (Louvain 1516)

Ambrosius Holbein's* woodcut of Utopia, as it appeared in the 1518 Basel
edition of the text

a b c d e f g h i k l m n o p q r ſ t u x y

Ò Θ Φ Ϙ Θ Θ Ϩ Ꝿ Ꙅ Ꙇ Ꙅ Ꙇ Ⳃ Ⳁ Ⳁ Ⳁ Ⳁ Ⳁ Ⳁ Ⳁ

TETRASTICHON VERNACVLA VTO/
PIENSIVM LINGVA.

Vtopos   ha   Boccas   peula   chama.

Bargol   he   maglomi   baccan

soma   gymnoſophaon

Agrama   gymnoſophon   labarem

bacha   bodamilomin

Voluala   barchin   heman   la

lauoluola   dramme   pagloni.

HORVM VERSVVM AD VERBVM HAEC
EST SENTENTIA.

Vtopus me dux ex non inſula fecit inſulam.
Vna ego terrarum omnium abſcȝ philoſophia.
Ciuitatem philoſophicam expreſſi mortalibus.
Libenter impartio mea, non grauatim accipio meliora.

b 3

The Utopian alphabet, as it appeared in the 1518 Basel edition of the text

Io.Clemens. Hythlodæus. Tho.Morus. Pet.Aegid.

SERMONIS QVEM

RAPHAEL HYTHLODAEVS VIR EXIMIVS,
de optimo reipublicæ ſtatu habuit, liber primus, per il
luſtrem uirū Thomam Morum inclytæ Britannia
rū urbis Londini & ciuem, & uicecomitem.

VVM NON EXIGVI MO
mẽti negocia quædam in
uictiſſim⁹ Angliæ rex HEN
RICVS eius nominis octa
uus, omnibus egregij princi
pis artibus ornatiſſimus, cũ
ſereniſſimo Caſtellæ princi
pe CAROLO controuerſa
d nuper ha

The opening paragraph of Book One from the 1518 Basel edition of *Utopia*
showing a woodcut (possibly by Ambrosius Holbein), of Hythloday, More,
and Peter Giles talking on the bench covered with 'turves', with John
Clements, More's page, attending them on the left

APPENDIX

Ancillary Materials From Other Early Editions of *Utopia*

Jerome Busleyden to Thomas More:* Greeting

It was not enough, my accomplished friend More, that you formerly spent all your care, labour and study upon the interests and advantage of individuals; but you must bestow them (such is your kindness and generosity) on the community at large. You thought that this benefit of yours, whatever it might be, deserved the greater indulgence, courted the greater favour, and aimed at the higher renown, on this very account, that it was likely to profit the more, the more widely it was diffused and the more there were to share it. To confer this benefit has always been your object on other occasions, and of late you have, with singular good fortune, been most successful in attaining it: I mean, in that 'afternoon's talk', which you have reduced to writing and published, about the right and good constitution, that all must long for, of the Utopian commonwealth.

In your happy description of that fair institution, we nowhere miss either the highest learning or consummate knowledge of the world. Both those qualities are blended together in the work, meeting on such equal terms that neither yields to the other, but both contend on an equality for the palm.* The truth is, you are the able possessor of such varied learning, and on the other hand of so wide and exact a knowledge of the world, that, whatever you write you assert from full experience, and, whatever assertion you have decided to make, you write most learnedly. A felicity this as rare as it is admirable! What makes it rarer is that it withholds itself from the many, and only imparts itself to the few;—to such above all as have the candour to wish, the knowledge to understand, the credit which will qualify, and the influence which will enable them to consult the common interest as dutifully, justly, and providently as you now plainly do. For, deeming yourself born not for yourself alone, but for the whole world, you have thought fit by this fair service to make the whole world itself beholden to you.

And this result you would not have been able to effect so well and rightly by any other means, as by delineating for rational beings themselves an ideal commonwealth, a pattern and finished model of conduct, than which there has never been seen in the world one more wholesome in its institution, or more perfect, or to be thought more desirable. For it far surpasses and leaves a long way behind the many famous states, that we have heard so much about, of Sparta and Athens and Rome. Had these been inaugurated under the same favourable conditions, with the same institutions, laws, enactments and rules of life to control them as this commonwealth of yours, they would not, we may be sure, have by this time been lying in ruins, levelled with the ground, and now, alas, obliterated beyond all hope of renewal. On the contrary, they would have been still unfallen, still fortunate and prosperous, leading a happy existence, mistresses of the world meanwhile, and dividing a widespread empire by land and sea.

Of these commonwealths you compassionated the unhappy lot. And so you wished to save other states in like manner, which now hold the supreme power, from undergoing a like vicissitude, by your picture of a perfect state; one which directed its chief energies not so much to framing laws as to appointing the most approved magistrates. (And with good reason: for otherwise, without them, even the best laws, if we take Plato's word for it,* would all be counted dead.) Magistrates these, above all after whose likeness, pattern of uprightness, example of conduct, and mirror of justice, the whole state and right course of any perfect commonwealth whatever ought to be modelled; wherein should unite, above all things, prudence in the rulers, courage in the soldiers, temperance in the private individuals, and justice in all.*

And since the commonwealth you make so famous is manifestly formed, in fairest manner, of these principles it is no wonder if on this account it comes not only as an object of fear to many, but also of reverence to all nations, and one for all generations to tell of; the more so, that in it all competition for ownership is taken away, and no one has any private property at all. For the rest, all men have all things in common, with a view to the commonwealth itself; so that every matter, every action, however unimportant, whether public or private, instead of being directed to the greed of many or the caprice of a few, has sole reference to the upholding of one uniform justice, equality and communion. When that is made the entire object of every action, there must needs be a clearance of all that serves as matter and fuel and feeder of intrigue, of luxury, envy, and wrong; to which mankind are hurried on, even at times against their will, either by the possession of private property, or by the burning thirst of gain, and that most pitiable of all things, ambition, to their own great and immeasurable loss. For it is from these things that there often suddenly arise divisions of feeling, taking up of arms, and wars worse than civil; whereby not only is the flourishing state of wealthy republics utterly overthrown, but the renown they won in other days, the triumphs celebrated, the splendid trophies, the rich spoils so often won from conquered enemies, are all utterly effaced.

If on these matters the words I write should chance to be less convincing than I desire, there will at any rate be ready at hand the most sufficient witnesses for me to refer you to: I mean, the many great cities formerly laid waste, the states destroyed, the republics overthrown, the villages burnt and consumed. As scarce any relics or traces of their great calamity are to be seen at this day, so neither are their names preserved by any history, however ancient it be, and however far back its records extend.

These memorable disasters, devastations, overthrows, and other calamities of war our states, whatever they be, will easily succeed in escaping, if they only adapt themselves exactly to the one pattern of the Utopian commonwealth, and do not deviate a hair's-breadth from it. By so acting alone, they will at length most fully recognize by the result how greatly they have profited by this service you have rendered them; especially since by its acquisition they have learnt to preserve their own state in safety, unharmed, and victorious. It follows that their debt to you, their present deliverer, will be no less than is the just due of those, who have saved—I do not say some one member of a state, but the whole state itself.

Meanwhile farewell. Go on and prosper, ever devising, carrying out and perfecting something, the bestowal of which on your country may give it long continuance and yourself immortality. Farewell, learned and courteous More, glory of your island, and ornament of this world of ours.

From my house at Mechlin,* 1516.

Thomas More sends his Best Wishes to his own Peter Giles*

I have been highly delighted, my dearest Peter, with the criticism, which has come also to your ears, of that very clever man* who in regard to my *Utopia* employs the following dilemma. 'If it is supposed to be true, I consider some details to be rather absurd; if fictitious, I should like to know More's real opinion about some of the matters he relates.'

Whoever this man may be, Peter (and I suspect him to be learned and feel sure he is a friend), I am most grateful to him. Indeed I do not know that anyone, since the book was published, has given me such pleasure as he has by his candid criticism. First of all it is gratifying to find that, whether out of friendship to me or out of real interest in the book, he has not wearied of the task of reading it to the very end. Nor has he read it cursorily or hastily, as priests read their breviaries (those, that is to say, who read them at all), but so slowly and carefully that he weighs carefully every point as he proceeds. Then by the very fact that he disagrees with certain points, he makes it sufficiently evident that his agreement with the rest is not rash but considered. Lastly, by the very terms which he employs to blame me, he confers on me, indirectly, much more praise than have those who have tried to flatter me. For a man who, on reading something faulty that I may have written, complains that he has been disappointed, clearly shows what a high opinion he has conceived of me. As for myself, on the other hand, if out of all that I have written some few details at least should not be entirely absurd, it is much more than I ventured to hope for.

But (for I want, in my turn, to be equally open with him) I do not see why he should pride himself on being so sharp-sighted (or, as the Greeks call it, '*oxyderches*') as to find some of the Utopian customs rather absurd, or to consider that I have unwisely contrived certain features in my commonwealth, as if nowhere else in the world were there any absurdity, or as if out of all the philosophers no one, in laying down regulations for the State, the ruler, or the private house, had ever suggested anything that could be improved upon. As to which, if I were not restrained by the reverence I bear to the memory, consecrated by age, of great men, I could from any one of them extract propositions which everyone would surely agree with me in condemning.

But now as he doubts whether Utopia is real or imaginary, I in turn demand his real opinion. I do not indeed deny that if I had determined to write about a commonwealth, and the idea of one had formed itself in my mind, I would not perhaps have thought it a sin to add fictitious details so that the truth, thus coated with honey, might be more palatable to my readers. But in that case even if I had wished to abuse the ignorance of the unlearned, I should certainly not have omitted to insert indications by which scholars would easily have been able to see through my design. If I had done nothing else I should at least have given such names to the prince, the river, the city, the island, as would have warned the skilful reader that the island exists nowhere, that the city is of shadows, the river without water, and the prince without people. It would not have been difficult to do and would have been much more witty. Unless truth had compelled me, I should certainly not have been so stupid as to use those outlandish, meaningless names, Utopia, Anyder, Amaurote, Ademus.

But, dear Giles, some men are so cautious. Whereas we, in simple faith, wrote out all that Hythloday narrated, they are so wary, so hard to satisfy, that they can scarcely be persuaded to believe it. At any rate, whatever they may think of the story, I am glad to think that they cannot call into question my own veracity, for I can say of my offspring what Mysis in Terence* says to prove that the son of Glycery was not supposititious, 'Thank God there were reputable witnesses present at the birth.' For it has, indeed, turned out most fortunately for me that Raphael not only said what he did to you and to me, but to many other men of dignity and credit he said at least as much if not indeed more. Or if they are so unbelieving as not to trust even these, let them go to Hythloday himself, for he is yet living. Only recently I heard from some who had just come from Portugal that on March 1 last he was as well and strong as ever. Let them ask him, let them worm out the truth from him, if they please, by their questions, but let them understand that all I can do is to reproduce the story faithfully, not to guarantee the truth of what I was told.

Farewell, my dearest Peter, with your delightful wife and clever daughter, to whom my wife sends her best wishes.

Guillaume Budé to his English friend
Thomas Lupset:* Greeting

I owe you many thanks, my learned young friend Lupset, for having sent me Thomas More's *Utopia*, and so drawn my attention to what is very pleasant, and likely to be very profitable, reading.

It is not long ago since you prevailed upon me (your entreaties seconding my own strong inclination) to read the six books of Galen *On the Preservation of the Health*, to which that master of the

Greek and Latin tongues, Dr Thomas Linacre, has lately rendered the service (or rather, paid the compliment) of translating them from the extant originals into Latin.* So well has the task been performed, that if all that author's works (which I consider worth all other medical lore put together) be in time translated, the want of a knowledge of Greek is not likely to be seriously felt by our schools of medicine.

I have hastily skimmed over that work, as it stands in Linacre's papers (for the courteous loan of which, for so long a time, I am very greatly indebted to you) with the result that I deem myself much benefited by the perusal. But I promise myself still greater profit when the book itself, on the publication of which at the presses of this city you are now busily engaged, shall have appeared in print.

While I thought myself already under a sufficient obligation to you on this account, here you have presented to me More's *Utopia*, as an appendix or supplement to your former kindness. He is a man of the keenest discernment, of a pleasant disposition, well versed in knowledge of the world. I have had the book by me in the country, where my time was taken up with running about and giving directions to workpeople (for you know something, and have heard more, of my having been occupied for more than a twelvemonth on business connected with my country-house); and was so impressed by reading it, as I learnt and studied the manners and customs of the Utopians, that I well-nigh forgot, nay, even abandoned, the management of my family affairs. For I perceived that all the theory and practice of domestic economy, all care whatever for increasing one's income, was mere waste of time.

And yet, as all see and are aware, the whole race of mankind is goaded on by this very thing, as if some gadfly were bred within them to sting them. The result is that we must needs confess the object of nearly all legal and civil qualification and training to be this: that with jealous and watchful cunning, as each one has a neighbour with whom he is connected by ties of citizenship, or even at times of relationship, he should be ever conveying or abstracting something from him; should pare away, repudiate, squeeze, chouse, chisel, cozen, extort, pillage, purloin, thieve, filch, rob, and (partly with the connivance, partly with the sanction of the laws) be ever plundering and appropriating.

This goes on all the more in countries where the civil and canon law, as they are called, have greater authority in the two courts. For it is evident that their customs and institutions are pervaded by the principle, that those are to be deemed the high-priests of Law and Equity, who are skilled in *caveats* (or *capias*, rather); men who hawk at their unwary fellow-citizens; artists in formulas, that is, in gudgeon-traps; adepts in concocted law; getters up of cases; juris-consults of a controverted, perverted, inverted *jus*. These are the only fit persons to give opinions as to what is fair and good; nay, what is far more, to settle with plenary power what each one is to be allowed to have, and what not to have, and the extent and limit of his tenure. How deluded must public opinion be to have determined matters thus!

The truth is that most of us, blind with the thick rheum of ignorance in our eyes, suppose that each one's cause, as a rule, is *just*, in proportion to its accordance with the requirements of the *law*, or to the way in which he has based his claim on the *law*. Whereas, were we agreed to demand our rights in accordance with the rule of truth, and what the simple Gospel prescribes, the dullest would understand, and the most senseless admit, if we put it to them, that, in the decrees of the canonists, the divine law differs as much from the human; and, in our civil laws and royal enactments, true equity differs as much from law; as the principles laid down by Christ, the founder of human society, and the usages of His dis-ciples, differ from the decrees and enactments of those who think the *summum bonum* and perfection of happiness to lie in the money-bags of a Croesus or a Midas.* So that, if you chose to define Justice nowadays, in the way that early writers liked to do, as the power who assigns to each his due, you would either find her non-existent in public, or, if I may use such a comparison, you would have to admit that she was a kind of kitchen stewardess: and this, alike whether you regard the character of our present rulers, or the dis-position of fellow-citizens and fellow-countrymen one towards another.

Perhaps indeed it may be argued, that the law I speak of has been derived from that inherent, world-old justice called *natural* law; which teaches that the stronger a man is, the more he should possess; and, the more he possesses, the more eminent among his countrymen he ought to be: with the result that now we see it an accepted principle in the Law of Nations, that persons who are unable to help their fellows by any art or practice worth mentioning, if only they are adepts in those complicated knots and stringent bonds, by which men's properties are tied up (things accounted a mixture of Gordian knots and charlatanry, with nothing very wonderful about them, by the ignorant multitude, and by scholars living, for the sake of recreation or of investigating the truth, at a distance from the Courts),—that these persons, I say, should have an income equal to that of a thousand of their countrymen, nay, even of a whole state, and sometimes more than that; and that they should then be greeted with the honourable titles of wealthy men, thrifty men, makers of splendid fortunes. Such in truth is the age in which we live; such our manners and customs; such our national character. These have pronounced it lawful for a man's credit and influence to be high, in proportion to the way in which he has been the architect of his own fortunes and of those of his heirs: an influence, in fact, which goes on increasing, according as their descendants in turn, to the remotest generation, vie in heaping up with fine additions the property gained by their ancestors; which amounts to saying, according as they have ousted more and more extensively their connections, kindred, and even their blood relations.

But the founder and regulator of all property, Jesus Christ, left among His followers a Pythagorean communion* and love; and ratified it by a plain example, when Ananias* was condemned to death for breaking this law of communion. By laying down this principle, Christ seems to me to have abolished, at any rate among his followers, all the voluminous quibbles of the civil law, and still more of the later canon law; which latter we see at the present day holding the highest position in jurisprudence, and controlling our destiny.

As for the island of Utopia, which I hear is also called 'Udepo-tia',* it is said (if we are to believe the story), by what must be owned a singular good fortune, to have adopted Christian usages both in public and in private; to have imbibed the wisdom thereto belonging; and to have kept it undefiled to this very day. The reason is, that it holds with firm grip to three divine institutions:—namely, the absolute equality, or, if you prefer to call it so, the civil communication, of all things good and bad among fellow-citizens; a settled and unwavering love of peace and quietness; and a contempt for gold and silver. Three things these, which overturn, one may say, all fraud, all imposture, cheating, roguery, and unprincipled deception. Would that Providence, on its own behalf, would cause these three principles of Utopian law to be fixed in the minds of all men by the rivets of a strong and settled conviction. We should soon see pride, covetousness, insane competition, and almost all other deadly weapons of our adversary the Devil, fall powerless; we should see the interminable array of law-books, [the work of] so many excellent and solid understandings, that occupy men till the very day of their death, consigned to bookworms, as mere hollow and empty things, or else given up to make wrapping-paper for shops.*

Good heavens! what holiness of the Utopians has had the power of earning such a blessing from above, that greed and covetousness have for so many ages failed to enter, either by force or stealth, into that island alone? that they have failed to drive out from it, by wanton effrontery, justice and honour?

Would that great Heaven in its goodness had dealt so kindly with the countries which keep, and would not part with, the appellation they bear, derived from His most holy name! Of a truth, greed, which perverts and sinks down so many minds, otherwise noble and elevated, would be gone from hence once for all, and the Golden Age* of Saturn would return. In Utopia one might verily suppose that there is a risk of Aratus* and the early poets having been mistaken in their opinion, when they made Justice depart from earth, and placed her in the Zodiac. For, if we are to believe Hythloday, she must needs have stayed behind in that island, and not yet made her way to heaven.

But in truth I have ascertained by full inquiry, that Utopia lies outside the bounds of the known world. It is in fact one of the Fortunate Isles,* perhaps very close to the Elysian Fields; for More himself testifies that Hythloday has not yet stated its position definitely. It is itself divided into a number of cities, but all uniting or confederating into one state, named Hagnopolis;* a state contented with its own customs, its own goods, blest with innocence, leading a kind of heavenly life, on a lower level indeed than heaven, but above the defilements of this world we know, which amid the endless pursuits of mankind, as empty and vain as they are keen and eager, is being hurried in a swollen and eddying tide to the cataract.

It is to Thomas More, then, that we owe our knowledge of this island. It is he who, in our generation, has made public this model of a happy life and rule for leading it, the discovery, as he tells us, of Hythloday: for he ascribes all to him. For while Hythloday has built the Utopians their state, and established for them their rites and customs; while, in so doing, he has borrowed from them and brought home for us the representation of a happy life; it is beyond question More, who has set off by his literary style the subject of that island and its customs. He it is who has perfected, as by rule and square, the City of the Hagnopolitans itself, adding all those touches by which grace and beauty and weight accrue to the noble work; even though in executing that work he has claimed for himself only a common mason's share. We see that it has been a matter of conscientious scruple* with him, not to assume too important a part in the work, lest Hythloday should have just cause for complaint, on the ground of More having plucked the first flowers of that fame, which would have been left for him, if he had himself ever decided to give an account of his adventures to the world. He was afraid, of course, that Hythloday, who was residing of his own choice in the island of Udepotia, might some day come in person upon the scene, and be vexed and aggrieved at this unkindness on his part, in leaving him the glory of this discovery with the best flowers plucked off. To be of this persuasion is the part of good men and wise.

Now while More is one who of himself carries weight, and has great authority to rest upon, I am led to place unreserved confidence in him by the testimony of Peter Giles of Antwerp. Though I have never made his acquaintance in person (apart from recommendations of his learning and character that have reached me), I love him on account of his being the intimate friend of the illustrious Erasmus, who has deserved so well of letters of every kind, whether sacred or profane; with whom personally I have long corresponded and formed ties of friendship.

Farewell, my dear Lupset. Greet for me, at the first opportunity, either by word of mouth or by letter, Linacre, that pillar of the British name in all that concerns good learning; one who is now, as I hope, not more yours than ours. He is one of the few whose good opinion I should be very glad, if possible, to gain. When he was himself known to be staying here, he gained in the highest degree the good opinion of me and of Jehan Ruelle,* my friend and the sharer in my studies. And his singular learning and careful industry I should be the first to look up to and strive to copy.

Greet More also once and again for me, either by message, as I said before, or by word of mouth. As I think and often repeat, Minerva* has long entered his name on her selectest album; and I love and revere him in the highest degree for what he has written about this isle of the New World, Utopia.

In his history our age and those which succeed it will have a nursery, so to speak, of polite and useful institutions; from which men may borrow customs, and introduce and adapt them each to his own state. Farewell.

From Paris, the 31st of July.

Erasmus of Rotterdam to his Dear Gossip
John Froben:* Greeting

I have hitherto been pleased beyond measure with all that my friend More has written, but felt some distrust of my own judgment, by reason of the close friendship between us. But now that I see learned men to be all unanimously of my opinion, even outdoing me in the warmth of their admiration for his transcendant genius (a proof of their greater discernment, though not of their greater affection), I am quite satisfied that I am in the right, and shall not shrink in future from openly expressing what I think. What would not such marvellous natural gifts have accomplished, if his intellect had been trained in Italy; if it were wholly devoted to literature; if it had had time to ripen for its proper harvest, its own autumn? While quite young, he amused himself with composing epigrams, many of them written when he was a mere boy. He has never gone out of his native Britain, save once or twice, when acting as ambassador for his sovereign in the Netherlands.* He is married, and has the cares of a family; he has the duties of a public office to discharge, and is immersed in the business of the law-courts; with so many important affairs of state distracting him besides, that you would wonder at his having leisure even to think of books.

So I have sent you his *Prolusions** and *Utopia*. If you think fit, let them go forth to the world and to posterity with the recommendation of being printed by you. For such is the reputation of your press, that for a book to be known to have been published by Froben, is a passport to the approbation of the learned.

Farewell, and greet for me your good father-in-law, your charming wife, and the darling children. Mind you bring up in good learning my little godson Erasmus, in whom I have a claim as well as you; for learning has rocked his cradle.

Louvain: Aug. 25th, 1517.

Appendix

To the right honourable, and his very singular good master,
Master William Cecil, esquire, one of the two principal
secretaries to the King his most excellent majesty,
Ralph Robinson wisheth continuance of health with
daily increase of virtue and honour*

Upon a time when tidings came to the city of Corinth that King Philip, father to Alexander surnamed the Great, was coming thitherward with an army royal to lay siege to the city, the Corinthians being forthwith stricken with great fear, began busily and earnestly to look about them and to fall to work on all hands.* Some to scour and trim up harness, some to carry stones, some to amend and build higher the walls, some to rampire and fortify the bulwarks and fortresses, some one thing and some another for the defending and strengthening of the city. The which busy labour and toil of theirs when Diogenes the philosopher saw, having no profitable business whereupon to set himself on work (neither any man required his labour and help as expedient for the commonwealth in that necessity), immediately girded about him his philosophical cloak, and began to roll and tumble up and down hither and thither upon the hillside that lieth adjoining to the city his great barrel or tun, wherein he dwelled, for other dwelling-place would he have none. This seeing one of his friends, and not a little musing thereat, came to him: and, 'I pray thee, Diogenes,' quoth he, 'why dost thou thus, or what meanest thou hereby?' 'Forsooth I am tumbling my tub too,' quoth he, 'because it were no reason that I only should be idle, where so many be working.'*

In semblable manner, right honourable sir, though I be, as I am indeed, of much less ability than Diogenes was to do anything that shall or may be for the advancement and commodity of the public wealth of my native country; yet I, seeing every sort and kind of people in their vocation and degree busily occupied about the commonwealth's affairs, and especially learned men daily putting forth in writing new inventions and devices to the furtherance of the same, thought it my bounden duty to God and to my country so to tumble my tub: I mean so to occupy and exercise myself in bestowing such spare hours as I (being at the beck and commandment of others), could conveniently win to myself, that though no commodity of that my labour and travail to the public weal should arise, yet it might by this appear that mine endeavour and goodwill hereunto was not lacking. To the accomplishment, therefore, and fulfilling of this my mind and purpose, I took upon me to turn and translate out of Latin into our English tongue the fruitful and profitable book which Sir Thomas More, knight, compiled and made of the new isle Utopia, containing and setting forth the best state and form of a public weal, a work (as it appeareth) written almost forty years ago by the said Sir Thomas More the author thereof. The which man, forasmuch as he was a man of late time, yea almost of this our days, and for the excellent qualities where-with the great goodness of God had plentifully endowed him, and for the high place and room whereunto his prince had most gra-ciously called him, notably well known, not only among us his countrymen, but also in foreign countries and nations; therefore I have not much to speak of him. This only I say: that it is much to be lamented of all, and not only of us Englishmen, that a man of so incomparable wit, of so profound knowledge, of so absolute learning, and of so fine eloquence was yet nevertheless so much blinded, rather with obstinacy than with ignorance, that he could not or rather would not see the shining light of God's holy truth in certain principal points of Christian religion; but did rather choose to persevere and continue in his wilful and stubborn obstinacy even to the very death.*

This I say is a thing much to be lamented. But letting this matter pass, I return again to Utopia. Which (as I said before) is a work not only for the matter that it containeth fruitful and profitable, but also for the writer's eloquent Latin style pleasant and delectable. Which he that readeth in Latin, as the author himself wrote it, perfectly understanding the same, doubtless he shall take great pleasure and delight both in the sweet eloquence of the writer and also in the witty invention and fine conveyance or disposition of the matter, but most of all in the good and wholesome lessons which be there in great plenty and abundance. But now I fear greatly that in this my simple translation, through my rudeness and ignorance in our English tongue, all the grace and pleasure of the eloquence where-with the matter in Latin is finely set forth, may seem to be utterly excluded and lost, and therefore the fruitfulness of the matter itself much peradventure diminished and appaired. For who knoweth not, which knoweth anything, that an eloquent style setteth forth and highly commendeth a mean matter? Whereas on the other side rude and unlearned speech defaceth and disgraceth a very good matter.

According as I heard once a wise man say, a good tale evil told

were better untold, and an evil tale well told needeth none other
solicitor. This thing I, well pondering and weighing with myself,
and also knowing and acknowledging the barbarous rudeness of my
translation, was fully determined never to have put it forth in print,
had it not been for certain friends of mine, and especially one whom
above all other I regarded, a man of sage and discreet wit and in
worldly matters by long use well experienced, whose name is
George Tadlowe, an honest citizen of London, and in the same city
well accepted and of good reputation. At whose request and
instance I first took upon my weak and feeble shoulders the heavy
and weighty burden of this great enterprise. This man with divers
other, but this man chiefly (for he was able to do more with me than
many other), after that I had once rudely brought the work to an
end, ceased not by all means possible continually to assault me until
he had at the last, what by the force of his pithy arguments and
strong reasons, and what by his authority so persuaded me, that he
caused me to agree and consent to the imprinting hereof. He therefore, as the chief persuader, must take upon him the danger which
upon this bold and rash enterprise shall ensue. I, as I suppose, am
herein clearly acquit and discharged of all blame.

Yet, honourable sir, for the better avoiding of envious and malicious tongues, I (knowing you to be a man not only profoundly
learned and well affected towards all such as either can or will take
pains in the well bestowing of that poor talent which GOD hath
endued them with, but also for your godly disposition and virtuous
qualities not unworthily now placed in authority and called to honour) am the bolder humbly to offer and dedicate unto your good
mastership this my simple work. Partly that under the safe conduct
of your protection it may the better be defended from the obloquy
of them which can say well by nothing that pleaseth not their fond
and corrupt judgements, though it be else both fruitful and godly,
and partly that by the means of this homely present I may the better
renew and revive (which of late, as you know, I have already begun
to do) that old acquaintance that was between you and me in the
time of our childhood, being then schoolfellows together. Not
doubting that you for your native goodness and gentleness will
accept in good part this poor gift, as an argument or token that mine
old goodwill and hearty affection towards you is not, by reason of
long tract of time and separation of our bodies, anything at all
quailed and diminished, but rather (I assure you) much augmented
and increased. This verily is the chief cause that hath encouraged

me to be so bold with your mastership, else truly this my poor present is of such simple and mean sort, that it is neither able to recompense the least portion of your great gentleness to me, of my part undeserved, both in the time of our old acquaintance and also now lately again bountifully showed, neither yet fit and meet for the very baseness of it to be offered to one so worthy as you be. But almighty God (who therefore ever be thanked) hath advanced you to such fortune and dignity, that you be of ability to accept thankfully as well a man's goodwill as his gift. The same God grant you and all yours long and joyfully to continue in all godliness and prosperity.

FRANCIS BACON

NEW ATLANTIS

NEW ATLANTIS

A Work Unfinished

To the Reader.

This fable my Lord devised, to the end that he might exhibit therein a model or description of a college instituted for the interpreting of nature and the producing of great and marvellous works for the benefit of men, under the name of Salomon's House, or the College of the Six Days' Works. And even so far his Lordship hath proceeded, as to finish that part. Certainly the model is more vast and high than can possibly be imitated in all things; notwithstanding most things therein are within men's power to effect. His Lordship thought also in this present fable to have composed a frame of Laws, or of the best state or mould of a commonwealth; but foreseeing it would be a long work, his desire of collecting the Natural History diverted him, which he preferred many degrees before it. This work of the *New Atlantis* (as much as concerneth the English edition) his Lordship designed for this place;* in regard it hath so near affinity (in one part of it) with the preceding Natural History.

W. Rawley*

We sailed from Peru, (where we had continued by the space of one whole year), for China and Japan, by the South Sea;* taking with us victuals for twelve months; and had good winds from the east, though soft and weak, for five months' space and more. But then the wind came about, and settled in the west for many days, so as we could make little or no way, and were sometimes in purpose to turn back. But then again there arose strong and great winds from the south, with a point east; which carried us up (for all that we could do) towards the north: by which time our victuals failed us, though we had made good spare of them. So that finding ourselves in the midst of the greatest wilderness of waters in the world, without victual, we gave ourselves for lost men, and prepared for death. Yet we did lift up our hearts and voices to God above, who 'showeth his wonders in the deep';* beseeching him of his mercy, that as in the beginning he discovered the face of the deep, and brought forth dry land,* so he would now discover land to us, that we might not perish.

And it came to pass that the next day about evening, we saw within a kenning before us, towards the north, as it were thick clouds, which did put us in some hope of land; knowing how that part of the South Sea was utterly unknown; and might have islands or continents, that hitherto were not come to light. Wherefore we bent our course thither, where we saw the appearance of land, all that night; and in the dawning of the next day, we might plainly discern that it was a land; flat to our sight, and full of boscage; which made it show the more dark. And after an hour and a half's sailing, we entered into a good haven, being the port of a fair city; not great indeed but well built, and that gave a pleasant view from the sea: and we thinking every minute long till we were on land, came close to the shore, and offered to land. But straightways we saw divers of the people, with bastons in their hands, as it were forbidding us to land; yet without any cries or fierceness, but only as warning us off by signs that they made. Whereupon being not a little discomforted, we were advising with ourselves what we should do. During which time there made forth to us a small boat, with about eight persons in it; whereof one of them had in his hand a tipstaff of a yellow cane, tipped at both ends with blue, who came aboard our ship, without any show of distrust at all. And when he saw one of our number present himself somewhat afore the rest, he drew forth a little scroll of parchment (somewhat yellower than our parchment, and shining like the leaves of writing tables, but otherwise soft and flexible), and delivered it to our foremost man.* In which scroll were written in ancient Hebrew and in ancient Greek, and in good Latin of the School,* and in Spanish, these words; 'Land ye not, none of you; and provide to be gone from this coast within sixteen days, except you have further time given you. Meanwhile, if you want fresh water, or victual, or help for your sick, or that your ship needeth repair, write down your wants, and you shall have that which belongeth to mercy.' This scroll was signed with a stamp of cherubins' wings,* not spread but hanging downwards, and by them a cross. This being delivered, the officer returned, and left only a servant with us to receive our answer.

Consulting hereupon amongst ourselves, we were much perplexed. The denial of landing and hasty warning us away troubled us much; on the other side, to find that the people had languages* and were so full of humanity, did comfort us not a little. And above all, the sign of the cross to that instrument* was to us a great rejoicing, and as it were a certain presage of good. Our answer was in the Spanish tongue; 'That for our ship, it was well; for we had rather met with calms and contrary winds than any tempests. For our sick, they were many, and in very ill case; so that if they were not permitted to land, they ran danger of their lives.' Our other wants we set down in particular; adding, 'that we had some little store of merchandise, which if it pleased them to deal for, it might supply our wants without being chargeable unto them.'* We offered some reward in pistolets unto the servant, and a piece of crimson velvet to be presented to the officer; but the servant took them not, nor would scarce look upon them; and so left us, and went back in another little boat which was sent for him.

About three hours after we had dispatched our answer, there came towards us a person (as it seemed) of place. He had on him a gown with wide sleeves, of a kind of water chamolet, of an excellent azure colour, far more glossy than ours; his under-apparel was green; and so was his hat, being in the form of a turban, daintily made, and not so huge as the Turkish turbans; and the locks of his hair came down below the brims of it. A reverend man was he to behold. He came in a boat, gilt in some part of it,* with four persons more only in that boat; and was followed by another boat, wherein were some twenty. When he was come within a flight-shot of our ship, signs were made to us that we should send forth some to meet him upon the water; which we presently did in our ship-boat, sending the principal man amongst us save one, and four of our number with him.

When we were come within six yards of their boat, they called to us to stay, and not to approach farther; which we did. And thereupon the man whom I before described stood up, and with a loud voice in Spanish, asked, 'Are ye Christians?' We answered, 'We were;' fearing the less, because of the cross we had seen in the subscription. At which answer the said person lifted up his right hand towards heaven, and drew it softly to his mouth (which is the gesture they use when they thank God), and then said: 'If ye will swear (all of you) by the merits of the Saviour that ye are no pirates, nor have shed blood lawfully nor unlawfully within forty days past, you may have licence to come on land.' We said, 'We were all ready to take that oath.' Whereupon one of those that were with him, being (as it seemed) a notary, made an entry of this act. Which done, another of the attendants of the great person, which was with him in the same boat, after his lord had spoken a little to him, said aloud; 'My lord would have you know, that it is not of pride or greatness that he cometh not aboard your ship; but for that in your answer you declare that you have many sick amongst you, he was warned by the Conservator of Health of the city that he should keep a distance.' We bowed ourselves towards him, and answered, 'We were his humble servants; and accounted for great honour and singular humanity towards us that which was already done;* but hoped well that the nature of the sickness of our men was not infectious.' So he returned; and a while after came the notary to us aboard our ship; holding in his hand a fruit of that country, like an orange,* but of colour between orange-tawny and scarlet, which cast a most excellent odour. He used it (as it seemeth) for a preservative against infection. He gave us our oath; 'By the name of Jesus and his merits:' and after told us that the next day by six of the clock in the morning we should be sent to, and brought to the Strangers' House (so he called it), where we should be accommodated of things both for our whole and for our sick. So he left us; and when we offered him some pistolets, he smiling said, 'He must not be twice paid for one labour:'* meaning (as I take it) that he had salary sufficient of the state for his service. For (as I after learned) they call an officer that taketh rewards, 'twice paid'.

The next morning early, there came to us the same officer that came to us at first with his cane, and told us, he came to conduct us to the Strangers' House; and that he had prevented the hour,* because we might have the whole day before us for our business. 'For,' said he, 'if you will follow my advice, there shall first go with me some few of you, and see the place, and how it may be made convenient for you; and then you may send for your sick, and the rest of your number which ye will bring on land.' We thanked him, and said, 'That this care which he took of desolate strangers God would reward.' And so six of us went on land with him: and when we were on land, he went before us, and turned to us, and said, 'He was but our servant, and our guide.' He led us through three fair streets; and all the way we went there were gathered some people on both sides standing in a row; but in so civil a fashion, as if it had been not to wonder at us but to welcome us; and divers of them, as we passed by them, put their arms a little abroad;* which is their gesture when they bid any welcome.

The Strangers' House is a fair and spacious house, built of brick, of somewhat a bluer colour than our brick; and with handsome windows, some of glass, some of a kind of cambric oiled.* He brought us first into a fair parlour above stairs, and then asked us, 'What number of persons we were? And how many sick?' We answered, 'We were in all (sick and whole) one and fifty persons, whereof our sick were seventeen.' He desired us to have patience a little, and to stay till he came back to us; which was about an hour after; and then he led us to see the chambers which were provided for us, being in number nineteen: they having cast it (as it seemeth) that four of those chambers, which were better than the rest, might receive four of the principal men of our company, and lodge them alone by themselves; and the other fifteen chambers were to lodge us two and two together. The chambers were handsome and cheerful chambers, and furnished civilly. Then he led us to a long gallery, like a dorture, where he showed us all along the one side (for the other side was but wall and window) seventeen cells, very neat ones, having partitions of cedar wood. Which gallery and cells, being in all forty (many more than we needed), were instituted as an infirmary for sick persons. And he told us withal, that as any of our sick waxed well, he might be removed from his cell to a chamber; for which purpose there were set forth ten spare chambers, besides the number we spake of before. This done, he brought us back to the parlour, and lifting up his cane a little, (as they do when they give any charge or command), said to us, 'Ye are to know that the custom of the land requireth, that after this day and to-morrow, (which we give you for removing of your people from your ship), you are to keep within doors for three days. But let it not trouble you, nor do not think yourselves restrained, but rather left to your rest and ease. You shall want nothing, and there are six of our people appointed to attend you, for any business you may have abroad.' We gave him thanks with all affection and respect, and said, 'God surely is manifested in this land.' We offered him also twenty pistolets; but he smiled, and only said; 'What? twice paid!' And so he left us.

Soon after our dinner was served in; which was right good viands, both for bread and meat: better than any collegiate diet* that I have known in Europe. We had also drink of three sorts, all wholesome and good; wine of the grape; a drink of grain, such as is with us our ale, but more clear; and a kind of cider made of a fruit of that country; a wonderful pleasing and refreshing drink. Besides, there were brought in to us great store of those scarlet oranges for our sick; which (they said) were an assured remedy for sickness taken at sea. There was given us also a box of small grey or whitish pills, which they wished our sick should take, one of the pills every night, before sleep; which (they said) would hasten their recovery.

The next day, after that our trouble of carriage and removing of our men and goods out of our ship was somewhat settled and quiet, I thought good to call our company together; and when they were assembled said unto them; 'My dear friends, let us know ourselves, and how it standeth with us. We are men cast on land, as Jonas was out of the whale's belly,* when we were as buried in the deep: and now we are on land, we are but between death and life; for we are beyond both the old world and the new; and whether ever we shall see Europe, God only knoweth. It is a kind of miracle hath brought us hither: and it must be little less that shall bring us hence. Therefore in regard of our deliverance past, and our danger present and to come, let us look up to God, and every man reform his own ways. Besides we are come here amongst a Christian people, full of piety and humanity: let us not bring that confusion of face upon ourselves,* as to show our vices or unworthiness before them. Yet there is more. For they have by commandment (though in form of courtesy) cloistered us within these walls for three days: who knoweth whether it be not to take some taste of our manners and conditions?* and if they find them bad, to banish us straightways; if good, to give us further time. For these men that they have given us for attendance may withal have an eye upon us. Therefore for God's love, and as we love the weal of our souls and bodies, let us so behave ourselves as we may be at peace with God, and may find grace in the eyes of this people.' Our company with one voice thanked me for my good admonition, and promised me to live soberly and civilly, and without giving any the least occasion of offence. So we spent our three days joyfully and without care, in expectation what would be done with us when they were expired. During which time, we had every hour joy of the amendment of our sick; who thought themselves cast into some divine pool of healing,* they mended so kindly and so fast.

The morrow after our three days were past, there came to us a new man that we had not seen before, clothed in blue as the former was, save that his turban was white, with a small red cross on the top. He had also a tippet of fine linen. At his coming in, he did bend to us a little, and put his arms abroad. We of our parts saluted him in a very lowly and submissive manner; as looking that* from him we should receive sentence of life or death. He desired to speak with some few of us: whereupon six of us only stayed, and the rest avoided the room. He said, 'I am by office governor of this House of Strangers, and by vocation I am a Christian priest; and therefore am come to you to offer you my service, both as strangers and chiefly as Christians. Some things I may tell you, which I think you will not be unwilling to hear. The state hath given you licence to stay on land for the space of six weeks: and let it not trouble you if your occasions ask further time, for the law in this point is not precise; and I do not doubt but myself shall be able to obtain for you such further time as may be convenient. Ye shall also understand, that the Strangers'

House is at this time rich, and much aforehand; for it hath laid up revenue these thirty-seven years; for so long it is since any stranger arrived in this part: and therefore take ye no care; the state will defray you all the time you stay; neither shall you stay one day the less for that. As for any merchandise ye have brought, ye shall be well used, and have your return either in merchandise or in gold and silver: for to us it is all one. And if you have any other request to make, hide it not. For ye shall find we will not make your coun- tenance to fall by the answer ye shall receive. Only this I must tell you, that none of you must go above a *karan*' (that is with them a mile and an half) 'from the walls of the city, without especial leave.'

We answered, after we had looked awhile one upon another, admiring this gracious and parent-like usage; 'That we could not tell what to say: for we wanted words to express our thanks; and his noble free offers left us nothing to ask. It seemed to us that we had before us a picture of our salvation in heaven, for we that were awhile since in the jaws of death, were now brought into a place where we found nothing but consolations. For the commandment laid upon us, we would not fail to obey it, though it was impossible but our hearts should be inflamed* to tread further upon this happy and holy ground.' We added; 'That our tongues should first cleave to the roofs of our mouths, ere we should forget either his reverend person or this whole nation in our prayers.'* We also most humbly besought him to accept of us as his true servants, by as just a right as ever men on earth were bounden; laying and presenting both our persons and all we had at his feet. He said; 'He was a priest, and looked for a priest's reward: which was our brotherly love and the good of our souls and bodies.' So he went from us, not without tears of tender- ness in his eyes; and left us also confused with joy and kindness, saying amongst ourselves, 'That we were come into a land of angels, which did appear to us daily and prevent us with comforts, which we thought not of, much less expected.'

The next day, about ten of the clock, the governor came to us again, and after salutations said familiarly, 'That he was come to visit us': and called for a chair, and sat him down: and we, being some ten of us (the rest were of the meaner sort, or else gone abroad), sat down with him. And when we were set, he began thus: 'We of this island of Bensalem,'* (for so they call it in their language), 'have this;

that by means of our solitary situation, and of the laws of secrecy which we have for our travellers, and our rare admission of strangers, we know well most part of the habitable world, and are ourselves unknown. Therefore because he that knoweth least is fittest to ask questions, it is more reason, for the entertainment of the time,* that ye ask me questions, than that I ask you.'

We answered; 'That we humbly thanked him that he would give us leave so to do: and that we conceived by the taste we had already, that there was no worldly thing on earth more worthy to be known than the state of that happy land. But above all', (we said), 'since that we were met from the several ends of the world,* and hoped assuredly that we should meet one day in the kingdom of heaven (for that we were both parts Christians),* we desired to know (in respect that land was so remote, and so divided by vast and unknown seas, from the land where our Saviour walked on earth), who was the apostle of that nation, and how it was converted to the faith?' It appeared in his face that he took great contentment in this our question: he said, 'Ye knit my heart to you, by asking this question in the first place; for it showeth that you "first seek the kingdom of heaven";* and I shall gladly and briefly satisfy your demand.

'About twenty years after the ascension of our Saviour, it came to pass that there was seen by the people of Renfusa,* (a city upon the eastern coast of our island), within night (the night was cloudy and calm), as it might be some mile into the sea, a great pillar of light;* not sharp, but in form of a column or cylinder, rising from the sea a great way up towards heaven: and on the top of it was seen a large cross of light, more bright and resplendent than the body of the pillar. Upon which so strange a spectacle, the people of the city gathered apace together upon the sands, to wonder; and so after put themselves into a number of small boats, to go nearer to this marvellous sight. But when the boats were come within about sixty yards of the pillar, they found themselves all bound, and could go no further; yet so as they might move to go about, but might not approach nearer: so as the boats stood all as in a theatre, beholding this light as an heavenly sign. It so fell out, that there was in one of the boats one of the wise men of the society of Salomon's House; which house or college (my good brethren) is the very eye of this kingdom; who having awhile attentively and devoutly viewed and contemplated this pillar and cross, fell down upon his face; and then raised himself upon his knees, and lifting up his hands to heaven, made his prayers in this manner:

'"Lord God of heaven and earth, thou hast vouchsafed of thy grace to those of our order,* to know thy works of creation, and the secrets of them; and to discern (as far as appertaineth to the generations of men) between divine miracles, works of nature, works of art, and impostures and illusions of all sorts.* I do here acknowledge and testify before this people, that the thing which we now see before our eyes is thy Finger* and a true Miracle; and forasmuch as we learn in our books that thou never workest miracles but to a divine and excellent end (for the laws of nature are thine own laws, and thou exceedest them not but upon great cause), we most humbly beseech thee to prosper this great sign, and to give us the interpretation and use of it in mercy; which thou dost in some part secretly promise by sending it unto us."

'When he had made his prayer, he presently found the boat he was in moveable and unbound; whereas all the rest remained still fast; and taking that for an assurance of leave to approach, he caused the boat to be softly and with silence rowed towards the pillar. But ere he came near it, the pillar and cross of light brake up, and cast itself abroad, as it were, into a firmament of many stars;* which also vanished soon after, and there was nothing left to be seen but a small ark or chest of cedar, dry, and not wet at all with water, though it swam. And in the fore-end of it, which was towards him, grew a small green branch of palm;* and when the wise man had taken it with all reverence into his boat, it opened of itself, and there were found in it a Book and a Letter; both written in fine parchment, and wrapped in sindons of linen. The Book contained all the canonical books of the Old and New Testament, according as you have them, (for we know well what the Churches with you receive); and the Apocalypse itself, and some other books of the New Testament which were not at that time written,* were nevertheless in the Book. And for the Letter, it was in these words:

'"I Bartholomew,* a servant of the Highest, and Apostle of Jesus Christ, was warned by an angel that appeared to me in a vision of glory, that I should commit this ark to the floods of the sea. Therefore I do testify and declare unto that people where God shall ordain this ark to come to land, that in the same day is come unto them salvation and peace and good-will, from the Father, and from the Lord Jesus."

'There was also in both these writings, as well the Book as the Letter, wrought a great miracle, conform to that of the Apostles in the original Gift of Tongues.* For there being at that time in this land Hebrews, Persians, and Indians, besides the natives, every one read upon the Book and Letter, as if they had been written in his own language. And thus was this land saved from infidelity (as the remain of the old world was from water) by an ark, through the apostolical and miraculous evangelism of St. Bartholomew.' And here he paused, and a messenger came, and called him from us. So this was all that passed in that conference.

The next day, the same governor came again to us immediately after dinner, and excused himself, saying, 'That the day before he was called from us somewhat abruptly, but now he would make us amends, and spend time with us, if we held his company and conference agreeable.' We answered, 'That we held it so agreeable and pleasing to us, as we forgot both dangers past and fears to come, for the time we heard him speak; and that we thought an hour spent with him, was worth years of our former life.' He bowed himself a little to us, and after we were set again, he said: 'Well, the questions are on your part.'

One of our number said, after a little pause, 'That there was a matter we were no less desirous to know, than fearful to ask, lest we might presume too far. But encouraged by his rare humanity towards us (that could scarce think ourselves strangers, being his vowed and professed servants), we would take the hardiness to propound it: humbly beseeching him, if he thought it not fit to be answered, that he would pardon it, though he rejected it.' We said, 'We well observed those his words, which he formerly spake,* that this happy island where we now stood was known to few, and yet knew most of the nations of the world; which we found to be true, considering they had the languages of Europe, and knew much of our state and business; and yet we in Europe (notwithstanding all the remote discoveries and navigations of this last age*), never heard any of the least inkling or glimpse of this island. This we found wonderful strange; for that all nations have inter-knowledge one of another either by voyage into foreign parts, or by strangers that come to them: and though the traveller into a foreign country doth commonly know more by the eye, than he that stayeth at home can by relation of the traveller; yet both ways suffice to make a mutual knowledge, in some degree, on both parts. But for this island, we never heard tell of any ship of theirs that had been seen to arrive upon any shore of Europe; no, nor of either the East or West Indies; nor yet of any ship of any other part of the world that had made return from them. And yet the marvel rested not in this. For the situation of it (as his lordship said) in the secret conclave of such a vast sea might cause it. But then that they should have knowledge of the languages, books, affairs, of those that lie such a distance from them, it was a thing we could not tell what to make of; for that it seemed to us a condition and propriety of divine powers and beings, to be hidden and unseen to others, and yet to have others open and as in a light to them.'

At this speech the governor gave a gracious smile, and said; 'That we did well to ask pardon for this question we now asked; for that it imported as if we thought this land a land of magicians, that sent forth spirits of the air into all parts, to bring them news and intelligence of other countries.' It was answered by us all, in all possible humbleness, but yet with a countenance taking knowledge* that we knew that he spake it but merrily, 'That we were apt enough to think there was somewhat supernatural in this island; but yet rather as angelical than magical. But to let his lordship know truly what it was that made us tender and doubtful to ask this question, it was not any such conceit, but because we remembered he had given a touch in his former speech, that this land had laws of secrecy touching strangers.' To this he said; 'You remember it aright; and therefore in that I shall say to you I must reserve some particulars, which it is not lawful for me to reveal; but there will be enough left to give you satisfaction.

'You shall understand (that which perhaps you will scarce think credible) that about three thousand years ago, or somewhat more, the navigation of the world (specially for remote voyages) was greater than at this day. Do not think with yourselves that I know not how much it is increased with you within these six-score years:* I know it well, and yet I say greater then than now; whether it was, that the example of the ark, that saved the remnant of men from the universal deluge, gave men confidence to adventure upon the waters; or what it was; but such is the truth. The Phoenicians, and especially the Tyrians, had great fleets. So had the Carthaginians, their colony, which is yet further west. Toward the east, the shipping of Egypt and of Palestina was likewise great. China also, and the great Atlantis (that you call America), which have now but junks and canoes, abounded then in tall ships.* This island (as appeareth by faithful registers of those times) had then fifteen hundred strong ships, of great content. Of all this there is with you sparing memory, or none; but we have large knowledge thereof.

'At that time, this land was known and frequented by the ships and vessels of all the nations before named. And (as it cometh to pass) they had many times men of other countries that were no sailors, that came with them; as Persians, Chaldeans, Arabians; so as almost all nations of might and fame resorted hither; of whom we have some stirps and little tribes with us at this day. And for our own ships, they went sundry voyages, as well to your Straits, which you call the Pillars of Hercules, as to other parts in the Atlantic and Mediterranean Seas; as to Paguin (which is the same with Cambaline) and Quinzy, upon the Oriental Seas, as far as to the borders of the East Tartary.*

'At the same time, and an age after, or more, the inhabitants of the great Atlantis did flourish. For though the narration and description which is made by a great man with you,* that the descendants of Neptune* planted there; and of the magnificent temple, palace, city, and hill; and the manifold streams of goodly navigable rivers, (which, as so many chains, environed the same site* and temple); and the several degrees of ascent whereby men did climb up to the same, as if it had been a *scala coeli*; be all poetical and fabulous: yet so much is true, that the said country of Atlantis, as well that of Peru, then called Coya, as that of Mexico, then named Tyrambel,* were mighty and proud kingdoms in arms, shipping, and riches: so mighty, as at one time (or at least within the space of ten years) they both made two great expeditions; they of Tyrambel through the Atlantic to the Mediterranean Sea; and they of Coya through the South Sea upon this our island. And for the former of these, which was into Europe, the same author amongst you (as it seemeth) had some relation from the Egyptian priest whom he citeth.* For assuredly such a thing there was. But whether it were the ancient Athenians that had the glory of the repulse and resistance of those forces, I can say nothing: but certain it is, there never came back either ship or man from that voyage. Neither had the other voyage of those of Coya upon us had better fortune, if they had not* met with enemies of greater clemency. For the king of this island (by name Altabin*), a wise man and a great warrior, knowing well both his own strength and that of his enemies, handled the matter so, as he cut off their land-forces from their ships; and entoiled both their navy and their camp with a greater power than theirs, both by sea and land; and compelled them to render themselves without striking stroke: and after they were at his mercy, contenting himself only with their oath that they should no more bear arms against him, dismissed them all in safety.

'But the Divine Revenge* overtook not long after those proud enterprises. For within less than the space of one hundred years, the great Atlantis was utterly lost and destroyed: not by a great earthquake, as your man saith (for that whole tract is little subject to earthquakes), but by a particular deluge or inundation; those countries having, at this day, far greater rivers and far higher mountains to pour down waters, than any part of the old world.* But it is true that the same inundation was not deep; not past forty foot, in most places, from the ground: so that although it destroyed man and beast generally, yet some few wild inhabitants of the wood escaped. Birds also were saved by flying to the high trees and woods. For as for men, although they had buildings in many places higher than the depth of the water, yet that inundation, though it were shallow, had a long continuance; whereby they of the vale that were not drowned, perished for want of food and other things necessary.

'So as marvel you not at the thin population of America, nor at the rudeness and ignorance of the people; for you must account your inhabitants of America* as a young people; younger a thousand years, at the least, than the rest of the world; for that there was so much time between the universal flood and their particular inundation. For the poor remnant of human seed which remained in their mountains peopled the country again slowly, by little and little; and being simple and savage people, (not like Noah and his sons, which was the chief family of the earth), they were not able to leave letters, arts, and civility* to their posterity; and having likewise in their mountainous habitations been used (in respect of the extreme cold of those regions) to clothe themselves with the skins of tigers, bears, and great hairy goats,* that they have in those parts; when after they came down into the valley, and found the intolerable heats which are there, and knew no means of lighter apparel, they were forced to begin the custom of going naked, which continueth at this day. Only they take great pride and delight in the feathers of birds,* and this also they took from those their ancestors of the mountains, who were invited unto it by the infinite flights of birds that came up to the high grounds, while the waters stood below. So you see, by this main accident of time, we lost our traffic with the Americans, with whom of all others, in regard they lay nearest to us, we had most commerce.

'As for the other parts of the world, it is most manifest that in the ages following (whether it were in respect of* wars, or by a natural revolution of time),* navigation did everywhere greatly decay; and specially far voyages (the rather by the use of galleys, and such vessels as could hardly brook the ocean), were altogether left and omitted.* So then, that part of intercourse which could be from other nations to sail to us,* you see how it hath long since ceased; except it were by some rare accident, as this of yours. But now of the cessation of that other part of intercourse, which might be by our sailing to other nations, I must yield you some other cause. For I cannot say (if I shall say truly), but our shipping, for number, strength, mariners, pilots, and all things that appertain to navigation, is as great as ever: and therefore why we should sit at home, I shall now give you an account by itself: and it will draw nearer to give you satisfaction to your principal question.*

'There reigned in this island, about nineteen hundred years ago, a King, whose memory of all others we most adore; not superstitiously, but as a divine instrument, though a mortal man; his name was Solamona: and we esteem him as the law-giver of our nation. This king had a "large heart", inscrutable for good;* and was wholly bent to make his kingdom and people happy. He therefore, taking into consideration how sufficient and substantive this land was to maintain itself without any aid at all of the foreigner;* being five thousand six hundred miles in circuit, and of rare fertility of soil in the greatest part thereof; and finding also the shipping of this country might be plentifully set on work, both by fishing and by transportations from port to port, and likewise by sailing unto some small islands that are not far from us, and are under the crown and laws of this state; and recalling into his memory the happy and flourishing estate wherein this land then was, so as it might be a thousand ways altered to the worse, but scarce any one way to the better; thought nothing wanted to his noble and heroical intentions, but only (as far as human foresight might reach) to give perpetuity to that which was in his time so happily established. Therefore amongst his other fundamental laws of this kingdom, he did ordain the interdicts and prohibitions which we have touching entrance of strangers; which at that time (though it was after the calamity of America) was frequent; doubting novelties, and commixture of manners.* It is true, the like law against the admission of strangers without licence is an ancient law in the kingdom of China, and yet continued in use. But there it is a poor thing; and hath made them a curious, ignorant, fearful, foolish nation.* But our lawgiver made his law of another temper. For first, he hath preserved all points of humanity, in taking order and making provision for the relief of strangers distressed; whereof you have tasted.'

At which speech (as reason was*) we all rose up, and bowed ourselves. He went on. 'That king also, still desiring to join humanity and policy together; and thinking it against humanity to detain strangers here against their wills, and against policy that they should return and discover their knowledge of this estate, he took this course: he did ordain that of the strangers that should be permitted to land, as many (at all times) might depart as would; but as many as would stay should have very good conditions and means to live from the state. Wherein he saw so far, that now in so many ages since the prohibition, we have memory not of one ship that ever returned; and but of thirteen persons only, at several times, that chose to return in our bottoms. What those few that returned may have reported abroad I know not. But you must think, whatsoever they have said could be taken where they came but for a dream. Now for our travelling from hence into parts abroad, our Lawgiver thought fit altogether to restrain it. So is it not in China. For the Chineses sail where they will or can; which showeth that their law of keeping out strangers is a law of pusillanimity and fear. But this restraint of ours hath one only exception, which is admirable; preserving the good which cometh by communicating with strangers, and avoiding the hurt; and I will now open it to you. And here I shall seem a little to digress, but you will by and by find it pertinent.

'Ye shall understand (my dear friends) that amongst the excellent acts of that king, one above all hath the preeminence. It was the erection and institution of an Order or Society which we call "Salomon's House"; the noblest foundation (as we think) that ever was upon the earth; and the lanthorn of this kingdom. It is dedicated to the study of the Works and Creatures of God. Some think it beareth the founder's name a little corrupted, as if it should be Solamona's House. But the records write it as it is spoken. So as I take it to be denominate of the King of the Hebrews,* which is famous with you, and no stranger to us. For we have some parts of his works which with you are lost; namely, that Natural History which he wrote, of all plants, from the "cedar of Libanus" to the "moss that groweth out of the wall", and of all "things that have life and motion".* This maketh me think that our king, finding himself to symbolize in many things with that king of the Hebrews (which lived many years before him), honoured him with the title of this foundation. And I am the rather induced to be of this opinion, for that I find in ancient records this Order or Society is sometimes called Salomon's House, and sometimes the College of the Six Days Works; whereby I am satisfied that our excellent king had learned from the Hebrews that God had created the world and all that therein is within six days; and therefore he instituting that House for the finding out of the true nature of all things (whereby God might have the more glory in the workmanship of them, and men the more fruit in the use of them) did give it also that second name.

'But now to come to our present purpose. When the king had forbidden to all his people navigation into any part that was not under his crown, he made nevertheless this ordinance; That every twelve years there should be set forth out of this kingdom two ships, appointed to several voyages; That in either of these ships there should be a mission of three of the Fellows or Brethren of Salomon's House; whose errand was only to give us knowledge of the affairs and state of those countries to which they were designed, and especially of the sciences, arts, manufactures, and inventions of all the world; and withal to bring unto us books, instruments, and patterns in every kind; That the ships after they had landed the brethren, should return; and that the brethren should stay abroad till the new mission. These ships are not otherwise fraught, than with store of victuals, and good quantity of treasure to remain with the brethren, for the buying of such things and rewarding of such persons as they should think fit. Now for me to tell you how the vulgar sort of mariners are contained from being discovered at land; and how they that must be put on shore for any time, colour themselves under the names of other nations; and to what places these voyages have been designed; and what places of "rendez-vous" are appointed for the new missions; and the like circumstances of the practique; I may not do it: neither is it much to your desire. But thus you see we maintain a trade, not for gold, silver, or jewels; nor for silks; nor for spices; nor any other commodity of matter;* but only for God's first creature, which was *Light*: to have *light* (I say) of the growth of all parts of the world.'*

And when he had said this, he was silent; and so were we all. For indeed we were all astonished to hear so strange things so probably told. And he, perceiving that we were willing to say somewhat but had it not ready, in great courtesy took us off, and descended* to ask us questions of our voyage and fortunes; and in the end concluded, that we might do well to think with ourselves* what time of stay we would demand of the state; and bade us not to scant ourselves; for he would procure such time as we desired. Whereupon we all rose up, and presented ourselves to kiss the skirt of his tippet; but he would not suffer us; and so took his leave. But when it came once amongst our people that the state used to offer conditions to strangers that would stay, we had work enough to get any of our men to look to our ship, and to keep them from going presently to the governor to crave conditions. But with much ado we refrained them, till we might agree what course to take.

We took ourselves now for free men, seeing there was no danger of our utter perdition; and lived most joyfully, going abroad and seeing what was to be seen in the city and places adjacent within our tedder; and obtaining acquaintance with many of the city, not of the meanest quality; at whose hands we found such humanity, and such a freedom and desire to take strangers as it were into their bosom, as was enough to make us forget all that was dear to us in our own countries:

and continually we met with many things right worthy of observation and relation; as indeed, if there be a mirror in the world worthy to hold men's eyes, it is that country.

One day there were two of our company bidden to a Feast of the Family, as they call it. A most natural, pious, and reverend custom it is, showing that nation to be compounded of all goodness. This is the manner of it. It is granted to any man that shall live to see thirty persons descended of his body alive together, and all above three years old, to make this feast; which is done at the cost of the state. The Father of the Family, whom they call the *Tirsan,** two days before the feast, taketh to him three of such friends as he liketh to choose; and is assisted also by the governor of the city or place where the feast is celebrated; and all the persons of the family, of both sexes, are summoned to attend him. These two days the Tirsan sitteth in consultation concerning the good estate of the family. There, if there be any discord or suits between any of the family, they are compounded and appeased. There, if any of the family be distressed or decayed,* order is taken for their relief and competent means to live. There, if any be subject to vice, or take ill courses, they are reproved and censured. So likewise direction is given touching marriages, and the courses of life which any of them should take, with divers other the like orders and advices. The governor assisteth, to the end to put in execution by his public authority the decrees and orders of the Tirsan, if they should be disobeyed; though that seldom needeth; such reverence and obedience they give to the order of nature. The Tirsan doth also then ever choose one man from amongst his sons, to live in house with him: who is called ever after the Son of the Vine. The reason will hereafter appear.

On the feast-day, the Father or Tirsan cometh forth after divine service into a large room where the feast is celebrated; which room hath an half-pace at the upper end. Against the wall, in the middle of the half-pace, is a chair placed for him, with a table and carpet before it. Over the chair is a state, made round or oval, and it is of ivy; an ivy somewhat whiter than ours, like the leaf of a silver asp, but more shining; for it is green all winter. And the state is curiously wrought with silver and silk of divers colours, broiding or binding in the ivy; and is ever of the work of some of the daughters of the family; and veiled over at the top with a fine net of silk and silver. But the substance of it is true ivy;* whereof, after it is taken down, the friends of the family are desirous to have some leaf or sprig to keep.

The Tirsan cometh forth with all his generation or lineage, the males before him, and the females following him; and if there be a mother from whose body the whole lineage is descended, there is a traverse placed in a loft above on the right hand of the chair, with a privy door, and a carved window of glass, leaded with gold and blue; where she sitteth but is not seen. When the Tirsan is come forth, he sitteth down in the chair; and all the lineage place themselves against the wall, both at his back and upon the return of the half-pace, in order of their years without difference of sex; and stand upon their feet. When he is set; the room being always full of company, but well kept and without disorder; after some pause there cometh in from the lower end of the room a *Taratan* (which is as much as an herald) and on either side of him two young lads; whereof one carrieth a scroll of their shining yellow parchment; and the other a cluster of grapes of gold, with a long foot or stalk. The herald and children are clothed with mantles of sea-water-green satin; but the herald's mantle is streamed with gold,* and hath a train.

Then the herald with three curtesies, or rather inclinations, cometh up as far as the half-pace; and there first taketh into his hand the scroll. This scroll is the King's Charter, containing gift of revenew, and many privileges, exemptions, and points of honour, granted to the Father of the Family; and is ever styled and directed, 'To such an one our well-beloved friend and creditor': which is a title proper only to this case. For they say the king is debtor to no man, but for propagation of his subjects. The seal set to the king's charter is the king's image, imbossed or moulded in gold; and though such charters be expedited of course, and as of right, yet they are varied by discretion, according to the number and dignity of the family.* This charter the herald readeth aloud; and while it is read, the father or Tirsan standeth up, supported by two of his sons, such as he chooseth. Then the herald mounteth the half-pace, and delivereth the charter into his hand: and with that there is an acclamation by all that are present in their language, which is thus much: 'Happy are the people of Bensalem'.

Then the herald taketh into his hand from the other child the cluster of grapes, which is of gold, both the stalk and the grapes. But the grapes are daintily enamelled; and if the males of the family be the greater number, the grapes are enamelled purple, with a little sun set on the top, if the females, then they are enamelled into a greenish yellow, with a crescent on the top. The grapes are in number as many as there are descendants of the family. This golden cluster the herald delivereth also to the Tirsan; who presently delivereth it over to that son that he had formerly chosen to be in house with him: who beareth it before his father as an ensign of honour when he goeth in public, ever after; and is thereupon called the Son of the Vine.

After this ceremony ended, the father or Tirsan retireth; and after some time cometh forth again to dinner, where he sitteth alone under the state, as before; and none of his descendants sit with him, of what degree or dignity soever, except he hap to be of Salomon's House. He is served only by his own children, such as are male; who perform unto him all service of the table upon the knee; and the women only stand about him, leaning against the wall. The room below the half-pace hath tables on the sides for the guests that are bidden; who are served with great and comely order; and towards the end of dinner (which in the greatest feasts with them lasteth never above an hour and an half) there is an hymn sung, varied according to the invention of him that composeth it (for they have excellent poesy), but the subject of it is (always) the praises of Adam and Noah and Abraham; whereof the former two peopled the world, and the last was the Father of the Faithful:* concluding ever with a thanksgiving for the nativity of our Saviour, in whose birth the births of all are only blessed.*

Dinner being done, the Tirsan retireth again; and having withdrawn himself alone into a place where he maketh some private prayers, he cometh forth the third time, to give the blessing; with all his descendants, who stand about him as at the first. Then he calleth them forth by one and by one, by name, as he pleaseth, though seldom the order of age be inverted. The person that is called (the table being before removed) kneeleth down before the chair, and the father layeth his hand upon his head, or her head, and giveth the blessing in these words: 'Son of Bensalem (or Daughter of Bensalem), thy father saith it; the man by whom thou hast breath and life speaketh the word; The blessing of the everlasting Father, the Prince of Peace, and the Holy Dove be upon thee, and make the days of thy pilgrimage* good and many.' This he saith to every of them;* and that done, if there be any of his sons of eminent merit and virtue, (so they be not above two),* he calleth for them again; and saith, laying his arm over their shoulders, they standing; 'Sons, it is well ye are born, give God the praise, and persevere to the end.' And withal delivereth to either of them a jewel, made in the figure of an ear of wheat, which they ever after wear in the front of their turban or hat. This done, they fall to music and dances, and other recreations, after their manner, for the rest of the day. This is the full order of that feast.

By that time six or seven days were spent, I was fallen into strait acquaintance with a merchant of that city, whose name was Joabin.* He was a Jew, and circumcised: for they have some few stirps of Jews yet remaining among them, whom they leave to their own religion. Which they may the better do, because they are of a far differing disposition from the Jews in other parts. For whereas they hate the name of Christ, and have a secret inbred rancour against the people amongst whom they live: these (contrariwise) give unto our Saviour many high attributes, and love the nation of Bensalem extremely. Surely this man of whom I speak would ever acknowledge that Christ was born of a Virgin, and that he was more than a man; and he would tell how God made him ruler of the Seraphims which guard his throne; and they call him also the 'Milken Way',* and the *Eliah* of the *Messiah*;* and many other high names; which though they be inferior to his divine Majesty, yet they are far from the language of other Jews. And for the country of Bensalem, this man would make no end of commending it: being desirous, by tradition among the Jews there, to have it believed that the people thereof were of the generations of Abraham, by another son, whom they call Nachoran; and that Moses by a secret cabala ordained the laws of Bensalem which they now use; and that when the Messiah should come, and sit in his throne at Hierusalem,* the king of Bensalem should sit at his feet, whereas other kings should keep a great distance. But yet setting aside these Jewish dreams, the man was a wise man, and learned, and of great policy, and excellently seen in the laws and customs of that nation.

Amongst other discourses, one day I told him I was much affected with the relation I had from some of the company, of their custom in holding the Feast of the Family; for that (methought) I had never heard of a solemnity wherein nature did so much preside. And because propagation of families proceedeth from the nuptial copulation, I desired to know of him what laws and customs they had concerning marriage; and whether they kept marriage well; and whether they were tied to one wife? For that where population is so much affected, and such as with them it seemed to be, there is commonly permission of plurality of wives. To this he said, 'You have reason for to commend that excellent institution of the Feast of the Family. And indeed we have experience, that those families that are partakers of the blessing of that feast do flourish and prosper ever after in an extraordinary manner. But hear me now, and I will tell you what I know. You shall understand that there is not under the heavens so chaste a nation as this of Bensalem; nor so free from all pollution or foulness. It is the virgin of the world. I remember I have read in one of your European books, of an holy hermit amongst you that desired to see the Spirit of Fornication; and there appeared to him a little foul ugly Ethiop.* But if he had desired to see the Spirit of Chastity of Bensalem, it would have appeared to him in the likeness of a fair beautiful Cherubin. For there is nothing amongst mortal men more fair and admirable, than the chaste minds of this people.

'Know therefore, that with them there are no stews, no dissolute houses, no courtesans, nor any thing of that kind. Nay they wonder (with detestation) at you in Europe, which permit such things. They say ye have put marriage out of office: for marriage is ordained a remedy for unlawful concupiscence; and natural concupiscence seemeth as a spur to marriage. But when men have at hand a remedy more agreeable to their corrupt will, marriage is almost expulsed. And therefore there are with you seen infinite men that marry not, but choose rather a libertine and impure single life, than to be yoked in marriage; and many that do marry, marry late, when the prime and strength of their years is past. And when they do marry, what is marriage to them but a very bargain; wherein is sought alliance, or portion, or reputation, with some desire (almost indifferent) of issue; and not the faithful nuptial union of man and wife, that was first instituted.* Neither is it possible that those that have cast away so basely so much of their strength, should greatly esteem children (being of the same matter*), as chaste men do. So likewise during marriage, is the case much amended, as it ought to be if those things were tolerated only for necessity? No, but they remain still as a very affront to marriage. The haunting of those dissolute places, or resort to courtesans are no more punished in married men than in bachelors. And the depraved custom of change, and the delight in meretricious embracements (where sin is turned into art), maketh marriage a dull thing, and a kind of imposition or tax.

'They hear you defend these things, as done to avoid greater evils; as advoutries, deflowering of virgins, unnatural lust, and the like. But they say this is a preposterous wisdom; and they call it "Lot's offer",* who to save his guests from abusing, offered his daughters: nay they say farther that there is little gained in this; for that the same vices and appetites do still remain and abound; unlawful lust being like a furnace, that if you stop the flames altogether, it will quench; but if you give it any vent, it will rage. As for masculine love,* they have no touch of it; and yet there are not so faithful and inviolate friendships in the world again as are there; and to speak generally (as I said before), I have not read of any such chastity in any people as theirs. And their usual saying is, that "whosoever is unchaste cannot reverence himself"; and they say, that "the reverence of a man's self is, next religion, the chiefest bridle of all vices".'

And when he had said this, the good Jew paused a little; whereupon I, far more willing to hear him speak on than to speak myself, yet thinking it decent that upon his pause of speech I should not be altogether silent, said only this; 'That I would say to him, as the widow of Sarepta said to Elias;* that he was come to bring to memory our sins; and that I confess the righteousness of Bensalem was greater than the righteousness of Europe.' At which speech he bowed his head and went on in this manner: 'They have also many wise and excellent laws touching marriage. They allow no polygamy. They have ordained that none do intermarry or contract,* until a month be passed from their first interview. Marriage without consent of parents they do not make void, but they mulct it in the inheritors: for the children of such marriages are not admitted to inherit above a third part of their parents' inheritance. I have read in a book of one of your men, of a Feigned Commonwealth, where the married couple are permitted, before they contract, to see one another naked.* This they dislike; for they think it a scorn to give a refusal after so familiar knowledge. But because of many hidden defects in men and women's bodies, they have a more civil way; for they have near every town a couple of pools, (which they call "Adam and Eve's pools"), where it is permitted to one of the friends of the man, and another of the friends of the woman, to see them severally bathe naked.'

And as we were thus in conference, there came one that seemed to be a messenger, in a rich huke, that spake with the Jew: whereupon he turned to me and said; 'You will pardon me, for I am commanded away in haste.' The next morning he came to me again, joyful as it seemed, and said, 'There is word come to the governor of the city, that one of the Fathers of Salomon's House will be here this day seven-night: we have seen none of them this dozen years. His coming is in state; but the cause of his coming is secret. I will provide you and your fellows of a good standing to see his entry.' I thanked him, and told him, 'I was most glad of the news.'

The day being come, he made his entry. He was a man of middle stature and age, comely of person, and had an aspect as if he pitied men. He was clothed in a robe of fine black cloth, with wide sleeves and a cape. His under garment was of excellent white linen down to the foot, girt with a girdle of the same; and a sindon or tippet of the same about his neck. He had gloves that were curious, and set with stone; and shoes of peach-coloured velvet. His neck was bare to the shoulders. His hat was like a helmet, or Spanish Montera, and his locks curled below it decently: they were of colour brown. His beard was cut round, and of the same colour with his hair, somewhat lighter. He was carried in a rich chariot without wheels, litter-wise;* with two horses at either end, richly trapped in blue velvet embroidered; and two footmen on each side in the like attire. The chariot was all of cedar, gilt, and adorned with crystal; save that the fore-end had panels of sapphires, set in borders of gold, and the hinder-end the like of emeralds of the Peru colour.* There was also a sun of gold, radiant, upon the top, in the midst; and on the top before, a small cherub of gold, with wings displayed. The chariot was covered with cloth of gold tissued upon blue.* He had before him fifty attendants, young men all, in white satin loose coats to the mid-leg; and stockings of white silk; and shoes of blue velvet; and hats of blue velvet; with fine plumes of divers colours, set round like hat-bands. Next before the chariot went two men, bare-headed, in linen garments down to the foot, girt, and shoes of blue velvet; who carried the one a crosier, the other a pastoral staff like a sheep-hook; neither of them of metal, but the crosier of balm-wood, the pastoral staff of cedar. Horsemen he had none, neither before nor behind his chariot: as it seemeth, to avoid all tumult and trouble. Behind his chariot went all the officers and principals of the Companies of the City.* He sat alone, upon cushions of a kind of excellent plush, blue: and under his foot curious carpets of silk of divers colours, like the Persian, but far finer. He held up his bare hand as he went, as blessing the people, but in silence. The street was wonderfully well kept: so that there was never any army had their men stand in better battle-array, than the people stood. The windows likewise were not crowded, but every one stood in them as if they had been placed.*

When the show was passed, the Jew said to me; 'I shall not be able to attend you as I would, in regard of some charge the city hath laid upon me, for the entertaining of this great person.' Three days after, the Jew came to me again, and said, 'Ye are happy men; for the Father of Salomon's House taketh knowledge of your being here, and commanded me to tell you that he will admit all your company to his presence, and have private conference with one of you that ye shall choose: and for this hath appointed the next day after to-morrow. And because he meaneth to give you his blessing, he hath appointed it in the forenoon.'

We came at our day and hour, and I was chosen by my fellows for the private access. We found him in a fair chamber, richly hanged, and carpeted under foot, without any degrees to the state.* He was set upon a low throne richly adorned, and a rich cloth of state over his head, of blue satin embroidered. He was alone, save that he had two pages of honour, on either hand one, finely attired in white. His under-garments were the like that we saw him wear in the chariot; but instead of his gown, he had on him a mantle with a cape, of the same fine black, fastened about him. When we came in, as we were taught, we bowed low at our first entrance; and when we were come near his chair, he stood up, holding forth his hand ungloved, and in posture of blessing; and we every one of us stooped down, and kissed the hem of his tippet. That done, the rest departed, and I remained. Then he warned the pages forth* of the room, and caused me to sit down beside him, and spake to me thus in the Spanish tongue:

'God bless thee, my son; I will give thee the greatest jewel I have. For I will impart unto thee, for the love of God and men, a relation of the true state of Salomon's House. Son, to make you know the true state of Salomon's House, I will keep this order. First, I will set forth unto you the end of our foundation. Secondly, the preparations and instruments we have for our works. Thirdly, the several employments and functions whereto our fellows are assigned. And fourthly, the ordinances and rites which we observe.

'The End of our Foundation is the knowledge of Causes, and secret motions of things; and the enlarging of the bounds of Human Empire, to the effecting of all things possible.

'The Preparations and Instruments are these. We have large and deep caves of several depths: the deepest are sunk six hundred fathom; and some of them are digged and made under great hills and mountains: so that if you reckon together the depth of the hill and the depth of the cave, they are (some of them) above three miles deep. For we find that the depth of a hill, and the depth of a cave from the flat, is the same thing; both remote alike from the sun and heaven's beams, and from the open air. These caves we call the Lower Region. And we use them for all coagulations, indurations, refrigerations, and conservations of bodies. We use them likewise for the imitation of natural mines;* and the producing also of new artificial metals, by compositions and materials which we use, and lay there for many years. We use them also sometimes (which may seem strange) for curing of some diseases, and for prolongation of life in some hermits that choose to live there, well accommodated of all things necessary; and indeed live very long; by whom also we learn many things.

'We have burials in several earths, where we put divers cements, as the Chineses do their porcelain.* But we have them in greater variety, and some of them more fine. We have also great variety of composts, and soils, for the making of the earth fruitful.

'We have high towers; the highest about half a mile in height; and some of them likewise set upon high mountains; so that the vantage of the hill with the tower is in the highest of them three miles at least. And these places we call the Upper Region: accounting the air between the high places and the low, as a Middle Region. We use these towers, according to their several heights and situations, for insolation, refrigeration, conservation; and for the view of divers meteors; as winds, rain, snow, hail; and some of the fiery meteors also. And upon them, in some places, are dwellings of hermits, whom we visit sometimes, and instruct what to observe.

'We have great lakes both salt and fresh, whereof we have use for the fish and fowl. We use them also for burials of some natural bodies: for we find a difference in things buried in earth or in air below the earth, and things buried in water. We have also pools, of which some do strain fresh water out of salt; and others by art do turn fresh water into salt. We have also some rocks in the midst of the sea, and some bays upon the shore for some works wherein is required the air and vapour of the sea. We have likewise violent streams and cataracts, which serve us for many motions, and likewise engines for multiplying and enforcing of winds, to set also on going divers motions.*

'We have also a number of artificial wells and fountains, made in imitation of the natural sources and baths; as tincted upon vitriol,* sulphur, steel, lead, brass, nitre, and other minerals. And again we have little wells for infusions of many things, where the waters take the virtue* quicker and better than in vessels or basins. And amongst them we have a water which we call Water of Paradise, being, by that we do to it, made very sovereign* for health, and prolongation of life.

'We have also great and spacious houses, where we imitate and demonstrate meteors; as snow, hail, rain, some artificial rains of bodies and not of water, thunders, lightnings; also generations of bodies in air; as frogs, flies, and divers others.*

'We have also certain chambers, which we call Chambers of Health, where we qualify the air as we think good and proper for the cure of divers diseases, and preservation of health.

'We have also fair and large baths, of several mixtures, for the cure of diseases, and the restoring of man's body from arefaction: and others for the confirming of it in strength of sinews, vital parts, and the very juice and substance of the body.

'We have also large and various orchards and gardens, wherein we do not so much respect beauty, as variety of ground and soil, proper for divers trees and herbs: and some very spacious, where trees and berries are set whereof we make divers kinds of drinks, besides the vineyards. In these we practise likewise all conclusions of grafting and inoculating, as well of wild-trees as fruit-trees, which produceth many effects. And we make (by art) in the same orchards and gardens, trees and flowers to come earlier or later than their seasons; and to come up and bear more speedily than by their natural course they do. We make them also by art greater much than their nature; and their fruit greater and sweeter and of differing taste, smell, colour, and figure, from their nature. And many of them we so order, as they become of medicinal use.

'We have also means to make divers plants rise by mixtures of earths without seeds; and likewise to make divers new plants, differing from the vulgar; and to make one tree or plant turn into another.

'We have also parks and inclosures of all sorts of beasts and birds, which we use not only for view or rareness, but likewise for dissections and trials; that thereby we may take light what may be wrought upon the body of man. Wherein we find many strange effects; as continuing life in them, though divers parts, which you account vital, be perished and taken forth; resuscitating of some that seem dead in appearance; and the like. We try also all poisons and other medicines upon them, as well of chirurgery as physic. By art likewise, we make them greater or taller than their kind is; and contrariwise dwarf them, and stay their growth: we make them more fruitful and bearing than their kind is; and contrariwise barren and not generative. Also we make them differ in colour, shape, activity, many ways. We find means to make commixtures and copulations of different kinds; which have produced many new kinds, and them not barren, as the general opinion is. We make a number of kinds of serpents, worms, flies, fishes, of putrefaction;* whereof some are advanced (in effect) to be perfect creatures, like beasts or birds; and have sexes, and do propagate. Neither do we this by chance, but we know beforehand of what matter and commixture what kind of those creatures will arise.

'We have also particular pools, where we make trials upon fishes, as we have said before of beasts and birds.

'We have also places for breed and generation of those kinds of worms and flies which are of special use; such as are with you your silk-worms and bees.

'I will not hold you long with recounting of our brewhouses, bake-houses, and kitchens, where are made divers drinks, breads, and meats, rare and of special effects. Wines we have of grapes; and drinks of other juice of fruits, of grains, and of roots: and of mixtures with honey, sugar, manna, and fruits dried and decocted. Also of the tears or woundings of trees, and of the pulp of canes. And these drinks are of several ages, some to the age or last of forty years. We have drinks also brewed with several herbs, and roots, and spices; yea with several fleshes, and white meats; whereof some of the drinks are such, as they are in effect meat and drink both: so that divers, especially in age, do desire to live with them, with little or no meat or bread. And above all, we strive to have drinks of extreme thin parts, to insinuate into the body, and yet without all biting, sharpness, or fretting;* insomuch as some of them put upon the back of your hand will, with a little stay, pass through to the palm, and yet taste mild to the mouth. We have also waters which we ripen in that fashion, as they become nourishing; so that they are indeed excellent drink; and many will use no other. Breads we have of several grains, roots, and kernels; yea and some of flesh and fish dried; with divers kinds of leavenings and seasonings: so that some do extremely move appetites; some do nourish so, as divers do live of them, without any other meat; who live very long. So for meats, we have some of them so beaten and made tender and mortified, yet without all corrupting, as a weak heat of the stomach will turn them into good chylus, as well as a strong heat would meat otherwise prepared. We have some meats also and breads and drinks, which taken by men enable them to fast long after; and some other, that used make the very flesh of men's bodies sensibly more hard and tough, and their strength far greater than otherwise it would be.*

'We have dispensatories, or shops of medicines. Wherein you may easily think, if we have such variety of plants and living creatures more than you have in Europe (for we know what you have), the simples, drugs, and ingredients of medicines, must likewise be in so much the greater variety. We have them likewise of divers ages, and long fermentations. And for their preparations, we have not only all manner of exquisite distillations and separations, and especially by gentle heats and percolations through divers strainers, yea and substances; but also exact forms of composition, whereby they incorporate almost, as they were natural simples.*

'We have also divers mechanical arts, which you have not; and stuffs made by them; as papers, linen, silks, tissues; dainty works of feathers of wonderful lustre, excellent dyes, and many others; and shops likewise, as well for such as are not brought into vulgar use amongst us as for those that are.* For you must know that of the things before recited, many of them are grown into use throughout the kingdom; but yet if they did flow from our invention, we have of them also for patterns and principals.*

'We have also furnaces of great diversities, and that keep great diversity of heats; fierce and quick; strong and constant; soft and mild; blown, quiet; dry, moist; and the like. But above all, we have heats in imitation of the sun's and heavenly bodies' heats, that pass divers inequalities and (as it were) orbs, progresses, and returns,* whereby we produce admirable effects. Besides, we have heats of dungs, and of bellies and maws of living creatures, and of their bloods and bodies; and of hays and herbs laid up moist; of lime unquenched;* and such like. Instruments also which generate heat only by motion. And farther, places for strong insolations; and again, places under the earth, which by nature or art yield heat. These divers heats we use, as the nature of the operation which we intend requireth.

'We have also perspective-houses, where we make demonstrations of all lights and radiations; and of all colours; and out of things uncoloured and transparent, we can represent unto you all several colours; not in rain-bows, as it is in gems and prisms, but of themselves single. We represent also all multiplications of light, which we carry to great distance, and make so sharp as to discern small points and lines; also all colorations of light: all delusions and deceits of the sight, in figures, magnitudes, motions, colours: all demonstrations of shadows. We find also divers means, yet unknown to you, of producing of light originally from divers bodies.* We procure means of seeing objects afar off; as in the heaven and remote places; and represent things near as afar off, and things afar off as near; making feigned distances. We have also helps for the sight, far above spectacles and glasses in use. We have also glasses and means to see small and minute bodies perfectly and distinctly;* as the shapes and colours of small flies and worms, grains and flaws in gems, which cannot otherwise be seen; observations in urine* and blood, not otherwise to be seen. We make artificial rain-bows, halos, and circles about light. We represent also all manner of reflections, refractions, and multiplications of visual beams of objects.

'We have also precious stones of all kinds, many of them of great beauty, and to you unknown; crystals likewise; and glasses of divers kinds; and amongst them some of metals vitrificated, and other materials besides those of which you make glass. Also a number of fossils,* and imperfect minerals, which you have not. Likewise lode-stones* of prodigious virtue; and other rare stones, both natural and artificial.

'We have also sound-houses, where we practise and demonstrate all sounds, and their generation. We have harmonies which you have not, of quarter-sounds, and lesser slides of sounds. Divers instruments of music likewise to you unknown, some sweeter than any you have; together with bells and rings that are dainty and sweet. We represent small sounds as great and deep; likewise great sounds extenuate and sharp; we make divers tremblings and warblings of sounds, which in their original are entire. We represent and imitate all articulate sounds and letters, and the voices and notes of beasts and birds. We have certain helps which set to the ear do further the hearing greatly. We have also divers strange and artificial echoes, reflecting the voice many times, and as it were tossing it: and some that give back the voice louder than it came; some shriller, and some deeper; yea, some rendering the voice differing in the letters or articulate sound from that they receive. We have also means to convey sounds in trunks and pipes, in strange lines and distances.

'We have also perfume-houses; wherewith we join also practices of taste. We multiply smells, which may seem strange. We imitate smells, making all smells to breathe out of other mixtures than those that give them. We make divers imitations of taste likewise, so that they will deceive any man's taste. And in this house we contain also a confiture-house; where we make all sweet-meats, dry and moist, and divers pleasant wines, milks, broths, and sallets, far in greater variety than you have.

'We have also engine-houses, where are prepared engines and instruments for all sorts of motions. There we imitate and practise to make swifter motions than any you have, either out of your muskets or any engine that you have; and to make them and multiply them more easily, and with small force, by wheels and other means: and to make them stronger, and more violent than yours are; exceeding your greatest cannons and basilisks. We represent also ordnance and instruments of war, and engines of all kinds: and likewise new mixtures and compositions of gun-powder, wildfires burning in water,* and unquenchable. Also fire-works of all variety both for pleasure and use. We imitate also flights of birds, we have some degrees of flying in the air; we have ships and boats for going under water,* and brooking of seas;* also swimming-girdles and supporters. We have divers curious clocks, and other like motions of return, and some perpetual motions.* We imitate also motions of living creatures, by images of men, beasts, birds, fishes, and serpents.* We have also a great number of other various motions, strange for equality, fineness, and subtlety.

'We have also a mathematical-house, where are represented all instruments, as well of geometry as astronomy, exquisitely made.

'We have also houses of deceits of the senses; where we represent all manner of feats of juggling, false apparitions, impostures, and illusions; and their fallacies. And surely you will easily believe that we that have so many things truly natural which induce admiration, could in a world of particulars deceive the senses,* if we would disguise those things and labour to make them seem more miraculous. But we do hate all impostures and lies: insomuch as we have severely forbidden it to all our fellows, under pain of ignominy and fines, that they do not show any natural work or thing, adorned or swelling; but only pure as it is, and without all affectation of strangeness.*

'These are (my son) the riches of Salomon's House.

'For the several employments and offices of our fellows; we have twelve that sail into foreign countries, under the names of other nations (for our own we conceal); who bring us the books, and abstracts, and patterns of experiments of all other parts. These we call Merchants of Light.

'We have three that collect the experiments which are in all books. These we call Depredators.

'We have three that collect the experiments of all mechanical arts;

and also of liberal sciences; and also of practices which are not brought into arts.* These we call Mystery-men.

'We have three that try new experiments, such as themselves think good. These we call Pioners or Miners.

'We have three that draw the experiments of the former four into titles and tables, to give the better light for the drawing of observations and axioms out of them. These we call Compilers.

'We have three that bend themselves, looking into the experiments of their fellows, and cast about how to draw out of them things of use and practice for man's life, and knowledge as well for works as for plain demonstration of causes, means of natural divinations, and the easy and clear discovery of the virtues and parts of bodies.* These we call Dowry-men or Benefactors.

'Then after divers meetings and consults of our whole number, to consider of the former labours and collections, we have three that take care, out of them, to direct new experiments, of a higher light,* more penetrating into nature than the former. These we call Lamps.

'We have three others that do execute the experiments so directed, and report them. These we call Inoculators.

'Lastly, we have three that raise the former discoveries by experiments into greater observations, axioms, and aphorisms. These we call Interpreters of Nature.

'We have also, as you must think, novices and apprentices, that the succession of the former employed men do not fail; besides a great number of servants and attendants, men and women. And this we do also: we have consultations, which of the inventions and experiences which we have discovered shall be published, and which not: and take all an oath of secrecy, for the concealing of those which we think fit to keep secret: though some of those we do reveal sometimes to the state, and some not.

'For our ordinances and rites: we have two very long and fair galleries: in one of these we place patterns and samples of all manner of the more rare and excellent inventions: in the other we place the statues of all principal inventors. There we have the statue of your Columbus, that discovered the West Indies: also the inventor of ships: your monk that was the inventor of ordnance and of gunpowder:* the inventor of music: the inventor of letters: the inventor of printing: the inventor of observations of astronomy: the inventor of works in metal: the inventor of glass: the inventor of silk of the worm: the inventor of wine: the inventor of corn and bread: the inventor of sugars:* and all these by more certain tradition than you have. Then have we divers inventors of our own, of excellent works; which since you have not seen, it were too long to make descriptions of them; and besides, in the right understanding of those descriptions you might easily err. For upon every invention of value, we erect a statue to the inventor, and give him a liberal and honourable reward. These statues are some of brass; some of marble and touchstone; some of cedar and other special woods gilt and adorned: some of iron; some of silver; some of gold.

'We have certain hymns and services, which we say daily, of laud and thanks to God for his marvellous works: and forms of prayers, imploring his aid and blessing for the illumination of our labours, and the turning of them into good and holy uses.

'Lastly, we have circuits or visits of divers principal cities of the kingdom; where, as it cometh to pass, we do publish such new profitable inventions as we think good. And we do also declare natural divinations* of diseases, plagues, swarms of hurtful creatures, scarcity, tempests, earthquakes, great inundations, comets, temperature of the year,* and divers other things; and we give counsel thereupon what the people shall do for the prevention and remedy of them.'

And when he had said this, he stood up; and I, as I had been taught, kneeled down; and he laid his right hand upon my head, and said; 'God bless thee, my son, and God bless this relation which I have made. I give thee leave to publish it for the good of other nations; for we here are in God's bosom, a land unknown.' And so he left me; having assigned a value of about two thousand ducats, for a bounty to me and my fellows. For they give great largesses where they come upon all occasions.

[The rest was not perfected.]*

MAGNALIA NATURAE,
PRAECIPUE QUAD USUS HUMANOS.*

The prolongation of life.
The restitution of youth in some degree.

The retardation of age.

The curing of diseases counted incurable.

The mitigation of pain.

More easy and less loathsome purgings.

The increasing of strength and activity.

The increasing of ability to suffer torture or pain.

The altering of complexions, and fatness and leanness.

The altering of statures.

The altering of features.

The increasing and exalting of the intellectual parts.

Versions of bodies into other bodies.

Making of new species.

Transplanting of one species into another.

Instruments of destruction, as of war and poison.

Exhilaration of the spirits, and putting them in good disposition.

Force of the imagination, either upon another body, or upon the body itself.

Acceleration of time in maturations.

Acceleration of time in clarifications.

Acceleration of putrefaction.

Acceleration of decoction.

Acceleration of germination.

Making rich composts for the earth.

Impressions of the air, and raising of tempests.

Great alteration; as in induration, emollition, &c.

Turning crude and watery substances into oily and unctuous substances.

Drawing of new foods out of substances not now in use.

Making new threads for apparel; and new stuffs; such as paper, glass, &c.

Natural divinations.

Deceptions of the senses.

Greater pleasure of the senses.

Artificial minerals and cements.

HENRY NEVILLE

THE ISLE OF PINES

Two Letters Concerning the Island of Pines*
to a Credible Person in Covent Garden

Amsterdam, June the 29th, 1668

It is written by the last post from Rochelle,* to a merchant in this city, that there was a French ship arrived, the Master and Company of which reports that about two or three hundred leagues northwest from Cape Finis Terre,* they fell in with an Island, where they went on shore and found about 2000 English people without clothes, only some small coverings about their middle, and that they related to them that at their first coming to this Island (which was in Queen Elizabeth's time) they were but five in number, men and women, being cast ashore by distress or otherwise, and had there remained ever since, without having any correspondence with any other people, or any ship coming to them. This story seems very fabulous, yet the letter is come to a known merchant, and from a good hand in France, so that I thought fit to mention it. It may be that there may be some mistake in the number of the leagues, as also of the exact point of the compass, from Cape Finis Terre; I shall enquire more particularly about it. Some English here suppose is may be the Island of Brasile* which have been so oft sought for, southwest from Ireland: if true, we shall hear further about it.

Your friend and brother,
    Abraham Keek.

Amsterdam, July the 6th, 1668

It is said that the ship that discovered the Island of which I hinted to you in my last is departed from Rochelle on her way to Zealand:* several persons here have writ thither to enquire for the said vessel, to know the truth of this business. I was promised a copy of the letter that came from France, advising the discovery of the island above-said, but it's not yet come to my hand; when it cometh, or any further news about this Island, I shall acquaint you with it.

Your friend and brother,
    A. Keek.

THE ISLE OF PINES

Discovered near to the coast of *Terra Australis Incognita**
by Henry Cornelius Van Sloetten,* in a letter to a
friend on London declaring the truth of his voyage
to the East Indies.*

Sir,

I received your letter of this second instant, wherein you desire me
to give you a further account concerning the Land of Pines, on
which we were driven by distress of weather the last summer. I also
perused the printed book thereof you sent me, the copy of which was
surreptitiously taken out of my hands, else should I have given you a
more fuller account upon what occasion we came thither, how we
were entertained, with some other circumstances of note wherein
that relation is defective. To satisfy therefore your desires I shall
briefly yet fully give you a particular account thereof, with a true
copy of the relation itself, desiring you to bear with my blunt
phrases, as being more a seaman than a scholar.

April the 26th 1667. We set sail from Amsterdam intending for the
East Indies; our ship had to name the place from whence we came:
the 'Amsterdam', burthen 350 tun. And having a fair gale of wind,
on the 27 of May following we had a sight of the high peak of
Tenerife belonging to the Canaries. We have touched at the island
Palma, but having endeavoured it twice, and finding the winds contrary, we steered on our course by the isles of Cape Verd, or Insulae
Capitis Veridis,* where at St James's we took in fresh water, with
some few goats and hens, wherewith that island doth plentifully
abound.

June the 14 we had sight of Madagascar, or the island of St
Lawrence, an island of 4000 miles in compass, and situate under the
Southern Tropic.* Thither we steered our course, and trafficked with
the inhabitants for knives, beads, glasses and the like, having
exchanged thereof cloves and silver. Departing from thence we were
encountered with a violent storm, and the winds holding contrary
for the space of a fortnight brought us back almost as far as the Isle

del Principe;* during which time many of our men fell sick, and some died, but at the end of that time it pleased God the wind favoured us again, and we steered on our course merrily for the space of ten days, when on a sudden we were encountered with such a violent storm as if all the four winds together had conspired for our destruction, so that the stoutest spirit of all of us quailed, expecting every hour to be devoured by that merciless element of water. Sixteen days together did this storm continue, though not with such violence as at the first, the weather being so dark all the while and the sea so rough that we knew not in what place we were. At length all on a sudden the wind ceased and the air cleared, the clouds were all dispersed and a very serene sky followed, for which we gave hearty thanks to the Almighty, it being beyond our expectation that we should have escaped the violence of that storm.

At length one of our men, mounting the main mast, espied fire, an evident sign of some country near adjoining, which presently after we apparently discovered, and steering our course more nigher, we saw several persons promiscuously running about the shore, as it were wondering and admiring at what they saw. Being now near to the land, we manned out our long boat with ten persons, who, approaching the shore, asked them in our Dutch tongue, 'Wat Eylant is dit?'* To which they returned this answer in English: 'that they knew not what we said.' One of our company named Jeremiah Hanzen who understood English very well, hearing their words discoursed to them in their own language, so that in fine we were very kindly invited on shore, great numbers of them flocking about us, admiring at our cloths which we did wear, as we on the other side did to find in such a strange place so many that could speak English and yet to go naked.

Four of our men returning back in the long boat to our ship's company could hardly make them believe the truth of what they had seen and heard, but when we had brought our ship into harbour you would have blessed yourself to see how the naked islanders flocked unto us, so wondering at our ship as if it have been the greatest miracle of nature in [the] whole world.

We were very courteously entertained by them, presenting us with such food as that country afforded, which indeed was not to be despised: we ate of the flesh both of beasts and fowls (which they had cleanly dressed, though with no great curiosity as wanting materials wherewithal to do it); and for bread we had the inside or kernel of a great nut as big as an apple,* which was very wholesome and sound for the body and tasted to the palate very delicious.

Having refreshed ourselves, they invited us to the palace of their prince or chief ruler, some two miles distant off from the place where we landed, which we found to be about the bigness of one of our ordinary village houses. It was supported with rough unhewn pieces of timber, and covered very artificially with boughs so that it would keep out the greatest showers of rain. The sides thereof were adorned with several sorts of flowers which the fragrant fields there do yield in great variety. The Prince himself (whose name was William Pine, the grandchild of George Pine that was first on shore on this island) came to his palace door and saluted us very courteously, for though he had nothing of majesty in him, yet he had a courteous, noble and debonair spirit, wherewith your English nation (especially those of the gentry) are very much indued.

Scarce had he done saluting us when his lady or wife came likewise forth of their house or palace attended on by two maid servants. She was a woman of an exquisite beauty, and had on her head, as it were, a chaplet of flowers, which being intermixed with several variety of colours became her admirably. Her privities were hid with some pieces of old garments, the relics of those cloths (I suppose) of them which first came hither, and yet being adorned with flowers those rags seemeth beautiful. And indeed modesty so far prevaileth all over the female sex of that island that with grass and flowers interwoven and made strong by the peelings of young elms (which grow there in plenty) they do plant together so many of them as serve to cover those parts which nature would have hidden.

We carried him as a present some few knives (of which we thought they had great need), an axe or hatchet to fell wood (which was very acceptable unto him, the old one which was cast on shore at the first, and the only one which they ever had, being now so quite blunt and dulled that it would not cut at all. Some other things we also gave him which he very thankfully accepted, inviting us into his house or palace, and causing us to sit down with him, where we refreshed our selves again with some more country viands which were no other than such we had tasted before, prince and peasant here faring alike.

Nor is there any difference betwixt their drink, being only fresh sweet water, which the rivers yield them in great abundance.

After some little pause our companion who could speak English by our request desired to know of him something concerning their original, and how that people speaking the language of such a remote country should come to inhabit there, having not, as we could see, any ships or boats amongst them the means to bring them thither, and which was more, altogether ignorant and mere strangers to ships or shipping, the main thing conducible to that means. To which request of ours, the courteous Prince thus replied: 'Friends (for so your actions declare you to be, and shall by ours find no less), know that we are inhabitants of this island of no great standing, my grandfather being the first that ever set foot on this shore, whose native country was a place called England, far distant from this our land, as he led us to understand. He came from that place upon the waters in a thing called a ship, of which no question but you may have heard. Several other persons were in his company, not intending to have come hither (as he said), but to a place called India, when tempestuous weather brought him and his company upon this coast, where falling among the rocks his ship split all in pieces, the whole company perishing in the waters, saving only him and four women, which by means of a broken piece of that ship, by Divine assistance got on land.

'What after passed', said he, 'during my Grandfather's life, I shall show you in a relation thereof written by his own hand which he delivered to my Father (being his eldest Son), charging him to have a special care thereof, and assuring him that time would bring some people or other thither to whom he would have him to impart it, that the truth of our first planting here might not be quite lost. Which his commands my Father dutifully obeyed, but no one coming, he at his death delivered the same with the like charge to me. And you being the first people which (besides ourselves) ever set footing in this island, I shall therefore, in obedience to my Grandfather's and Father's commands, willingly impart the same unto you.'

Then stepping into a kind of inner room, which as we conceived was his lodging chamber, he brought forth two sheets of paper fairly written in English (being the same relation which you had printed with you at London) and very distinctly read the same over unto us, which we harkened unto with great delight and admiration, freely proffering us a copy of the same, which we afterward took and brought away along with us: which copy hereafter followeth.*

~

A way to the East Indies being lately discovered by sea, to the south of Affric, by certain Portugals,* far more safe and profitable than had been heretofore, certain English merchants were encouraged by the great advantages arising from the Eastern commodities, to settle a factory there to the advantage of trade. And having to that purpose obtained the Queen's Royal Licence,* Anno Dom. 1589, 11 or 12 Eliz., furnished out for those parts four ships. My master being sent as a factor to deal and negotiate for them, and to settle there, took with him his whole family, that is to say, his wife, and one son of about twelve years of age, and one daughter of about fourteen years, two maidservants, one negro female slave, and myself, who went under him as his bookkeeper. With this company, on Monday the third of April next following, having all necessaries for housekeeping when we should come there, we embarked ourselves in the good ship called the *India Merchant*, of about four hundred and fifty tons burthen; and having a good wind, we on the fourteenth of May had sight of the Canaries, and not long after of the Isles of Cape Vert or Verd, where taking in such things as were necessary for our voyage, and some fresh provisions, we steering our course south, and a point east, about the first of August came within sight of the Island of St Helen,* where we took in some fresh water. We then set our faces for the Cape of Good Hope, where by God's blessing [we arrived,] after some sickness, whereof some of our company died, though none of our family. And hitherto we had met with none but calm weather, yet so it pleased God, when we were almost in sight of St Lawrence,* an island so called (one of the greatest in the world, as mariners say), we were overtaken and dispersed by a great storm of wind, which continued with such violence many days, that losing all hope of safety, being out of our own knowledge, and whether we should fall on flats or rocks, uncertain in the night, not having the least benefit of the light, we feared most, always wishing for day, and then for land: but it came too soon for our good. For about the first of October, our fears having made us forget how the time passed to a certainty, we about the break of day discerned land, but what we knew not. The land seemed high and rocky, and the sea continued still very stormy and tempestuous, insomuch as there seemed no hope of safety, but looked suddenly to perish.

As we drew near land, perceiving no safety in the ship, which we looked would suddenly be beat in pieces, the Captain, my master, and some others got into the long boat thinking by that means to save their lives, and presently after, all the seamen cast themselves overboard, thinking to save their lives by swimming. Only myself, my master's daughter, the two maids, and the negro were left on board, for we could not swim; but those that left might as well have tarried with us, for we saw them, or most of them perish, ourselves now ready after to follow their fortune. But God was pleased to spare our lives, as it were by miracle, though to further sorrow. For when we came against the rocks, our ship having endured two or three blows against the rocks, being now broken and quite foundered in the waters, we having with much ado gotten ourselves on the bowsprit, which being broken off, was driven by the waves into a small creek wherein fell a little river, which being encompassed by the rocks was sheltered from the wind, so that we had opportunity to land ourselves, (though almost drowned) in all four persons, beside the negro. When we were got upon the rock, we could perceive the miserable wreck to our great terror. I had in my pocket a little tinder-box, and steel, and flint to strike fire at any time upon occasion which served now to good purpose, for its being so close, preserved the tinder dry. With this, and with the help of some old rotten wood which we got together, we kindled a fire, and dried ourselves; which done, I left my female company, and went to see if I could find any of our ship's company that were escaped. But [I] could hear of none, though I hooted, and made all the noise I could; neither could I perceive the footsteps of any living creature, save a few birds and other fowls.

At length it drawing towards evening, I went back to my company, who were very much troubled for want of me. I being now all their stay in this lost condition, we were at first afraid that the wild people of the country might find us out, although we saw no footsteps of any, no not so much as a path, the woods round about being full of briars and brambles. We also stood in fear of wild beasts. Of such also we saw none, nor sign of any. But above all, and that we had greatest reason to fear, was to be starved to death for want of food. But God had otherwise provided for us, as you shall know hereafter. This done, we spent our time in getting some broken pieces of boards, and planks, and some of the sails and rigging on shore for shelter. I set up two or three poles, and drew two or three of the cords and lines from tree to tree, over which throwing some sail-cloths and having gotten wood by us, and three or four sea-gowns which we had dried, we took up our lodging for that night together. The blackamore being less sensible than the rest, we made our sentry. We slept soundly that night, as having not slept in three or four nights before, (our fears of what happened preventing us), neither could our hard lodging, fear, and danger, hinder us, we were so overwatched.

On the morrow, being well refreshed with sleep, the wind ceased, and the weather was very warm. We went down the rocks on the sands at low water, where we found great part of our lading, either on shore or floating near it. I, by the help of my company, dragged most of it on shore; what was too heavy for us [we] broke, and unbound the casks and chests, and, taking out the goods, secured all; for that we wanted no clothes, nor any other provisions necessary for housekeeping, to furnish a better house than any we were like to have; but no victuals (the salt water having spoiled all). Only one cask of biscuit (being lighter than the rest) was dry: this served for bread a while. And we found on land a sort of fowl about the bigness of a swan,* very heavy and fat, and by reason of their weight could not fly. Of these we found little difficulty to kill, so that was our present food. We carried out of England certain hens and cocks to eat by the way. Some of these when the ship was broken, by some means got to land, and bred exceedingly; so that in the future they were a great help unto us. We found also, by a little river, in the flags, store of eggs, of a sort of fowl much like our ducks, which were very good meat, so that we wanted nothing to keep us alive.

On the morrow, which was the third day, as soon as it was morning, seeing nothing to disturb us, I looked out a convenient place to dwell in, that we might build us a hut to shelter us from the weather, and from any other danger of annoyance from wild beasts, if any should find us out. So, close by a large spring which rose out of a high hill overlooking the sea, on the side of a wood, having a prospect towards the sea, by the help of an axe and some other implements (for we had all necessaries, the working of the sea having cast up most of our goods) I cut down all the straightest poles I could find, and which were enough for my purpose. By the help of the company (necessity being our master) I digged holes in the earth, setting my poles at an equal distance, and nailing the broken boards of the casks, chests, and cabins, and such like to them, making my door to the seaward. And having covered the top, with sail-clothes strained and nailed, I in the space of week had made a large cabin big enough to hold all our goods and ourselves in it. I also placed our hammocks for lodging, purposing (if it pleased God to send any ship that way), we might be transported home. But it never came to pass, the place wherein we were (as I conceived), being much out of the way.

We having lived in this manner four full months, and not so much as seeing or hearing of any wild people or of any of our company, more than ourselves (they being found now by experience to be all drowned), and the place as we after found, being a large island, and disjoined and out of sight of any other land, was wholly uninhabited by any people, neither was there any hurtful beast to annoy us. But on the contrary, the country so very pleasant, being always clothed in green, and full of pleasant fruits, and variety of birds, ever warm and never colder than in England in September. So that this place, had it the culture that skilful people might bestow on it, would prove a paradise.

The woods afforded us a sort of nuts, as big as a large apple, whose kernel being pleasant and dry, we made use of instead of bread, the fowl before mentioned, and a sort of water-fowl like ducks, and their eggs, and a beast about the size of a goat, and almost such a like creature, which brought two young ones at a time, and that twice a year, of which the low lands and woods were very full, being a very harmless creature and tame, so that we could easily take and kill them. Fish also, especially shellfish, which we could best come by, we had great store of; so that in effect, as to food we wanted nothing. And thus, and by such like helps, we continued six months, without any disturbance or want.

Idleness and a fullness of everything begot in me a desire for enjoying the women. Beginning now to grow more familiar, I had persuaded the two maids to let me lie with them, which I did at first in private; but after, custom taking away shame (there being none but us), we did it more openly, as our lusts gave us liberty. Afterwards my master's daughter was content also to do as we did. The truth is, they were all handsome women, when they had clothes, and well shaped, feeding well. For we wanted no food, and living idly, and seeing us at liberty to do our wills, without hope of ever returning home made us thus bold. One of the first of my consorts, with whom I first accompanied, the tallest and handsomest, proved presently with child. The second was my master's daughter. And the other also not long after fell into the same condition, none now remaining but my negro, who seeing what we did, longed also for her share. One night, I being asleep, my negro with the consent of the others got close to me, thinking it being dark to beguile me, but I awaking and feeling her, and perceiving who it was, yet willing to try the difference, satisfied myself with her, as well as with one of the rest. That night, although the first time, she proved also with child, so that in the year of our being there, all my women were with child by me; and they all coming at different seasons, were a great help to one another.

The first brought me a brave boy. My master's daughter was the youngest: she brought me a girl. So did the other maid, who, being somewhat fat, sped worse at her labour. The negro had no pain at all, brought me a fine white girl. So I had one boy and three girls. The women were soon well again, and the two first with child again before the two last were brought to bed, my custom being not to lie with any of them after they were with child till others were so likewise; and not with the black at all after she was with child, which commonly was the first time I lay with her (which was in the night and not else; my stomach would not serve me,* although she was one of the handsomest blacks I had seen, and her children as comely as any of the rest). We had no clothes for them, and therefore when they had sucked, we laid them in moss to sleep, and took no further care of them; for we knew, when they were gone more would come; the women never failing once a year at least. And none of the children, for all the hardship we put them to, were ever sick; so that wanting now nothing but clothes, nor them much neither, other than for decency, the warmth of the country and custom supplying that defect, we were now well satisfied with our condition. Our family beginning to grow large, there being nothing to hurt us, we many times lay abroad on mossy banks, under the shelter of some trees, or such like, for having nothing else to do, I had made me several arbors to sleep in with my women in the heat of the day. In these I and my women passed the time away, they never being willing to be out of my company.

And having now no thought of ever returning home as having resolved and sworn never to part or leave one another, or the place; having by my several wives forty-seven children, boys and girls, but most girls, and growing up apace; we were all of us very fleshy, the country so well agreeing with us, that we never ailed anything. My negro having had twelve, was the first that left bearing, so I never meddled with her more. My master's daughter, by whom I had most children being the youngest and the handsomest, was most fond of me, and I of her. Thus we lived for sixteen years, till perceiving my eldest boy to mind the ordinary work of nature, by seeing what we did, I gave him a mate; and so I did to all the rest, as fast as they grew up, and were capable. My wives having left bearing, my children began to breed apace, so we were like to be a multitude. My first wife brought me thirteen children, my second seven, my master's daughter fifteen, and the negro twelve, in all forty-seven.

After we had lived there twenty-two years, my negro died suddenly, but I could not perceive anything that ailed her. Most of my children being grown, as fast as we married them I sent and placed them over the river by themselves severally, because we would not pester one another. And now, they being all grown up and gone, and married after our manner, except some two or three of the youngest, for, growing myself into years, I liked not the wanton annoyance of young company.

Thus having lived to the sixtieth year of my age and the fortieth of my coming thither, at which time I sent for all of them to bring their children, and they were in number descended from me by these four women, of my children, grand-children, and great-grandchildren, five hundred and sixty of both sorts. I took off the males of one family, and married them to the females of another, not letting any to marry their sisters, as we did formerly out of necessity. So blessing God for his providence and goodness, I dismissed them. I having taught some of my children to read formerly, for I had left still the Bible, I charged it should be read once a month at a general meeting. At last one of my wives died, being sixty-eight years of age, which I buried in a place set out on purpose; and within a year after another; so I had none now left but my master's daughter, and we lived together twelve years longer. At length she died also, so I buried her also next the place where I purposed to be buried myself, and the tall maid, my first wife, next me on the other side, the negro next without her, and the other maid next my master's daughter. I had now nothing to mind, but the place whither I was to go, being very old, almost eighty years, I gave my cabin and furniture that was left, to my eldest son (after my decease), who had married my eldest daughter by my beloved wife; whom I made King and Governor of all the rest. I informed them of the manners of Europe, and charged them to remember the Christian religion, after the manner of them that spake the same language, and to admit no other, I hereafter any should come and find them out.

And now, once for all, I summoned them to come to me, that I might number them. Which I did, and found the estimate to contain, in or about the eightieth year of my age, and fifty-ninth of my coming there, in all, of all sorts, one thousand seven hundred eighty and nine. Thus praying God to multiply them, and send them the true light of the gospel, I last of all dismissed them. For being now very old, and my sight decayed, I could not expect to live long. I gave this narration, written with my own hand, to my eldest son, who now lived with me, commanding him to keep it, and if any strangers should come thither by chance, to let them see it, and take copy of it if they would, that our name be not lost from off the earth. I gave this people, descended from me the name of the 'English Pines' (George Pine being my name, and my master's daughter's name Sarah English). My two other wives were Mary Sparkes, and Elizabeth Trevor. So their several descendants are called the 'English', the 'Sparks', the 'Trevors', and the 'Phills', from the Christian name of the negro, which was Philippa, she having no surname. And the general name of the whole the 'English Pines': whom God bless with the dew of heaven, and the fat of the earth. Amen.*

~

After the reading and delivering unto us a copy of this Relation, then proceeded he on in his discourse.

'My grandfather when he wrote this was, as you hear, eighty years of age, there proceeding from his loins one thousand seven hundred eighty nine children which he had by them four women aforesaid. My father was his eldest son, and was named "Henry", begotten of his wife Mary Sparks, whom he appointed chief Governor and Ruler over the rest. And having given him a charge not to exercise tyranny over them, seeing they were his fellow brethren by [his] father's side (of which there could be no doubt made of double dealing therein), exhorting him to use justice and sincerity amongst them, and not to let religion die with him, but to observe and keep those precepts which he had taught them, he quietly surrendered up his soul, and was buried with great lamentation of all his children.

'My father coming to rule and the people growing more populous, made them to range further in the discovery of the country, which they found answerable to their desires, full both of fowl and beasts, and those not too hurtful to mankind, as if this country (on which we were by providence cast without arms or other weapons to defend ourselves or offend others), should by the same providence be so inhabited as not to have any need of such like weapons of destruction wherewith to preserve our lives.

'But as it is impossible, but that in multitudes disorders will grow, the stronger seeking to oppress the weaker, no tie of religion being strong enough to chain up the depraved nature of mankind, even so amongst them mischief began to rise, and they soon fell from those good orders prescribed them by my grandfather. The source from whence those mischiefs spring, was at first, I conceive, the neglect of hearing the Bible read, which according to my grandfather's prescription, was once a month at a general meeting, but now many of them wandering far up into the country, they quite neglected the coming to it, with all other means of Christian instruction, whereby the sense of sin being quite lost in them, they fell to whoredoms, incests, and adultery; so that what my grandfather was forced to do for necessity, they did for wantonness. Nay, not confining themselves within the bounds of any modesty, but brother and sister lay openly together; those who would not yield to their lewd embraces, were by force ravished, yea, many times endangered of their lives. To redress those enormities, my father assembled all the country near unto him, to whom he declared the wickedness of those their brethren; who with all one consent agreed that they should be severely punished. And so arming themselves with boughs, stones, and such like weapons, they marched against them, who having notice of their coming, and fearing their deserved punishment, some of them fled into woods, others passed over a great river which runneth through the heart of our country, hazarding drowning to escape punishment. But the greatest offender of them all was taken, whose name was John Phill, the second son of the Negro-woman that came with my grandfather into this island. He being proved guilty of divers ravishings and tyrannies committed by him, was adjudged guilty of death, and accordingly was thrown down from a high rock into the sea, where he perished in the waters. Execution being done upon him, the rest were pardoned for what was passed, which being notified abroad, they returned from those desert and obscure places wherein they were hidden.

'Now as seed being cast into stinking dung produceth good and wholesome corn for the sustentation of man's life, so bad manners produceth good and wholesome laws for the preservation of humane society. Soon after my father with the advice of some few others of his counsel, ordained and set forth these laws to be observed by them.*

1. That whosoever should blaspheme or talk irrelevantly of the name of God should be put to death.*

2. That who should be absent from the monthly assembly to hear the Bible read, without sufficient cause shown to the contrary, should for the first default be kept without any victuals or drink for the space of four days, and if he offend therein again, then to suffer death.

3. That who should force or ravish any maid or woman should be burnt to death, the party so ravished putting fire to the wood that should burn him.

4. Whosoever shall commit adultery,* for the first crime the male shall lose his privities, and the woman have her right eye bored out; if after that she was taken again in the act, she should die without mercy.

5. That who so injured his neighbour by laming of his limbs* or taking any thing away which he possesseth,* shall suffer in the same kind himself by loss of limb; and for defrauding his neighbour, to become servant to him, whilst he had made him double satisfaction.

6. That who should defame or speak evil of the Governor* or refuse to come before him on a summons, should receive a punishment by whipping with rods, and afterward be exploded from the society of the rest of the inhabitants.

'Having set forth these laws, he chose four several persons under him to see them put in execution, whereof one was of the Englishes, the offspring of Sarah English; another of his own tribe, the Sparks; a third of the Trevors, and a fourth of the Phills; appointing them every year at a certain time to appear before him, and give an account of what they had done in the prosecution of those laws.

'The country being thus settled, my father lived quiet and peaceable till he attained to the age of ninety and four years, when dying. I succeeded in his place, in which I have continued peaceably and quietly till this very present time.'

He having ended his speech, we gave him very heartily thanks for our information, assuring him we should not be wanting to him in any thing which lay in our powers, wherewith we could pleasure him in what he should desire, and thereupon proffered to depart, but before our going away, he would needs engage us to see him the next day, which was to be their great assembly or monthly meeting for the celebration of their religious exercises.

Accordingly the next day we came thither again, and were courteously entertained as before. In a short space there was gathered such a multitude of people together as made us to admire; and first there were several weddings celebrated, the manner whereof was thus. The bridegroom and bride appeared before him who was their priest or reader of the Bible, together with the parents of each party, or if any of their parents were dead, then the next relation unto them, without whose content as well as the parties to be married, the priest will not join them together. But being satisfied in those particulars, after some short orisons, and joining of hands together, he pronounces them to be man and wife. And with exhortations to them to live lovingly towards each other, and quietly towards their neighbours, he concludes with some prayers and so dismisses them.

The weddings being finished, all the people took their places to hear the Word read, the new married persons having the honour to be next unto the priest that day. After he had read three of four chapters he fell to expounding the most difficult places therein, the people being very attentive all that while. This exercise continued for two or three hours, which being done, with some few prayers he concluded, but all the rest of that day was by the people kept very strictly, abstaining from all manner of playing or pastimes, with which on other days they use to pass their time away, as having need of nothing but victuals, and that they have in such plenty as almost provided to their hands.

Their exercises of religion being over, we returned again to our ship, and the next day, taking with us two or three fowling pieces, leaving half of our company to guard the ship, the rest of us resolved to go higher into the country for a further discovery. All the way as we passed the first morning, we saw abundance of little cabins or huts of these inhabitants, made under trees, and fashioned up with boughs, grass, and such like stuff to defend them from the sun and the rain. And as we went along, they came out of them much wondering at our attire, and standing aloof off from us as if they were afraid. But our companion that spake English calling to them in their own tongue, and giving them good words, they drew nigher, some of them freely proffering to go along with us, which we willingly accepted. But having passed some few miles, one of our party espying a beast like unto a goat come gazing on him, he discharged his piece, sending a brace of bullets into his belly, which brought him dead upon the ground. These poor naked unarmed people, hearing the noise of the piece and seeing the beast lie tumbling in his gore, without speaking any words betook them to their heels, running back again as fast as they could drive. Nor could the persuasions of our company, assuring them they should have no hurt, prevail anything at all with them, so that we were forced to pass along without their company. All the way that we went we heard the delightful harmony of singing birds, the ground very fertile in trees, grass and such flowers as grow by the production of nature without the help of art. Many and several sorts of beasts we saw, who were not so much wild as in other countries: whether it were as having enough to satiate themselves without ravening upon others, or that they never before saw the sight of man, nor heard the report of murdering guns, I leave it to others to determine. Some trees bearing wild fruits we also saw, and of those some whereof we tasted, which were neither unwholesome nor distasteful to the palate. And no question, had but nature [had] the benefit of art added unto it, it would equal, if not exceed, many of our European countries: the valleys were everywhere intermixed with running streams, and no question but the earth hath in it rich veins of minerals, enough to satisfy the desires of the most covetous.

It was very strange to us to see that in such fertile country, which was as yet never inhabited, there should be notwithstanding such a free and clear passage to us, without the hindrance of bushes, thorns and such like stuff, wherewith most islands of the like nature are pestered, the length of the grass (which yet was very much intermixed with flowers) being the only impediment that we found.

Six days together did we thus travel, setting several marks in our ways as we went for our better return, not knowing whether we should have the benefit of the stars for our guidance in our going back, which we made use of in our passage. At last we came to the vast ocean on the other side to the island, and by our coasting it, conceive it to be of an oval form, only here and there shooting forth with some promontories. I conceive it hath but few good harbours belonging to it, the rocks in most places making it inaccessible. The length of it may be about two hundred, and the breadth one hundred, miles; the whole in circumference above five hundred miles.

It lieth about seventy-six degrees of longitude and twenty of latitude, being situate under the third climate,* the longest day being about thirteen hours and forty-five minutes. The weather, as in all Southern countries, is far more hot than with us in Europe, but what is by the sun parched in the day, the night refreshes again with cool pearly dews. The air is found to be very healthful by the long lives of the present inhabitants, few dying there till such time as they come to good years of maturity, many of them arriving to the extremity of old age.

And now speaking concerning the length of their lives, I think it will not be amiss in this place to speak something of their burials, which they used to do thus. When the party was dead, they stuck his carcass all over with flowers, and after carried him to the place appointed for burial, where, setting him down (the priest having given some godly exhortations concerning the frailty of life), then do they take stones (a heap being provided there for that purpose) and the nearest of the kin begins to lay the first stone upon him. Afterwards the rest follows, they never leaving till they have covered the body deep in stones, so that no beast can possibly come to him. And this shift were they forced to make, having no spades or shovels wherewith to dig them graves; which want of theirs we espying, bestowed a pick-axe and two shovels upon them.

Here might I add their way of christening children, but that being little different from yours in England, and taught to them by George Pines at first, which they have since continued, I shall therefore forebear to speak thereof.

After our return back from the discovery of the country, the wind not being fit for our purpose, and our men also willing thereto, we got all our cutting instruments on land, and fell to hewing down of trees with which, in a little time (many hands making light work) we built up a palace for this William Pines the Lord of that country, which though much inferior to the houses of your gentry in England, yet to them (which never had seen better), it appeared a very lordly place. This deed of ours was beyond expression acceptable unto him, loading us with thanks for so great a benefit, of which he said he should never be able to make a requital.

And now acquainting him that upon the first opportunity we were resolved to leave the island, as also how that we were near neighbours to the country of England from whence his ancestors came, he seemed upon the news to be much discontented that we would leave him, desiring, if it might stand with our commodity, to continue still with him. But seeing he could not prevail, he invited us to dine with him the next day, which we promised to do, against which time he provided, very sumptuously (according to his estate) for us. And now was he attended after a more royal manner than ever we saw him before, both for a number of servants and multiplicity of meat, on which we fed very heartily. But he having no other beverage for us to drink than water, we fetched from our ship a case of brandy, presenting some of it to him to drink, but when he had tasted of it he would by no means be persuaded to touch thereof again, preferring (as he said) his own country water before all such liquors whatsoever. After we had dined, we were invited out into the fields to behold their country dancing, which they did with great agility of body, and though they had no other then only vocal music (several of them singing all that while) yet did they trip it very neatly, giving sufficient satisfaction to all that beheld them.

The next day we invited the Prince William Pines aboard our ship, where there was nothing wanting in what we could to entertain him. He had about a dozen of servants to attend on him; he much admired at the tacklings of our ship; but when we came to discharge a piece or two of ordnance, it struck him into a wonder and amazement to behold the strange effects of powder. He was very sparing in his diet, neither could he or any of his followers be induced to drink anything but water. We there presented him with several things (as much as we could spare,) which we thought would any ways conduce to their benefit, all which he very gratefully received, assuring us of his real love and goodwill whensoever we should come thither again.

And now we intended the next day to take our leaves, the wind standing fair, blowing with a gentle gale south and by east. But as we were hoisting of our sails and weighing anchor, we were suddenly alarmed with a noise from the shore; the prince, W. Pines, imploring our assistance in an insurrection which had happened amongst them, of which this was the cause. Henry Phill, the chief ruler of the tribe or family of the Phills, being the offspring of George Pines which he had by the negro-woman; this man had ravished the wife of one of the principal of the family of the Trevors, which act being made known, the Trevors assembled themselves altogether to bring the offender unto justice. But he, knowing his crime to be so great as extended to the loss of life, fought to defend that by force which he had as unlawfully committed, whereupon the whole island was in a great hurly-burly, they being two great potent factions, the bandying of which against each other threatened a general ruin to the whole state.

The governor William Pine had interposed in the matter, but found his authority too weak to repress such disorders; for where the hedge of government is once broken down, the most vile bear the greatest rule. Whereupon he desired our assistance, to which we readily condescended, and arming out twelve of us, went on shore, rather as to a surprise than fight, for what could nakedness do to encounter with arms? Being conducted by him to the force of our enemy, we first entered into parley, seeking to gain them rather by fair means than force. But that not prevailing, we were necessitated to use violence, for this Henry Phill being of an undaunted resolution, and having armed his fellows with clubs and stones, they sent such a peal amongst us, as made us at the first to give back, which encouraged them to follow us on with great violence. But we discharging off three or four guns, when they saw some of themselves wounded, and heard the terrible reports which they gave, they ran away with greater speed than they came. The band of the Trevors (who were joined with us), hotly pursued them, and having taken their captain returned with great triumph to their Governor, who sitting in judgement upon him, he was adjudged to death and thrown off a steep rock into the sea, the only way they have of punishing any by death, except burning.

And now at least we took our solemn leaves of the Governor and departed from thence, having been there in all, the space of three weeks and two days. We took with us good store of the flesh of a beast which they call there *'reval'*,* being in taste different either from beef or swine's flesh, yet very delightful to the palate, and exceeding nutrimental. We took also with us alive divers fowl which they call *'marde'*,* about the bigness of a pullet, and yet not different in taste. They are very swift of flight, and yet so fearless of danger that they will stand still till such time as you catch them. We had also sent us in by the governor about two bushels of eggs, which as I conjecture were the *mardes'* eggs, very luscious in taste, and strengthening to the body.

June 8. We had a sight of Cambaia, a part of the East Indies, but under the government of the great Cham of Tartary;* here our vessel springing a leak we were forced to put to shore, receiving much damage in some of our commodities. We were forced to ply the pump for eighteen hours together, which, had that miscarried, we had inevitably had perished. Here we stayed five days mending our ship and drying some of our goods, and then hoisting sail, in four days' time more we came to Calicut.*

This Calicut is the chief mart town and staple of all the Indian traffic. It is very populous and frequented by merchants of all nations. Here we unloaded a great part of our goods, and taking in others, which caused us to stay there a full month, during which space at leisure times I went abroad to take a survey of the city, which I found to be large and populous, lying for three miles together upon the sea-shore. Here is a great many of those persons whom they call Brachmans,* being their priests or teachers whom they much reverence. It is a custom here for the King to give to some of those Brachmain, the handling of his Nuptial Bed, for which cause, not the Kings, but the King's sisters' sons succeed in the Kingdom,* as being more certainly known to be of the true Royal blood. And these sisters of his choose what Gentleman they please on whom to bestow their Virginities: and if they prove not in a certain time to be with child, they betake themselves to these Brachman Stallions, who never fail of doing their work.

The people are indifferently civil and ingenious. Both men and women imitate a majesty in their train and apparel (which they sweeten with oils and perfumes), adorning themselves with jewels and other ornaments befitting each rank and quality of them.

They have many odd customs amongst them which they observe very strictly; as first, not knowing their wives after they have born them two children; secondly, not accompanying them, if after five years' cohabitation they can raise no issue by them, but taking others in their rooms; thirdly, never being rewarded for any military exploit, unless they bring with them an enemy's head in their hand, but that which is strangest, and indeed most barbarous, is that when any of their friends falls sick, they will rather choose to kill him than that he should be withered by sickness. Thus you see there is little employment there for doctors, when to be sick, is the next way for to be slain, or perhaps the people may be of the mind rather to kill themselves, then to let the doctors do it.

Having dispatched our business, and freighted again our ship, we left Calicut and put forth to sea, and coasted along several of the islands belonging to India. At Camboia I met with our old friend Mr David Prire, who was overjoyed to see me, to whom I related our discovery of the Island of Pines, in the same manner as I have related it to you. He was then but newly recovered of a fever, the air of that place not being agreeable to him. Here we took in good store of aloes, and some other commodities, and victualled our ship for our return home.

After four days sailing we met with two Portugal ships which came from Lisbon, one whereof had in a storm lost its top-mast, and was forced in part to be towed by the other. We had no bad weather in eleven day's space, but then a sudden storm of wind did us much harm in our tacklings, and swept away one of our sailors off from the forecastle. November the sixth had like to have been a fatal day unto us, our ship striking twice upon a rock, and at night was in danger of being fired by the negligence of a boy leaving a candle carelessly in the gunroom. The next day we were chased by a pirate of Argiere,* but by the swiftness of our sails we outran him. December the first we came again to Madagascar, where we put in for a fresh recruit of victuals and water.

During our abode here, there happened a very great earthquake, which tumbled down many houses. The people of themselves are very unhospitable and treacherous, hardly to be drawn to traffic with any people; and now, this calamity happening upon them, so enraged them against the Christians (imputing all such calamities to the cause of them), that they fell upon some Portugals and wounded them, and we, seeing their mischievous actions, with all the speed we could put forth to sea again and sailed to the Island of St Helens.

Here we stayed all the Christmas Holy-days, which was very much celebrated by the Governor there under the King of Spain. Here we furnished ourselves with all necessaries which we wanted; but upon our departure, our old acquaintance Mr Petrus Ramazina, coming in a skiff out of the Isle del Principe, or the Prince's Island, retarded our going for the space of two days, for both my self and our purser had emergent business with him, he being concerned in those affairs of which I wrote to you in April last. Indeed, we cannot but acknowledge his courtesies unto us, of which you know he is never sparing.

January the first, we again hoisted sail, having a fair and prosperous gale of wind, we touched at the Canaries, but made no tarriance, desirous now to see our native country. But the Winds was very cross unto us for the space of a week. At last we were favoured with a gentle gale, which brought us on merrily, though we were on a sudden stricken again into a dump: a sailor from the main mast discovering five ships, which put us all in a great fear, we being richly laden, and not very well provided for defence. But they bearing up to us, we found them to be Zealanders and our friends. After many other passages concerning us, not so much worthy of note, we at last safely arrived at home, May 26, 1668.

Thus Sir, have I given you a brief, but true relation of our voyage. Which I was the more willing to do, to prevent false copies which might be spread of this nature. As for the Island of Pines itself, which caused me to write this relation, I suppose it is a thing so strange as will hardly be credited by some. Although perhaps knowing persons, especially considering our last age being so full of discoveries, that this place should lie dormant for so long a space of time, others I know, such Nullifidians as will believe nothing but what they see, applying that proverb unto us, 'That Travellers may lie by authority'.* But Sir, in writing to you, I question not but to give credence, you knowing my disposition so hateful to divulge falsities. I shall request you to impart this my relation to Mr W.W. and Mr P.L., remembering me very kindly unto them, not forgetting my old acquaintance, Mr J.P. and Mr J.B. No more at present, but only my best respects to you and your second self, I rest,

> Yours in the best of friendship,
> Henry Cornelius Van Sloetten.

July 22, 1668.

Postscript.
One thing concerning the Isle of Pines, I had almost quite forgot. We had with us an Irish man named Dermot Conelly who had formerly been in England, and had learned there to play on the bagpipes, which he carried to Sea with him. Yet so un-Englished he was, that he had quite forgotten your language, but still retained his art of bagpipe-playing, in which he took extraordinary delight. Being one day on land in the Isle of Pines, he played on them, but to see the admiration of those naked people concerning them, would have stricken you into admiration. Long time it was before we could persuade them that it was not a living creature, although they were permitted to touch and feel it. And yet are the people very

intelligible, retaining a great part of the ingenuity and gallantry of the English nation, though they have not that happy means to express themselves. In this respect we may account them fortunate, in that possessing little, they enjoy all things, as being contented with what they have, wanting those allurements to mischief which our European Countries are enriched with. I shall not dilate any further. No question but time will make this Island known better to the world; all that I shall ever say of it is that it is a place enriched with nature's abundance, deficient in nothing conducible to the sustentation of man's life, which were it manured by agriculture and gardening, as other of our European countries are, no question but it would equal, if not exceed many which now pass for praiseworthy.

FINIS

EXPLANATORY NOTES

UTOPIA

3 *the request of a friend . . . himself alone*: the friend was one George Tadlowe, of whom nothing is known. See Robinson's dedication to William Cecil (printed in the Appendix of Ancillary Materials) which was included in the first edition of Robinson's translation but dropped in the second.

more haste than good speed: Robinson is playing on the old meaning of 'good speed' = success, and implying that his haste led him to overlook errors.

the Latin proverb . . . whelps: from Erasmus's collection of classical proverbs *Adagia* (1500): *Canis festinans caecos ponit catulos* (quoting Aristotle and Galen).

this notable saying of Terence . . . corrigas: see the Roman comic dramatist Terence's *Adelphoe, or The Brothers*, ll. 739–41. The meaning of the lines is accurately explained by Robinson.

4 *More . . . sendeth greeting*: Peter Giles (also spelt 'Gilles') was a pupil and friend of Erasmus, born in Antwerp in 1586, and appointed Chief Secretary of the town in 1510. Erasmus introduced him to More in 1515. This letter originally appeared in the first edition of *Utopia*.

5 *Raphael*: Raphael Hythloday, who reports to More his visit to Utopia.

Truth . . . plainness: some of the marginal notes in this edition appear to have been written by Robinson. Others were translated from notes that appeared in the Latin editions of the text. Peter Giles claims credit for some of these in his letter to Busleyden (see below); elsewhere, however, they are attributed to Erasmus.

6 *John Clement, my boy*: Clement was a page in More's household and later married More's adopted daughter. He was a student of Colet at St Paul's School. In 1519 he became Reader at Oxford, and later in life was a well-known physician.

Hythloday: 'Hythloday' is from the Greek *huthlos* ('nonsense', 'trifles') and *daio* ('distribute', 'kindle'), thus 'peddlar of trifles', 'kindler of nonsense'. Raphael was one of God's archangels. R. M. Adams suggests that a 'trilingual pun could make the whole name mean "God heals [Heb. Raphael] through the nonsense [Gk. huthlos] of God [Lat. dei]"'. There has been some recent disagreement over the meaning of Hythloday's name, however. Halpern (1991: see Select Bibliography) suggests that 'nonsense' is an inaccurate translation of *huthlos*, and proposes instead that pleasurable, non-philosophical speech rather than falseness is what Hythloday peddles.

7 *late famous vicar of Croydon in Surrey*: possibly Rowland Phillips, Canon of St Paul's and Warden of Merton College Oxford. He was vicar of Croydon in 1497. As the marginal note makes clear, it is uncertain whether or not More was describing a real person here.

8 *danger of gunshot*: the proverb appears in Erasmus's *Adagia*.

10 *Raphael Hythloday*: see note to p. 6 above.

Henry the eighth . . . king of Castile: the future Charles V, who became Prince of Castile in 1516, and Holy Roman Emperor in 1519. The controversy to which More refers here concerns the wool trade: the English had prohibited the export of wool to the Netherlands after Charles's Dutch dominions had imposed strict import duties on English wool.

ambassador into Flanders . . . Master of the Rolls: the prohibition of wool sales to the Netherlands had adversely affected the English wool trade. A delegation, of which More was a part, was sent to Flanders to negotiate in 1515: More wrote Book Two of the *Utopia* while serving on this delegation (Book One was written after his return to England). Cuthbert Tunstall was also a member of the delegation to Flanders; greatly respected by More for his learning, he was appointed Master of the Rolls (Clerk of the Chancery Court) in 1516.

as the proverb saith: sayings similar to this appear in Erasmus's *Adagia*.

the Margrave . . . profoundly learned: the Margrave was the chief magistrate, or mayor; Bruges was an important port for the English wool trade. George Temsice, also a native of Bruges, and sometimes known as George (or Georges) de Themsecke (or Theimsecke), was, as More says, Provost, or Chief Magistrate, of Cassel.

but in reasoning . . . few fellows: whose debating skills were second to none, partly by virtue of his native intelligence, partly thanks to his extensive experience.

11 *Peter Giles*: see note to p. 4 above.

Our Lady's Church: the Gothic Cathedral of Notre Dame.

stricken in age: of advanced years.

12 *not as the mariner Palinurus . . . Plato*: Palinurus was the pilot of Aeneas in Virgil's *Aeneid*; Ulysses the hero of Homer's *Odyssey*. Plato was reported to have travelled widely in his search for knowledge. More seems to be drawing a distinction here between those who travel for money or glory and those who travel in pursuit of higher virtues; he may also expect his readers to remember that Palinurus lost his way in a storm, landing the ship on the island of Celaeno and her Harpies (see below), and later dropped asleep at the helm, fell overboard, and was murdered by the

inhabitants of the island he washed up upon (Virgil, *Aeneid*, iii. 202, v. 832, and vi. 340).

saving a few of Seneca's and Cicero's doings: Seneca was a Stoic; Cicero had Stoic sympathies.

for he is a Portugall born: the Portuguese were amongst the most tireless of early modern European explorers, reaching Cape Bojador in 1434, Gambia in 1446, the Congo in 1484, and India in 1498. They discovered, and for many years dominated, the Cape route to India and South East Asia.

Amerigo Vespucci . . . in every man's hands: born in 1451, Vespucci made four voyages between 1497 and 1504, the last two for the King of Portugal. He claimed to have discovered America (named after him) and published two accounts of his voyages (*New World* and *Quatuor Americi Vesputii Navigationes*, or *The Four Voyages of Amerigo Vespucci*) in the early years of the sixteenth century.

the twenty-four . . . the country of Gulike: Robinson has misunderstood More's Latin text here. More is referring to Vespucci's account of having left twenty-four men behind, in a fort: Robinson misunderstood the Latin for 'fort' as denoting the name of a town (Julich).

for his mind's sake: because he desired it.

these sayings: the first saying derives from Lucan (*Pharsalia*, vii. 819); the second from Cicero's *Tusculan Disputations*, i., xliii. 104.

Taprobane: an ancient name for Sri Lanka.

Calicut: a port in Southern India on the Malabar coast, which under the navigation of an Indian pilot was the first Indian port visited by Vasco de Gama in May 1498.

nothing less than looked for: completely unexpectedly.

14 *the lodestone . . . unknown*: magnets began to be extensively used in shipping from the fifteenth century.

as for monsters . . . incredible monsters: More alludes here to the reports of monsters that littered early modern travel narratives, which he compares with classical monsters (known to be purely mythical). Scylla was the monster (described by Homer as six-headed, by Virgil as having a woman's torso, a wolverine's belly, and a dolphin's tail) who lay in wait on one of the two rocks between Italy and Sicily (see Homer's *Odyssey*, xii; Virgil's *Aeneid*, iii. 426). Celaeno was a Harpy, a birdlike creature with the head of a woman (see Virgil's *Aeneid*, iii. 212). The Lestrygonians were cannibalistic giants who destroyed eleven of Odysseus' ships together with their crews (*Odyssey*, x).

16 *in bondage to . . . at your pleasure*: the distinction in the Latin is between *servias* (slave) and *inservias* (in service to); the Latin text has a sentence, omitted by Robinson, which draws attention to the pun. More himself hesitated over entering the service of the king.

16 *my mind . . . clean against*: completely counter to my principles and nature.

17 *So both the raven . . . fairest*: again a proverb which appears in Erasmus's *Adagia*.

Trip takers: those who trip up other men's arguments.

the insurrection . . . suppressed and ended: in 1497, after one tax too many, the Cornish rebelled, being brutally defeated at Blackheath. According to Hall's *Chronicle* the rebels lost more than 2,000 men in the battle.

18 *John Morton, Archbishop . . . I will say*: Morton was a statesman under Henry VI and Edward IV and was created Archbishop of Canterbury and Lord Chancellor by Henry VII. More served as a page in Morton's household between 1490 and 1492, and was encouraged by Morton to go to Oxford. Hythloday's admiration for Morton was not shared by a good deal of the English population, who hated him for devising a number of ingenious taxes. According to Bacon, the best-known of these was 'Morton's fork', which taxed those who spent on the grounds that they were rich, and those who did not spend on the grounds that they must have saved up money.

In the which . . . took great delectation: he took great delight in ready wit and bold spirit, since these were his own virtues too, just so long as those virtues were not accompanied with insolence.

that strait and rigorous . . . upon one gallows: The Latin text states that *sometimes* twenty would be hanged on one gallows. But the severity with which the death penalty was applied in England was notorious: according to Holinshed's *Chronicle*, for example, 7,200 thieves were hanged during the reign of Henry VIII alone.

19 *simple theft*: theft alone (i.e. not accompanied by actual or threatened violence).

Blackheath field . . . the wars in France: Blackheath field was the site of the bloody 1497 defeat of the Cornish rebels (see note to p. 17 above). Henry VII's wars with Charles VIII were terminated at the Treaty of Étaples in 1492. Henry VIII's troops also suffered heavy casualties in wars with France in 1512–13.

their tenants . . . raising their rents: 'poll and shave', i.e. exploit to the limit. Exploitative landlords purchased or leased property solely in order to raise the rents of sitting tenants, who had no protection under the law against such abuses.

idle and loitering serving men: such servants constituted the last vestiges of private armies retained by feudal noblemen, which had been broken up by Henry VII.

20 *Yet France . . . much sorer plague*: the French army was made up principally of mercenaries.

21 *of Sallust*: by the Roman historian Sallust, in *Catiline's War*, xvi. 3.

the examples of the Romans . . . manifestly declare: all these lost control of their armies, either because those armies were made up of slave labour, or because they employed, or fought against, mercenaries.

of their own armies . . . a readiness: by their own standing armies (which, being mercenaries or slaves, were ready to turn on them).

French soldiers . . . unpractised soldiers: England had achieved several large victories over the French, the most recent of which was Agincourt (1415).

picked and chosen men: handpicked, the very best.

22 *your sheep . . . very men themselves*: in pursuit of the considerable profits to be had from the wool trade, landowners were turning arable land into pasture for sheep, and enclosing large tracts of land previously held in common. In so doing they deprived commoners of their livelihoods, since they no longer had anywhere to graze their livestock, and since their skills in arable farming were no longer a means to employment when arable land was turned into pasture. (The Latin refers to this last consequence in a sentence which Robinson does not translate.) As a result, the peasantry was increasingly fragmented and atomized, forced from subsistence into destitution, from the land into the towns, and eventually, from being basically self-supporting smallholders into a mass of wage labourers.

certain abbots, holy men no doubt: the Church was frequently accused of enclosing common land; Cistercian monks, for instance, had practised sheep-farming on a large scale in the Pennines since the twelfth century.

cormorant: used figuratively to describe someone who was rapacious and insatiably greedy.

very little worth . . . the sale: which would be worth almost nothing even if its owners were able to sell it in the best possible market.

And yet . . . vagabonds: such 'vagabonds' came from a variety of sources. Some were disappropriated peasants, others ex-retainers from dismantled private armies. By the time Robinson produced his translation of the *Utopia*, the unemployed population had been swelled by Henry VIII's dissolution of the monasteries, since no provision was found for the considerable number of servants employed by the monks.

23 *no man . . . young store*: no one to devote himself to the breeding of young stock.

bred . . . brought up: bred more quickly than they are sold. This is the present state of affairs; Hythloday is anticipating what will happen when exploitative landlords turn their attentions to places so far untouched.

24 *unlawful games*: both Henry VII and Henry VIII passed various laws attempting to limit pastimes such as these.

24 *engross and forestall*: to monopolize commodities and hoard goods.

advance . . . felons: flatter yourselves that you do justice on your criminals.

25 *Hold your peace, quoth the Cardinal*: according to the marginalia in some early editions, Cardinal Morton did habitually curtail the garrulous.

what violence . . . to the mischief: what punishment (other than the death penalty) could prevent robbery from people who (are so base as to) believe that a reduction in the penalty is an invitation to the crime?

26 *And if any man . . . be lawful . . .*: if anyone should think that God's prohibition of killing only operates when it is not in conflict with killing sanctioned by the state . . .

after what sort: to what degree.

Moses law . . . clemency and mercy: for Mosaic, or Old Testament, law (as opposed to New Testament law with which More contrasts Mosaic law), see Exodus 19–24.

27 *did . . . please the Romans*: the Romans, like the Greeks, made considerable use of slave labour.

the Polylerites: from Greek *polus* ('much') and *léros* ('nonsense'), thus 'nonsensical people'.

28 *But if the thing . . . and children*: if the stolen item has disappeared, then its value is made up from the thief's own property, but apart from this, all the rest of his property is bestowed upon the thief's wife and children.

be not only tied . . . with stripes: in More's Latin text the convicts are flogged rather than imprisoned, not as well as.

29 *a coat of their own colour*: (they may receive) clothing (so long as) it is of the proper colour.

to him that openeth and uttereth . . . large gifts: informants are generously rewarded.

forasmuch as the end . . . for the same: inasmuch as the objective of their punishment is only to destroy vice and nurture virtue, by so treating and educating people that they cannot help but act virtuously, and use the rest of their lives to make amends for the harm they have done in the past.

taken with the manner: caught with the items.

30 *it is not to be thought . . . true and an honest man*: there is no need to worry that they would confide in one another, since they know this would endanger those who concealed such confidences and benefit those who informed upon them. On the other hand, no one is deprived of the hope of being freed for good behaviour.

the privileges of all sanctuaries: by tradition, criminals could take sanctuary in holy places such as churches and churchyards. The practice of sanctuary still applied in some places.

31 *to resemble and counterfeit the fool*: to play the fool.

the proverb . . . hit the mark: again, a similar proverb appears in Erasmus's *Adagia*.

For I had . . . good: for I would much prefer.

32 *distributed . . . religion*: forcibly placed in monasteries and convents.

lay brethren: people who took monastic vows, but who carried out only manual labour and were not admitted to orders.

friars: the distinction invoked is between monks and nuns, who lived and worked in monasteries and convents, and mendicant friars, who begged for their living.

scripture sayeth . . . your souls: see Luke 21: 19.

Be you angry, and sin not: see Psalms 4: 4.

33 *The zeal of thy house hath eaten me*: Psalms 69: 9.

The scorners of Elisha . . . zeal of the bald: 2 Kings 2: 23. Children mocked Elisha because he was bald; Elisha, in retaliation, made 'she bears' devour forty-two of the children.

For Solomon . . . be many bald men: for Elisha's story, see the previous note. For Solomon's proverb, see Proverbs 26: 5. Friars shaved their heads.

to hear his suitors: to attend to legal petitions brought before him.

34 *whereas your Plato . . . philosophy*: see the *Republic*, v. 473, where Plato maintains that civic good can only prosper when political power is informed by the wisdom of philosophy.

King Dionysius: Plato was called to Syracuse in 361 BC to instruct the dissolute Dionysius the Younger in philosophy, but was unsuccessful in the endeavour. The story is told in Diogenes Laertius' *Lives of Eminent Philosophers*, iii. 17 ff.

the French king: the following passage refers to the empire-building of French kings such as Charles VIII, Louis XII, and Francis I, and more generally to the attempts of various European magnates to annex for themselves the choicest possessions of their peers. Milan and Naples were both repeatedly conquered and lost by French kings between 1495 and 1515. Venice was divided between France, Spain, Austria, and the Pope in 1508. Flanders was part of the Austrian Netherlands as was Brabant; Burgundy was annexed to France, but its possessions passed to Austria. Various methods were utilized to achieve these ends, ranging from treaties whose terms were broken as soon as it became expedient to do so, to the use of German or Swiss mercenaries (the latter being so talented in the 'arts' of warfare that they were frequently paid not to fight). The emperor is Maximilian I of Austria; the King of Aragon is Ferdinand. Navarre (on the Franco-Spanish border) was coveted by both countries and annexed by Ferdinand in 1512.

35 *Lance knights*: 'lansquenets', i.e. German or Swiss mercenaries.

35 *his five eggs*: his two bits, his insignificant contribution.

to hook in . . . affinity or alliance: attempts to use marital alliances to acquire land, resolve conflict, or unite power were common.

the Scots must be had in a readiness: alliances between French and Scots against the English were frequent and long-standing.

some peer of England that is banished his country: covert support of rebels (such as Perkin Warbeck and Richard de la Pole, both of whom have been suggested as the referend of this passage) was (as it still is) a common tactic of nations aiming to destabilize their enemies.

36 *Achorians*: from *a* ('not', 'without') and *chora* ('place'), thus (like 'Utopians') 'those who live in a place that does not exist'.

37 *the valuation of money . . . gather any*: Edward IV and Henry VII frequently tampered with the value of coinage in the attempt to raise funds.

to feign war: in 1492 taxes levied by Henry VII for a war with France over Brittany were appropriated by the monarch for other uses when the conflict was settled instead by the Treaty of Étaples.

old and moth-eaten laws: Empson and Dudley, counsellors to Henry VII, had fined people for failure to observe laws until then largely forgotten. Morton also participated in the practice.

38 *to forbid many things . . . sustain loss and damage*: to prohibit many practices (especially those counter to public interest) under penalty of severe fines; and then to license those damaged by these new prohibitions so as to allow them to go on indulging in the practices now forbidden.

selling . . . licences: selling exemptions (from these new laws).

endanger unto . . . his side: to ensure that the judiciary remains on his side.

to take . . . in a trip: to catch his opponent out.

the king's indisputable prerogative: in fact, the question of the extent of monarchical privilege was a matter of growing debate.

the rich Crassus: Marcus Licinius Crassus, an enormously wealthy Roman. According to Cicero, Crassus declared that only those with enough money to maintain an army would be capable of taking part in government (Cicero, *On Duty*, i. 8).

39 *the office . . . himself*: see Ezekiel 34: 2 and Plato's *Republic*, i. 343, where Plato argues that a true ruler is he who only acts in the interests of his subjects. Diogenes Laertius also mentions Plato's views on the matter in his *Lives of Eminent Philosophers*, iii. 17.

Fabricius: Gaius Fabricius Luscinus, famous for his austerity and integrity. The saying attributed to him here is actually attributed (by Plutarch) to another Roman, Manius Curius Dentatus. See Plutarch's *Moralia*, 194, under the section on Manius Curius.

40 *Let him do cost not above his power*: spend only his income.

Macarians: from the Greek *makarios*, 'happy', 'blessed', thus 'happy people'.

41 *school philosophy*: academic philosophy, scholastic philosophy.

comedy of Plautus . . . Seneca disputeth with Nero: Plautus wrote farcical comedies, Seneca highly serious tragedies (amongst other works). Seneca did not write the tragedy *Octavia* (although it was handed down in his manuscripts), but appears as a character in it, arguing with the tyrant Nero about the evil of tyranny in the second act of the play.

the dumb person: a mute character in Greek drama.

42 *that Plato feigneth in his weal-public*: the *Republic*.

43 *those things . . . in open houses*: see Luke 12: 3 and Matthew 10: 27.

a rule of lead: a lead ruler was flexible and thus adaptable to curved surfaces; it was sometimes used as a metaphor for malleable ethics.

as Mitio saith in Terence: the reference is to a speech of Mitio's at the end of the first act of Terence's comedy *Adelphoe, or The Brothers*.

Wherefore Plato . . . commonwealth: 'Goodly similitude', i.e. fine analogy. Plato compares the man who wishes to do good to a traveller sheltering under a wall in a dust-storm. See the *Republic*, vi. 496.

44 *Plato . . . commodities*: Plato was invited to rule the Arcadians and the Thebans but declined when he learnt that they would not agree to equality of possessions. See Diogenes Laertius, *The Lives of the Eminent Philosophers*, iii. 23.

45 *a statute . . . sum of money*: laws limiting both land ownership and conspicuous consumption (the latter known as sumptuary laws) were enacted by several countries in early modern Europe.

offices should not . . . in their offices: once again, abuses such as the selling of offices were common in early modern England.

49 *receiveth in ships . . . the land*: allows ships to pass across it in the direction of any part of the land.

50 *King Utopus*: here and elsewhere, More's Latin does not refer to 'King Utopus' but simply to 'Utopus'; Robinson's later references to 'princes' are similarly misleading. Utopia is not a monarchy.

Abraxa: the derivation of this name is not known. Some suggest it is derived from 'Abraxas', a mystical term (whose numerical equivalent is 365) which might have meant 'Holy Name' or 'The Blessing', and referred to the highest heaven. Turner suggests instead that it comes from the Greek *a* (not) and *brakae* breeches: he 'translates' the term as 'Sanscullottia'. It is also possible that the Greek word *abrachos* may be another form of the word *abrochos* ('waterless'); if so, and given the context (Abraxa's attachment to the mainland), it seems likely that More may have had this in mind.

50 *Amaurote*: from the Greek *amauros* ('faint', 'dim', 'dark'), thus 'dim city', 'shadowy city'.

51 *Philarch*: from Greek *phularchos*, meaning 'head of the group'. There may also be a play on *phil* ('love') and *arché* ('rule'), thus 'loving ruler'.

53 *Anyder*: from the Greek *a* ('not') and *hudor* ('water'), thus 'dry', 'without water'.

54 *Whoso will may go in*: also a practice of Plato's republicans. See the conclusion of Book 3 of the *Republic*.

55 *the history of 1,760 years*: Logan and Adams note R. J. Schoeck's observation that 1,760 years before 1516 would be 244 BC, in which year Agis IV, who was eventually executed for attempting to effect egalitarian reforms, became King of Sparta.

fine linen . . . or amber: glass was rare in English windows until the seventeenth century. The inhabitants of the *New Atlantis* also have oiled cloth in their windows.

Syphogrant . . . Philarch: the derivation of these words is unknown. For the first syllables of syphogrant, some have suggested the Greek *sophos* ('wise'); others have proposed *supheos* ('of the pigsty'). It is also possible that the derivation might play on *suphar* ('a piece of old wrinkled skin'). For the second syllable of 'syphogrant' derivations suggested have included *gerontes* ('old men') and *krantor* ('ruler'). For the first syllables of 'tranibor' suggestions have included *tranos* ('clear', 'distinct') and *thranos* ('bench'); for the second, most commentators have used a variant of *bora* ('food'). Some of these suggestions stem from associations editors of the text have made between the practices used by the Utopians and the ritual dinners enjoyed by lawyers of the various Inns of Court in sixteenth-century England.

of the prince: the Latin has *princeps* ('ruler', 'leader'): More means something like 'chief magistrate of the city', not 'prince of the island'.

56 *counsels*: probably a misprint for 'councils'.

58 *the life of workmen . . . Utopia*: early modern agricultural workers had to work from daybreak to nightfall during autumn and winter, and from about 5 a.m. to about 8 p.m. during spring and summer.

dinner: unusually, the second edition introduces a misprint here, which is absent from the first edition of Robinson's translation, and which makes the text contradictory, since the total number of hours worked adds up to nine rather than six. The text should have read: '. . . assign only six of those hours to work; three before noon, upon which they go straight to dinner . . . then they work three . . .'

Dice-play . . . or a set field: 'dice-play', i.e. gambling. The 'battle of numbers' and the battle between vices and virtues seem to have been games invented by More.

59 *money . . . swing*: where money alone is valued.

60 *Barzanes . . . Adamus*: the derivation of Barzanes is uncertain. It may come from Mithrobarzanes (Menippus' guide to the Underworld in *Menippus* by the Greek comic writer Lucian), and hence have connotations of wisdom. Some have suggested that it means 'Son of Zeus', from the Hebrew *bar* ('son of'), plus *zanos*. 'Adamus' is Robinson's mistake, or a misprint: it should be 'Ademus' from the Greek *a* ('without') and *demos* ('people'), thus 'without people'.

61 *stood one man in much money*: cost one man a lot of money.

64 *meat markets*: food markets.

the number of their halls: the number of people in their halls.

the hospitals: the only English hospital at the time was St Bartholomew's, in London.

67 *They begin every dinner . . . virtue*: formerly the practice in monasteries, and the contemporary practice in universities, reading instructive literature aloud during meals was customary in More's own household.

69 *incontinent the lack . . . abundance of the other*: those who have immediately give up their excess to those who have not.

they sell for ready money . . . paid at a day: sell for hard cash or for promise of payment at a later date.

follow the credence of private men: trust individuals.

70 *be set together by the ears among themselves*: be set in conflict with one another.

72 *cast away nuts*: a Latin proverb for giving up childish things.

Anemolians: from the Greek *anemos* ('wind'), thus 'windy people'.

those three citizens . . . every city: i.e. those representatives from each city who come together to confer on matters relating to the commonwealth.

apparelled . . . colours: dressed in clothes of many different colours.

73 *Doubtful he calleth . . . very little worth*: in this marginal note Robinson appears to be uncertain how to translate More's Latin. His note means: 'More uses "doubtful" to qualify either the value of the counterfeit stones themselves, or the pleasure men take in them.'

74 *which selfsame wool . . . than a sheep*: see Lucian, *Demonax*, 41. For a story similar to that of the Anemolian ambassadors, see Lucian's *Nigrinus*.

as an augmentation . . . his money: as if he himself were a bonus prize over and above his wealth.

75 *pointed to of us*: pointed to by us.

our new logicians . . . with our finger: More here satirizes the academic discipline of logic, and its teaching in the schools and universities of medieval and early modern Europe. The *Small Logicals* was probably a logic textbook written by Petrus Hispanus (Peter of Spain), who later became Pope John XXI; 'restrictions', 'amplifications', and 'suppositions' were all terms for various logical procedures. 'First' and 'second' 'intentions' were terms used to distinguish between categories of perception. 'First intentions' referred to the mind's perception of a singular, material object; 'second intentions' to the mind's capacity to make distinctions between abstract notions of objects by comparing one with another, or categorizing them by their properties into species or other kinds of type. In this case, the distinction invoked is that between man as an individual, and 'Man' in the abstract, as a species.

75 *heavenly spheres*: Ptolemaic astronomical theory held that the earth is stable, and surrounded by a number of revolving spheres upon which were carried the planets.

deceitful divination by the stars: astrology.

76 *qualities of the soul . . . and of fortune*: see Plato's *Laws*, iii. 697; Aristotle's *Nichomachean Ethics*, I. viii. 2 and *Politics*, VII. i. 3–4. At numerous points in the ensuing dialogue Utopian thinking recapitulates, rejects, or is otherwise in dialogue with classical philosophy. For more extensive notes on this aspect of the *Utopia*, see the edition by Logan and Adams (in Select Bibliography).

the opinion of them . . . felicity to rest: such hedonism allies the Utopians with Epicurean ethics, and also, Logan and Adams suggest, with Vespucci's account of native peoples in his *Four Voyages*. Epicurean ethics underlie much of the Utopian thinking about pleasure.

79 *In this image . . . their own conceit*: those who take so much pleasure in giving themselves airs (just because their ancestors were noble) are themselves one of the greatest, and most ridiculous, examples of this kind of false pleasure.

80 *Nor they buy . . . and bare*: and they won't even buy (the stones) unless they first remove them from their settings, and strip off from them all the gold.

82 *the opinion of them . . . counted a pleasure*: for this discourse see Book 9 (582 ff.) of Plato's *Republic* and also the argument between Socrates and Callicles in Plato's *Gorgias*, 494b ff.

83 *that onwardness . . . refreshed*: the process of regaining one's proper strength generates in us the pleasure which refreshes us so much.

the own wealth and goodness: its own good.

For what man . . . that is not: anyone who is conscious is aware of his good health, unless he is ill.

chief part . . . conscience of good life: see Cicero, *On Old Age*, iii. 4.

84 *that man must needs . . . scratching and rubbing*: see Plato's *Gorgias*, 494c. More himself wore a hair shirt.

86 *Greek literature . . . and poets*: More himself thought that there was a great deal more of value in Greek literature than in Latin.

if the book were not false: so long as the text were not corrupt.

Theophrastus: a Greek naturalist and philosopher, Aristotle's pupil and friend, and his successor as head of the Lyceum, or Peripatetic school (Aristotle's school of philosophy in Athens). He is the reputed author of hundreds of works, most of which are now lost.

87 *Of them that have written the grammar . . . Galen's 'Microtechne'*: all of these authors had been recently published. Constantine Lascaris's *Erotemata* or *Grammatica Graeca* was one of the first books ever printed (at Milan, in 1476). Theodorus Gaza's Greek grammar was published at Venice in 1495. Hesychius's Greek lexicon was published in 1514. Pedanius Dioscorides did not write a dictionary; his *Materia Medica*, published in 1499, discussed the properties of drugs, herbs, and other substances. Four of Lucian's comic dialogues were translated by More into Latin. Nine of Aristophanes' comedies were published in 1498, seventeen of Euripides' plays in 1503, and the first edition of Sophocles in 1502. Most of these authors were published by the printing firm run by Aldus Pius Manutius and his two sons, which, renowned for its accuracy, was the first printing house to print Greek texts in Greek type. In 1502 Aldus's firm also published Thucydides and Herodotus, and in 1526 Hippocrates (to whom early medical writings were attributed). Galen was a famous Greek physician. The name of Hythloday's companion derives from the names of two towns in Apulia, Apina and Trica, said to have been sacked by Diomedes, and infamous for their insignificance. Thus 'Tricius Apinatus' implies 'trifler', or 'insignificant person'.

88 *such as they can get out of foreign countries*: the European slave trade was beginning in the early years of the sixteenth century. In 1509 the Bishop of Chiapas, Bartolomé de Las Casas, proposed that Spanish settlers should all try to import slaves from Africa to the New World; in 1518 a licence to import 4,000 African slaves to the Spanish New World was granted to Lorens de Gominot.

90 *actually*: the first edition of Robinson's translation has 'bodily'.

a custom which seemed to us very fond and foolish: if John Aubrey is to be believed, shortly after the publication of *Utopia* More had occasion to put Utopian theory into real practice on the betrothal of his eldest daughter Margeret to William Roper. 'Roper', Aubrey relates, 'came one morning, pretty early, to my Lord, with a proposal to marry one of his daughters. My Lord's daughters were then both together abed in a truckle-bed in their father's chamber asleep. He carries Sir William into the chamber and takes the sheete by the corner and suddenly whips it off. They lay on their Backs, and their smocks up as high as their armepitts. This awakened them, and immediately they turned on their bellies. Quoth Roper, I have seen both sides, and so gave a patt on the buttock he made a choice of sayeing, Thou art mine. Here was all the trouble of the wooeing.' (John Aubrey, *Aubrey's Brief Lives*, ed. Oliver Lawson Dick (Harmondsworth: Penguin, 1962), 283).

90 *in buying a colt*: the name of More's first wife was Jane Colt. But the comparison has a history: Horace also invokes it in defence of an argument for seeing women naked before sleeping with them. In his view congress with a prostitute is safer than adultery with a married woman, because prostitutes display their 'wares' openly, whilst married women do not (Horace, *Satires*, i. 2). Seneca also says that one uncovers a horse before buying it in order to expose its defects: he compares the practice to the buying of slaves (Seneca, *Moral Epistles*, 80). Plato suggests that boys and girls should dance naked together prior to marriage so that they can take a good look at each other (Plato, *Laws*, vi. 772).

91 *change and take another*: separation after adultery was permitted in More's England; remarriage was not.

   bringeth sickness . . . sickness itself: see the third act of Terence's *Phormio*.

92 *the open punishment . . . honest manners*: the example of a public punishment would encourage others to better behaviour.

93 *fools*: fools were employed by rich households: More's own fool, Henry Pattinson, appears in Holbein's portrait of More's family. This kind of fool, familiar to us from Shakespearean comedy, was witty and intelligent, but the word could also refer to the mentally disabled: it is the latter to whom More appears to be referring here.

   so to help the same with paintings: to use make-up.

   honest conditions and lowliness: honesty and humbleness.

94 *cap of maintenance*: a special headdress or hat made of crimson velvet lined with ermine and originally worn only by dukes.

   attorneys, proctors, and sergeants at the law: an attorney's duties were akin to those of a solicitor, as were those of the proctor, but the latter practised in the Ecclesiastical and Admiralty Courts. A sergeant at the law was the highest kind of barrister.

95 *they bring home again . . . their country*: they send home (to Utopia) with honour and praise, and replace them with new (Utopian) officials.

   where they take place . . . break justice: where they influence verdicts, forthwith incapacitate the power of justice.

   for here in Europe . . . the head bishops: the monarchs and pontiffs ('head bishops') of early modern Europe broke treaties all the time.

96 *because it shall not run at rovers*: so that it does not run off at a tangent.

97 *lest they should . . . need should require*: in case they should be ignorant of the art of warfare when the need arose.

   the contrary part: the other side.

98 *Which they do . . . under the colour of justice*: they do this not only when their friends' lands and possessions have been plundered by invading armies, but also, and more aggressively, when their friends' merchants have been cheated when trading abroad, either through the misapplication of good laws or the correct application of bad ones.

the Nephelogetes against the Alaopolitans: 'Nephelogetes' is from the Greek *nephelé* ('cloud'), thus 'cloudy people'; 'Alaopolitans' from the Greek *alaos* ('blind') and *polites* ('citizen') thus, 'blind men', 'blinkered people'.

their friends' merchant men: those with whom their friends trade.

101 *set in their necks*: make them obsessed with.

Zapoletes: from the Greek *za* (an intensifier) and *poletes* ('seller') thus 'arch-seller', 'those who will sell anything' (including themselves). More was probably referring to the Swiss here, Europe's most notorious mercenaries.

102 *be both private and out of office*: who secretly stand by in readiness.

103 *in set field*: in battle formation.

104 *spite of their teeth*: despite their most vehement opposition.

105 *them that keep watch . . . sudden adventures*: those who are posted in armour as sentinels over the trench, to warn of unexpected attacks.

106 *lay it upon their necks that be conquered*: make the conquered pay the costs.

107 *Mithra*: Mithras was a Persian god, worshipped as the sun-god in Rome, especially in the army.

108 *all things common . . . the rightest Christian communities*: for the disciples' communism see Acts 2: 44–5 and 4: 32–5. See also Mark 10: 21. The 'rightest Christian communities' are probably monasteries and convents.

one of our company: i.e. one of the Christians.

110 *suffer him not to dispute . . . among the common people*: he is prohibited from talking about his beliefs only with commoners, (being encouraged to discuss them with priests and scholars).

111 *that the dead be presently conversant among the quick*: that the dead are always present among the living.

112 *the praise thereof coming*: the praise of God which issues from the contemplation of nature.

For whatsoever unpleasant . . . embraiding others therewith: for they happily take upon themselves the distasteful and hard work whose difficulty and unpleasantness would scare others away, and, constantly labouring themselves, let others rest and never upbraid them for not working as hard as they.

from eating of flesh . . . of beasts: the distinction here is between meat, and the flesh of other kinds of animals (such as fish or poultry).

113 *Buthrescas*: from the Greek *bous* ('cow', used in compounds to indicate something of enormous size) and *threskos* ('religious'), thus 'very religious'.

by secret voices: by a secret ballot.

consecrate of their own company: ordained by the other priests.

it is their office . . . in divine matters: it is the priests' duty to offer encouragement and advice (concerning behaviour), whereas the duty of secular officials is to punish wrongdoing; the single exception being that the priests can excommunicate particularly incorrigible offenders, barring them from religious occasions.

115 *Cynemernes . . . Trapemernes*: 'Cynemernes' (which Robinson misprinted 'Lynermenes') is probably from the Greek *kun* ('dog') and *hemera* ('day'): the name probably derives from an association between dogs and Hecate, and from thence the beginning of the month, specifically, the night between the old moon and the new. *Trapemernes* is probably from *trepó* ('change') and *hemera* ('day'), thus 'changing day'.

116 *sacrifice*: ritual, since the Utopians have no sacrifice.

117 *not supposing this . . . the prayers of men*: not believing these items to be particularly useful to the divine being—any more than human prayers are.

in changeable colours: in many colours.

divers feathers of fowls: reports of tribes who wore feathers for decoration appear in a number of early modern travel narratives, including, Turner notes, Vespucci's *Quatuor Americi Vesputii Navigationes*, mentioned earlier by Peter Giles.

120 *goldsmith*: goldsmiths often acted as bankers.

the remembrance . . . killeth them up: the thought of poverty in their old age kills them off.

by common laws: possibly a reference to the Statute of Labourers, a series of laws with a long history which fixed the price of labour for the benefit of landowners and other employers. In 1373, for instance, the Statute of Labourers fixed the price of a reaper's labour at 2 or 3 pence per day; later the Statute fell into abeyance, but was revived in 1495–6 and again in 1514.

122 *So easily might men . . . should be opened*: men might live very easily if it were not for money, [since] money, invented to help us to survive, actually prevents us from making a living.

no jeopardy of domestical dissension: no danger of civil strife.

124 *To the Right Honourable . . . Health and Felicity*: Jerome Buslide, or Busleyden, was from Luxembourg; More met him in 1515. Arienn is Aire, a town near Calais; Charles was Prince of Castile. Busleyden was also canon of Brussels and Mechlin. He left money to fund the

teaching of Hebrew, Greek, and Latin at the University of Louvain. The letter first appeared in the first (Latin) edition of *Utopia* (1516). See the Appendix for Busleyden's response.

127 *A Metre of Four Verses*: the poem was originally published in 'Utopian' with a Latin 'translation', in the first edition of *Utopia*. The Utopian alphabet appeared with it. A facsimile of the alphabet as it first appeared is reprinted in the Appendix of Ancillary Materials.

A short metre of Utopia: again, this appeared in the first Latin edition of the text. 'Anemolius', as glossed above, means 'windy'. The poem is in part another variant on the central joke about Utopia: that it does not exist.

128 *Eutopie*: the first occasion of the pun on Greek *eu* ('good') being explicitly read into 'utopia'.

Gerard Noviomage: Gerhard Geldenhaur, called Novimage after his birthplace, Nimeguen in Guelderland. He was a teacher of philosophy in the University of Louvain, and served as chaplain to Charles of Austria. He later converted to Protestantism. The poem appeared in the first Latin edition of *Utopia*.

Cornelius Graphey: also known as Cornelius Grapheus or Cornelis de Schrijver. He lived in Antwerp and was a friend of Peter Giles.

129 *The Printer to the Reader*: appeared only in the 1556 edition of the text.

131 *Ambrosius Holbein*: the brother of Hans.

134 *Jerome Busleyden to Thomas More*: the letter appeared in the first edition. The translation is J. H. Lupton's.

for the palm: for the highest honour.

135 *Plato's word for it*: see Plato's *Laws*, vi. 715.

Magistrates . . . justice in all: see Plato's *Republic*, iv. 428–34.

136 *my house at Mechlin*: Busleyden had two country houses. The one at Mechlin was especially rich and sumptuous.

Thomas More . . . Peter Giles: this second letter from More to Giles only appeared in the second edition of *Utopia*. The translation is by Philip E. Hallett, from his edition of *Utopia* (London: Burns, Oates and Washbourne, 1937).

that very clever man: the identity of this person (if indeed he existed) is unknown.

138 *Mysis in Terence*: see Terence's *The Girl from Andros*, 786.

Guillaume Budé to . . . Lupset: Guillaume Budé was a famous French humanist, a close friend of Erasmus and Colet, and a courtier at the French court. Thomas Lupset was educated by Colet and Lily; he was at the time studying in Paris, and was involved in the printing of the second edition of *Utopia* (Paris 1517), where this letter first appeared. The translation is J. H. Lupton's.

139 *Linacre . . . Latin*: Linacre founded the Royal College of Physicians. Budé was involved in the printing of the books he mentions here.

140 *Croesus or a Midas*: like Croesus Midas was, in antiquity, of fabulous wealth.

141 *Jesus Christ . . . Pythagorean communion*: for the Christian tradition of communism see Acts 2: 44–5 and 4: 32–7. A communist lifestyle was also ascribed to the followers of Pythagoras.

Ananias: Ananias and his wife tried to trick God into thinking they had given him the entire value of their possessions when in fact they had offered him only a part. See Acts 5: 1–5.

Udepotia: from the Greek *oudepote* ('never'), thus 'Neverland'.

142 *wrapping-paper for shops*: to wrap commodities in (like newspaper for fish and chips).

the Golden Age: a mythical paradisiacal age, supposedly governed by Saturn.

Aratus: a Greek poet who said that Astraea (Justice) fled the earth as a consequence of human evil.

Fortunate Isles: a mythological paradise of the Blest, like the Elysian Fields, to which the virtuous dead were thought in mythology to go.

Hagnopolis: City of the Saints; Holy City. Budé may have intended to invoke Augustine's *City of God*.

143 *conscientious scruple*: see More's letter to Peter Giles, p. 5 above.

Jehan Ruelle: Johannes Ruellis, a physician and scholar.

Minerva: the Roman goddess of wisdom.

144 *Erasmus to . . . John Froben*: Erasmus, the great Dutch humanist, was More's great friend. Johann Froben was a printer in Basle; Erasmus was godfather to Froben's son Johann Erasmus (hence 'gossip', from 'god-sib', 'siblings in God'). Froben printed the third edition of *Utopia*, in which this letter first appeared. The translation is J. H. Lupton's.

never gone . . . Netherlands: More had in fact also been to Louvain and Paris. The trip Erasmus mentions here was the one during which More wrote Book Two of *Utopia*.

Prolusions: Youthful Exercises. these were translations into Latin of Greek epigrams by More and Lily, printed with *Utopia* in Froben's edition.

145 *William Cecil . . . honour*: Cecil was Robinson's patron. This was the preface to Robinson's first edition of *Utopia*. It was dropped in the second for reasons that are not clear.

Upon a time . . . all hands: the story is from Lucian; the Diogenes referred to Diogenes the Cynic (not Diogenes Laertius) who was said to have lived in an earthenware barrel.

'Forsooth . . . working': Rabelais uses the same story to illustrate

substantially the same point in his Prologue to *The Third Book of . . . Pantagruel*. This was published in 1546, so Robinson may well have read it.

146 *even to the very death*: Robinson refers to More's refusal to take the Oath of Supremacy (see Chronology of More's life).

NEW ATLANTIS

151 *this place*: the *New Atlantis* first appeared in 1627, at the end of the volume containing the *Sylva Sylvarum: or, A Natural History*.

W. Rawley: William Rawley was Bacon's chaplain, secretary, and literary executor.

152 *the South Sea*: the Pacific.

showeth . . . deep: a quotation from Psalms 107: 24. The preceding paragraph has many more indirect allusions to the same psalm.

as in the beginning . . . dry land: see Genesis 1: 9.

153 *foremost man*: leader.

Latin of the School: university Latin, Latin of the Scholastic philosophers.

cherubins' wings: biblical cherubim are non-human creatures, described as having various numbers of wings and faces, and associated with the ceaseless worship of God, and with his mercy.

had languages: spoke different (European) languages.

sign of the cross to that instrument: the symbol of the cross on that document.

some little store . . . chargeable unto them: some goods which, if they wished, we could offer in recompense for the services they offered us.

154 *gilt in some part of it*: painted gold in places.

accounted for . . . already done: considered the services already performed for us to be most honourable and of great humanity.

fruit . . . like an orange: oranges were used for the prevention and cure of scurvy, a disease particularly prevalent in sailors, induced by exposure and a diet too rich in salt, and caused by lack of vitamin C.

155 *twice paid for one labour*: Bacon was himself impeached for accepting bribes in 1621. There may be an allusion here to Plato, *Laws*, xii. 955.

prevented the hour: come early.

put their arms a little abroad: stretched their arms out a little to the side.

with handsome windows . . . cambric oiled: as in Utopia, and in early modern England, only the very rich had glass in their windows until well into the seventeenth century. Oiled cloth was used instead.

156 *collegiate diet*: institutional meal, as in a university.

156 *as Jonas . . . whale's belly*: see Jonah 1–2.

157 *let us not bring . . . ourselves*: 'confusion of face' is a biblical term meaning 'shame'. See Ezra 9: 7.

take some taste of our manners and conditions: observe our conduct and behaviour.

some divine pool of healing: the pool of Bethesda, a Biblical pool at Jerusalem whose waters sometimes healed the sick, and where Jesus made the cripple walk. See John 5: 2–4.

as looking that: believing that.

158 *it was impossible . . . inflamed*: we could not help but desire to.

our tongues . . . prayers: a direct quotation from Psalms 137: 6.

this island of Bensalem: 'Bensalem' could derive either from Hebrew or from Arabic. In Hebrew, *ben* means 'son' or 'offspring' and *Salem* is the early name for Jerusalem (see Genesis 14: 18, and Psalms 76). This would make the name mean 'Son of Jerusalem'. Etymologically, *Salem* derives from the root *shlm*, whose primary meaning is 'peace'. A similar connotation would be present given the possible Arabic roots of the word. In Arabic *ben* also means 'son of', and *salem*, 'safety' or 'peace'. This would make 'Bensalem' indicate 'someone who has been granted peace'. 'Salem' is also a man's name in Arabic, however, which might suggest that Bacon is playing with the similarity between 'Salem' and 'Solomon'. Such a view is given support by the fact that elsewhere in the text Bacon uses words which appear to be Arabic in structure, if not in meaning. See the notes to 'Altabin' and 'Tirsan' below.

159 *for the entertainment of the time*: for the efficient use of time.

we were met . . . of the world: we came from the opposite ends of the earth.

we were . . . Christians: we were on both sides Christians.

first seek the kingdom of heaven: a biblical injunction: in return for its fulfilment, God will clothe and feed the faithful. See Matthew 6: 33.

Renfusa: Weinberger suggests that the name is derived from the Greek *rhen* ('sheep') and *phusis* ('life', 'growth'), thus 'sheep-like', 'raised like sheep'.

pillar of light: God led Moses and the Israelites out of Egypt in the form of a pillar of fire (by night; by day a pillar of cloud). See Exodus 13: 21–2.

160 *those of our order*: of the order of Salomon's House.

impostures and illusions of all sorts: magical or deceptive ways of creating things, as opposed to divine, natural, or human ways.

thy Finger: thy own work.

cast itself . . . stars: dispersed itself into many tiny points of light.

a small green branch of palm: palm leaves are a biblical symbol of happiness and blessedness; they were waved by the people on Jesus's entry into Jerusalem.

canonical books . . . not at that time written: the 'canonical books' are those scriptures deemed authentic (the decision as to which these were had been controversial well into the Reformation); the 'Apocalypse' is 'The Revelation of St John', the last book in the Bible. Vickers points out that 'not yet written' would be true, since at the date at which this event is supposed to be happening (AD 49) most of the New Testament had not been written, although Bacon would not have known this.

Bartholomew: one of the twelve Apostles, reputed to have taken St Matthew's Gospel to the Indians.

161 *Gift of Tongues*: speaking in tongues. At Pentecost the Apostles, inspired by God, spoke to a crowd made up of many nationalities; each individual in the crowd heard the Apostles' words in his own particular language. See Acts 2: 1–11.

which he formerly spake: which he said before:

discoveries and navigations of this last age: just a few of these were: Dias rounding Africa and entering the Indian Ocean in 1487; Cabot rediscovering Newfoundland in 1497; Vasco da Gama reaching India in 1498; Cabral seeing the coast of Brazil in 1500; Magellan reaching the Philippines in 1521. Columbus discovered the Bahamas, Cuba, and Hispaniola in 1492, whilst searching for a western route to the Moluccas (the Spice Islands); it was not until Verrazzano's expedition in 1524 that America was understood to be a continent.

162 *with a countenance taking knowledge*: with an expression indicating.

how much it is increased . . . six-score years: see note on 'the discoveries . . . of the last age' above. Counting from 1492, this would make 1612 the date of the discovery of Bensalem.

163 *abounded then in tall ships*: in this and the following passages Bacon mentions a number of nations, both legendary and real, famous for their shipping and/or for their empires. The 'ark' is Noah's. The Phoenicians were great maritime traders between the twelfth and the sixth centuries BC, and much of the coastlines of what are now Morocco, Algeria, Tunisia, and Libya were under their control, as well as part of the Spanish and Portuguese coasts. The Tyrians were natives of Tyre, a Phoenician town; Carthage (now Tunis) was reputedly one of their colonies. Egypt was a major ancient power, as were China, Persia, and Mesopotamia (whose inhabitants were the Chaldeans).

Straits . . . East Tartary: the 'Straits' were those of Gibralter. Paguin and Cambaline were former names for Beijing (which Bacon apparently believed to be a seaport). Quinzy is Hangchow, and was visited by Marco Polo. East Tartary stretched from Turkey to Mongolia.

163 *narration and description which is made by a great man with you*: see Plato's *Timaeus*, 21–5, *Critias*, 113–21.

Neptune: the Roman god of the sea.

which, as so many chains, environed the same site: which, like chains of jewellery, encircled the location.

Peru . . . Tyrambel: Bacon invented these alternative names, though 'Coya' was the name for the chief wife of an Inca sovereign.

Egyptian priest . . . citeth: see Plato's *Timaeus*, 22.

164 *Neither had . . . if they had not*: the Coyan voyage would have fared no better had they not.

Altabin: Weinberger suggests that this is from the Latin *alta* ('high') and *bi* ('twice'), thus 'twice high', 'twice lofty'. But the word also has an Arabic structure: 'Al-tabin' could be an Arabic name.

Divine Revenge: nemesis.

not by a great earthquake . . . part of the old world: in Plato's account, Atlantis was destroyed by an earthquake (see *Timaeus*, 21–5); Bacon substitutes a flood of almost biblical proportions (although not the actual biblical flood, mentioned below as the 'universal flood'). See Bacon's essay 'On the Vicissitude of Things' for similar attempts to account for the differing technological expertise of various peoples, and for his contention that South America and the West Indies had no earthquakes.

your inhabitants of America: the inhabitants of America.

not able to leave . . . civility: not able to leave writings, skills, or civilization. See Plato's *Laws*, iii. 676–9.

165 *tigers, bears, and great hairy goats*: there are no tigers in the Americas though there are pumas and jaguars, as well as goats and bears. By 'great hairy goats' Bacon may have been thinking of the alpaca, or of llamas.

the feathers of birds: reports of native peoples' wearing of birds' feathers were common in the travel narratives of the early modern period. They may also, as noted earlier, have influenced Utopian ritual dress codes (see note to p. 117 above).

in respect of: because of.

a natural revolution of time: see Bacon's essay 'Of the Vicissitude of Things', for the Baconian concept of cyclical temporality.

and specially . . . left and omitted: and especially long voyages were not undertaken, since now they were only embarked upon by those in galleys and other ships which were hardly capable of sailing in the high seas.

So then . . . sail to us: so then, that contact with other nations that might come from others visiting us.

draw nearer . . . question: come closer to answering your main question.

his name was Solamona . . . inscrutable for good: the name of the King invokes the biblical Solomon, the lawgiver said to own 'largeness of heart', and 'wisdom and understanding exceeding much', in 1 Kings 4: 29 ff. Proverbs 25: 3 states that 'the heart of kings is unsearchable': by 'inscrutable for good' Bacon means that the king's goodness cannot be gauged or delimited. Solomon was described elsewhere by Bacon as the king who 'excelled in the glory of treasure and magnificent buildings, of shipping and navigations of service and attendance, of fame and reknown . . . yet he maketh no claim to any of those glories, but only to the glory of inquisition of truth; for so he saith expressly, "The glory of God is to conceal a thing, but the glory of the King is to find it out" as if, according to the innocent play of children, the Divine Majesty took delight to hide his works, to the end to have them found out; and as if kings could not obtain a greater honour than to be God's playfellows in that game' (*The Advancement of Learning* ed. Brian Vickers (see Select Bibliography), 151–2). But the precise relation between the biblical Solomon and King Salomona is left opaque in the text, as is the relation of the name of Salomon's House to both Solamona and Solomon.

how sufficient . . . of the foreigner: how the land was self-sufficient, and capable of being independent (economically and agriculturally) of any other country.

166 *doubting novelties . . . of manners*: frightened of (the potentially disruptive effect of) new ideas and the mixing of customs.

the like law . . . foolish nation: the Chinese were famous for their isolationism; they had little contact with the outside world, laws restricting the entry of foreigners had been in operation since ancient times, and they were supposedly profoundly ignorant of both the cultures and the geographies of the world beyond their borders. In fact though, and as Bacon notes below, the Chinese had in the past participated in the discovery of a complicated network of sea routes in South East Asia, and a couple of centuries previously, under the direction of Admiral Cheng-Ho, had sent out maritime expeditions which found their way through the Straits of Malacca to the Malabar coast of India, Persia, East Africa, and finally into the Red Sea, to Jedda in Arabia.

as reason was: as courtesy required.

167 *Solamona's House . . . King of the Hebrews*: see note to p. 165 above for the relation between Salomon's House, Solamona, and Solomon.

cedar of Libanus . . . life and motion: see 1 Kings 4: 33.

168 *commodity of matter*: material commodity.

God's first creature . . . of the world: see Genesis 1: 3. In Bacon's essay 'Of Truth' he describes God's 'first creature' as the 'light of sense' and his last as 'the light of reason'.

in great courtesy . . . and descended: politely changed the subject, and condescended.

168 *think with ourselves*: consider amongst ourselves.

169 *Tirsan*: as far as I know 'Tirsan' has no meaning. But it is, again, structured like an Arabic word.

distressed or decayed: fallen into poverty.

170 *true ivy*: real ivy.

streamed with gold: striped with gold lines.

and though such charters . . . of the family: and although these charters are issued in such cases as a matter of course, they are nevertheless varied in their natures, according to the size of the family and its importance in the community.

171 *the subject . . . Father of the Faithful*: Adam gave issue to the human race in the beginning; Noah to the human race after the flood. For the story of Abraham see Genesis 11–25; for his description as the Father of the Faithful see Romans 4: 16 and Galatians 3: 7.

in whose . . . only blessed: our own births, blessed only in the birth of Christ.

172 *days of thy pilgrimage*: see Genesis 47: 9.

every of them: every one of them.

so they be not above two: as long as there are not more than two of them.

Joabin: Weinberger suggests that Joabin is named after the biblical Joab, a nephew of David. Joab was a talented military commander and a ruthless murderer: ignoring David's instruction to spare his rebellious son Absalom, Joab stabbed him through the heart when he was entangled in an oak tree. After David's death Joab supported Adonijah, who plotted against Solomon; Solomon ordered him killed in retaliation for this, and also for two of his earlier murders. See 2 Samuel 11 and 18; 1 Kings 2. Another Joab is mentioned in 1 Chronicles 4: 14. This Joab is a craftsman.

the Milken Way: the Milky Way, believed by the Jews to flow from the throne of God.

the Eliah of the Messiah: Elijah (or Elias) the Prophet. See Malachi 4: 5; Matthew 17: 10.

the people thereof . . . at Hierusalem: 'Nachoran' is possibly suggestive of Abraham's brother Nahor, who had many sons. See Genesis 11; 22: 20–4. A *cabbala* is the Hebrew name for the tradition of mystical interpretation of the Old Testament, said to derive from Moses. For the second coming see Mark 13: 26–37; Matthew 14: 41–3; Mark 8: 38–9: 1.

173 *I have read . . . ugly Ethiop*: the book referred to is unknown. A similar (but later), story appears in La Motte Fouqué's *Sintram* (1820). 'Ethiop' was a racist byword for ugliness, as in Romeo's 'like a rich jewel in an Ethiop's ear', *Romeo and Juliet*, I. v. 50; racist anxieties about rapacious black sexuality were already in circulation. For a more extended performance of such anxieties see *The Isle of Pines*.

But when men have at hand . . . instituted: most aristocratic marriages in the early modern period were arranged, in order to promote the wealth or the power of the families involved. Although working partnerships often developed out of such marriages, the development of emotional ties between couples happened, if they did happen, after marriage, not before; such ties were therefore especially vulnerable to threat from adulterous liaisons.

being of the same matter: being of the same corrupt flesh.

174 *Lot's offer*: in the Bible Lot's action is virtuous, and rewarded by God: Lot offers his daughters to the Sodomites who are besieging his house in an attempt to rape his male guests, two of God's angels. See Genesis 19.

masculine love: homosexuality.

widow of Sarepta . . . Elias: Sarepta (New Testament name), or Zarephath (Old Testament name) is a Phoenician port; Elijah was given food and lodging there by a poor widow. See 1 Kings 17: 8–24.

intermarry or contract: marry each other or become engaged.

I have read in a book . . . one another naked: More's *Utopia*. See p. 90 and accompanying note.

175 *a rich . . . litter-wise*: in something akin to a sedan-chair, apparently carried by horses.

emeralds of the Peru colour: very green emeralds.

tissued upon blue: woven upon a blue background.

176 *the Companies of the City*: probably Merchants' guilds.

as if they had been placed: as if they had been put there, or instructed to stand there.

any degrees to the state: any steps up to the low throne.

warned the pages forth: asked the pages to leave.

177 *the imitation of natural mines*: the artificial production of natural mineral veins.

We have burials . . . porcelain: Chinese porcelain was thought to be obtained by a process which involved burying it underground.

178 *engines for multiplying . . . divers motions*: machines for increasing the intensity of winds, to bring about different movements.

as tincted upon vitriol: vitriol is the hydrous sulphate of a metal. 'Tincting upon vitriol' is the adding of vitriol to water to make mineral water.

take the virtue: absorb the property.

made very sovereign: rendered the very best, the most efficacious.

some artificial rains of bodies . . . and divers others: beliefs about various kinds of spontaneous generation were, in the absence of the microscope (see below), common in the early modern period. Below, Bacon refers to the generation of animals from decaying matter (putrefaction): it was thought that maggots, for instance, bred spontaneously in dung or dead animals. Here, Bacon rehearses the belief that swarms of insects are spontaneously generated in hot weather.

179 *We make a number . . . putrefaction*: see previous note.

180 *drinks of extreme thin parts . . . fretting*: drinks made up out of elements so tiny that they can be absorbed painlessly through the skin.

meats . . . otherwise it would be: native Peruvians chewed coca leaves to produce effects similar to those described here.

181 *exact forms of composition . . . natural simples*: exact methods of combining these substances, so that they fuse together almost entirely, as if they were originally and naturally one ingredient alone.

as well for such as are . . . those that are: for those things that are not commonly used, as well as for those that are.

but yet . . . patterns and principals: but in any case, of all those things that we invented ourselves, we keep examples to serve as blueprints or models (for future reference).

that pass divers . . . progresses, and returns: of diverse intensities, undergoing cyclical variations, increasing and diminishing.

lime unquenched: 'unquenched': unslaked, not hydrated. Lime generates heat only when it is slaked.

producing of light . . . divers bodies: making light originate from various substances.

means of seeing objects . . . distinctly: some lenses, such as the magnifying glass, had been in use since ancient times. Eyeglasses had been in use since the fourteenth century. The telescope was in use in some parts of Europe; it had been invented around 1600, perhaps by Hans Lippershey. Microscopes were a very recent, and still largely unknown invention (possibly invented by Zacharias Jansen, they were named by the naturalist John Faber in 1625). It was not until the publication of Robert Hooke's *Micrographia* in 1665 that the potential of the microscope was really recognized.

182 *observations in urine*: urine was analysed in order to diagnose disease: it was its colour which was thought to be the most significant indicator.

fossils: objects hidden in the earth, inorganic as well as organic.

lodestones: magnets had been known for centuries; the compass was a more recent invention. The Chinese had used magnetized needles as early compasses in shipping since about AD 1000, the Europeans since around the fifteenth century.

183 *wildfires burning in water*: naptha (liquid petroleum) had been used since ancient times for setting fire to enemy ships.

ships and boats for going under water: a submarine had been demonstrated in the Thames by the Dutch inventor Cornelis Drebbel in 1620.

brooking of seas: sailing over high waves.

clocks . . . perpetual motions: clocks telling the hour had been in use for centuries. The principle of isochronism (equal time of the pendulum's swing) was discovered by Galileo at the end of the sixteenth century, ushering in a period of rapid advance in the art of time-keeping, although the pendulum clock was not invented until the middle of the seventeenth century. Perpetual motion is an impossibility.

images of men . . . serpents: mechanical models of animals, automata.

could in a world . . . the senses: could trick the senses in lots of different ways.

they do not show . . . affectation of strangeness: they never exhibit any natural product or object in an exaggerated manner, but only exactly as it is in nature, without any attempt to make it more unusual than it really is.

184 *mechanical arts . . . brought into arts*: mechanical arts are those cultivated for profit, liberal sciences (or liberal arts) those pursued for the sake of knowledge. The third category comprises those skills and endeavours not comprehended by the first two.

knowledge as well for works . . . parts of bodies: for practical knowledge as well as theoretical, and also for knowledge of how to predict changes in nature, and understanding of the qualities of various parts of bodies and other objects.

of a higher light: of a more profound nature.

your monk . . . gunpowder: perhaps Roger Bacon (1210–92), a scholastic philosopher and Franciscan friar, traditionally thought to have invented gunpowder.

185 *the inventor of music . . . of sugars*: most of these things were discovered by cultures, not by individuals. In Old Testament mythology Jubal is said to be the father of music (see Genesis 4: 21); in Greek mythology Dionysus is the god of wine, and Triptolemus of agriculture.

declare natural divinations: draw attention to nature's warning signs.

temperature of the year: unusual changes to the weather normally expected at a given time of year.

The rest was not perfected: Rawley's note to the text.

Magnalia Naturae . . . humanos: 'The wonderful works of Nature, chiefly such as benefit mankind' (Vickers's translation). The list followed the *New Atlantis* in its first edition.

THE ISLE OF PINES

189 *Pines*: an anagram of 'penis'. But the word 'pine' also meant 'punishment',

'suffering' (especially the suffering of hell), and (as a verb) 'to lose one's vitality or vigour', as well as 'to languish with desire'.

189 *Rochelle*: the French port La Rochelle, an important commercial centre for overseas trade and also the site of Huguenot revolts in 1621–8.

Cape Finis Terre: the location of this Cape Finis Terre is uncertain. There are several places with this name in various countries of the world, but none seems to fit the location suggested in the text. This, however, may be Neville's 'deliberate' error, as Keek says below that 'there may be some mistake in the number of the leagues, as also of the exact point of the compass, from Cape Finis Terre'.

the Island of Brasile: not Brazil, which had been known since it was sighted by Cabral in 1500 and since settled, mostly by the Portuguese. 'Brasile' was the name given to a mythical island, supposedly situated in the Atlantic somewhere south-west of Ireland, and the subject of a pamphlet entitled *O Brasile*, which described an imaginary civilization there.

Zealand: Zeeland, a region in the Low Countries which had been one of the main locations for the Dutch revolt against Spanish rule in the sixteenth and early seventeenth centuries.

190 *Terra Australis Incognita*: Australia was unknown at the end of the seventeenth century. 'Terra Incognita Australis' (unknown southern land) was a term periodically used to designate unknown lands; it later became the title of a French utopia written by Gabriel de Foigny in 1692 and translated into English the following year.

Henry Cornelius Van Sloetten: the name has both English and Dutch resonances and would appear also to have parodic sexual significance. It has been suggested that 'Sloetten' may be derived from 'slut'. 'Cornelius' may be suspicious too, since the Latin for 'horn' is *cornu*, and horns were a symbol of cuckoldry.

the East Indies: the extraordinary wealth to be gained from exploiting the spice trade in the East Indies was one of the principal causes of the Anglo-Dutch War. By the mid-seventeenth century the Dutch had become dominant in the area, capturing Malacca from the Portuguese in 1641, and in 1623 massacring English traders at Amboina in the Moluccas. They had seized Macassar from the English in 1667.

isles of Cape Verd . . . Veridis: islands off the north-west (Senegambian) coast of Africa, a port for the Portuguese on the way to the East Indies. The Dutch developed a settlement at Goree on the mainland, the English a settlement slightly further south, at Cacheu.

under the Southern Tropic: Madagascar lies on the Tropic of Capricorn.

191 *Isle del Principe*: an island off the west coast of West Africa, below the Niger delta states, settled by the Portuguese.

Explanatory Notes

'*Wat Eylant is dit?*': in Dutch the question would be 'Welk Eiland is dat?'

192 *great nut . . . apple*: the *OED* records the first use of the term 'breadfruit' in 1697, where the author compares the tree that bears it to a European apple tree.

194 *hereafter followeth*: this point marks the first break between the framing narrative and Pine's narrative: see the introduction for a brief publishing history of the text.

A way . . . certain Portugals: the narrator is now George Pine, the time the 1590s, over a century prior to the narrative of Cornelius Van Sloetten. The Portuguese had first reached Malacca in 1509, and the Spice Islands (the Moluccas) in 1512–13.

the Queen's Royal Licence: one early edition of the text has a lengthy note at this point concerning Queen Elizabeth's insistence that the English East India Company (founded in 1600) should trade in English silver (which was not recognized in the East Indies) and not the coin of the Spanish (which was). The note is reprinted in Henderson's Everyman edition of the text.

the Island of St Helen: St Helena, in the Atlantic Ocean south-west of Angola, later a British colony.

St Lawrence: Madagascar.

196 *a sort of fowl . . . swan*: the bird has obvious similarities to the dodo, which lived in Mauritius.

198 *my stomach would not serve me*: I could not stomach it.

200 *Amen*: marks the end of Pine's narrative, which was inserted in the framing narrative in the third edition of the text (see introduction). From here, the narration returns to Cornelius Van Sloetten.

202 *these laws to be observed by them*: the laws are a condensation of Mosaic law, most saliently in principle (an eye for an eye, a tooth for a tooth, burning for burning, wound for wound, stripe for stripe). See Exodus 21: 23–5 and, more generally, 19–24.

blaspheme . . . put to death: see Exodus 20: 2, 7; 22: 20, 28.

commit adultery: see Exodus 21: 14, 17.

203 *laming of his limbs*: see Exodus 21: 12.

taking . . . possesseth: see Exodus 21: 15; 22: 4, 7.

defame . . . the Governor: see Exodus 22: 28.

205 *the third climate*: 'climate' in the obsolete sense of a 'belt of the earth's surface contained between two given parallels of latitude' (*OED*). Initially seven, by the end of the eighteenth century there were reckoned to be thirty lying between the equator and either pole.

208 *reval*: possibly derived from the French *rêve* ('dream').

marde: an anagram of 'dream'.

208 *Cambaia . . . the great Cham of Tartary*: European commercial and colonial interests often found themselves in competition not only with each other, but also with the complex network of cultures and empires that existed before the European arrival in South-East Asia. 'Tartary' refers to lands north of China; the 'great Cham' was the title given to the descendants of Genghis Khan, and more generally to potentates of Mongolia, Tartary, and China. Cambaia may be Cambay, a trading centre on the northernmost coast of India, under the control of the Mughal empire during the seventeenth century.

   Calicut: an important port on the Malabar coast of India.

209 *Brachmans*: Brahmins, i.e. high-caste Hindus.

   King's sisters' sons . . . Kingdom: this inheritance system is still practised in some parts of the world, property being passed from a man, not to his own sons (of whose paternity he can never be entirely certain), but to his sister's sons (with whom, he can be sure, he shares a genetic relation).

210 *Argiere*: Algiers. Pirates from the Corsair cities were greatly feared by European sailors.

211 *Although perhaps . . . lie by authority*: Neville's syntax is confusing here; the sentence means that intelligent people will believe his report, since they will have the sense to contextualize the tale within the knowledge of the discovery of many such new places in recent years, while stupidly sceptical people will not. A 'Nullifidian' is someone who has no faith or belief.

GLOSSARY

Words and phrases are glossed in the form in which they first appear in the text

a matter of the same seriousness
abate diminish
abide wait for
above stairs upstairs
abroad outside the home; out wide
abstracts summaries
abusing committing sodomy
accident catastrophe
admiring marvelling, wondering
advanced helped on
adventures unexpected events
advisement deliberation, consideration
advoutry adultery
affected impressed by; valued, desired
affection favouritism
affectioned attached
affiance confidence
afore in front of
aforehand in credit
aglets pendants, ornaments
alliance kindred
alliant akin, similar
allured drawn towards
amendment improvement
apace quickly
apostle missionary
apostolical connected with, relating to, the apostles
appaired impaired
apparel clothing
appertain belong
appertaineth be suitable for, proper to; belong to, be relevant to
applied to be consistent with
appointed laid out
approve prove, show
archdolts extreme idiots
arefaction action of drying
artificers skilled craftsmen
artificially skilfully constructed (as opposed to natural)
asp aspen

assaying attempting
assentation sycophantic agreement
assisteth is present
astonied deprived of sensation
at all adventures any old how, higgledy piggeldy
at the least way at least
attemper temper
avaled brought down, degraded
avaleth lowers
avaunt glory in, be proud of
aventures random events, chance
avoided left
avoutrers adulterers
balm-wood balsam wood (aromatic)
bands bonds, fetters
bare bore
basilisks large cannon
bastons truncheons
bawds pimps or panders (male before seventeenth century)
beams radiations
because that so that, in order that
because so that
beck signal
becometh suits
before in front
behated thoroughly hated
bend themselves apply themselves
bewrayed betrayed
blown (of heat) blown by bellows
bodies material substances
bondage enslavement
bondmen slaves, bonded labour
borderers neighbours, neighbouring countries
boscage woods, thickets
bottoms ships
bound transfixed
bounden indebted
brabbling arguments, contention
brazen brass

243

breed breeding

broiding braiding, plaiting

brook make use of, possess

brunt exertion; attack, onslaught

bryde up bring up, raise

bulls papal directives

by the purse with a fine

by course in turn

cambric fine white linen

came about turned around

capias writ enforcing arrest

carbuncles precious stones

careful troublesome; full of care, unhappy

cark trouble

cast gave off; arranged

cataracts waterfalls over precipices

cautel prevarication, device

cavillation quibble

cedar of Libanus cedar of Lebanon

cells cubicles

certes certainly

chaffare traffic, trade

chambers rooms

chamolet exotic and costly fabric made of Angora goat hair. Water chamolet had a wavy or watery surface

chases hunting grounds, unenclosed park land

children people

chirugery surgery

chouse cheat, swindler

chylus chyle

circuits tours

circumstance circumlocution

circumventions getting around something

civil applicable to real life, practical

clarifications purifications of liquids

cleped called (already archaic in More's time)

clerks scholars

cloth of gold cloth embroidered with gold thread

coagulations the thickening of liquids by methods such as evaporation and condensation

collier maker or transporter of coal

colour (false) reasoning; disguise

commendations recommendations, references

commissioners members of negotiating team, ambassadors

commodious beneficial; serviceable; easy

commodity convenience; comfort

common public

commonalty commonwealth

compassed encompassed, surrounded

compassionated granted out of, expressive of compassion

complexions bodily characteristics, humours

compositions components of metal

compounded settled

conceits skilfully cooked dishes; opinions, ideas

conclave secret location

conclusions results

condition quality

conduction direction, command

conform akin

confused astounded, overcome

consults consultations

contained prevented

continued stayed

contumely scornful rudeness

conversation interaction

corrupting rotting, going bad

countenance face, facial expression

countervail outprice, out-value

courages dispositions

covin deceit, treachery

crack boast

creatures creations

crosier a kind of staff, surmounted with a cross

curious finely wrought, elaborate

curtesies bowing of the body or head

damned condemned

danger power

dangerous reticent

dead lift lifting a dead weight; the pull of a horse at something beyond his power to move

debatement discussion

decocted concentrated by boiling

defray you pay for you

degrees steps; success, ability

demonstrations experiments

denominate of named after

denounced declared
depredators plunderers, pillagers
descended condescended
descried revealed
designed destined, directed
despite (at) contempt (for)
determination agreement about
dicers gamblers
direction instruction
disannulled abolished
discover uncover, disclose, reveal
discrepant different
dishonesty dishonour
dispensatories chemists, dispensaries
displayed outspread
displeasantly disagreeably
dispose place
disprove disapprove
dissident from at variance from
dissimulation pretending not to be the person that you are
dissolute houses brothels
divers different, several
diversities varieties
divinations forecasts; warnings
dizzards fools, jokers, blockheads
dors drones, idlers
dorture dormitory
doubtful hesitant
downstroke swordstroke made with the edge of the sword
dress prepare
drivel menial, drudge
earnest pressing
effeminated made feminine, emasculated
eftsoons soon after
either each
else by contrast, on the other hand
embraid upbraid
emollition softening
end aim
endeavour myself apply myself
engines machines
ensign badge of office
ensure assure
entered initiated
entire unbroken, intact
entoil entrap, ensnare
entreat treat; plead

espial spy
estate state, condition
esteem estimate the worth of, judge
ever always
evil willing unwilling
except unless
excogitated thought through, discovered
exemptions freedom from taxes or duties
exhilaration enlivening; raising
existimation estimation
experiences experiments
exploded expulsed, driven out
expulsed expelled
extenuate thin out
factor mercantile agent
fallacies refutations, disproofs
fantasy fancy, desire
fardel bundle, collection
fashion manner
fast securely
favour face, appearance
fear frighten; dissuade, put off
fearful frightening
feat knack
fells skins
flags bladed leaves
flight-shot flight-distance of an arrow
floods currents, waters
foin swordstroke made with point of the weapon towards one's enemy
for that because
forasmuch as inasmuch as
forby close by
fords shallows
fore castle fo'c'sle
fore-end front-end
forefeeling presentiment
foreseen provided
formerly previously
fossils objects dug from the soil, organic or inorganic
fraught laden, stocked up with
fray dissuade, put off
furnished equipped, stocked
gage deposit, security
gallant showy, fashionable
gallimaufry mish-mash, a thing of mixed genres

gather up recoup
gear things, doings, attire
generation production; ancestry
gilt painted gold
girt belted, girdled
glasses lenses
glebeland piece of cultivated land, field
go about turn around
goodman master of a household
goodwife mistress of a household
grains impurities
gramercy free, gratis
graved engraved, printed
greater more comprehensive
greatness high rank
grieved bored
gross fundamental
gudgeon small fish; a credulous person
guestwise as a visitor
guise habits, customs
gyves shackles
half-pace step or platform upon which something like a throne or altar is erected
handicrafts manual or skilled labour
handsome handy
handy manual, unskilled
hanged decorated with wall-hangings
hap happens
hapt dressed, attired
hardiness boldness, daring
harmless without being harmed
haunt habitation
haut high, lofty
head spring point where a river originates
helps remedies; hearing-aids
herborough shelter, lodging
Hierusalem Jerusalem
holden possessed, affected; detained
homely plainly, without refinement
honesty honour
huke cloak with a hood
husband cultivate, take care of
husbandry cultivation, agriculture, domestic economy
imbasing debasing
imbossed embossed
imported suggested

importune troublesome, pressing, persistent; inopportune
impressions atmospheric phenomena or pressures
impudency impudence
in aunters in case
in hazard at stake
in special especially
in fine in the end
inclinations bending forwards, bowing
incommodity inconvenience, damage
incontinent forthwith, straight away; wanting in restraint
indifferent moderately, moderate; impartial
indued endowed
induration hardening
indurations the hardening of solids
infamed disgraced
infidelity lack of Christian faith
infusion soaking something in water to infuse its qualities into the liquid
inoculating budding, grafting
insolation exposure to the sun's rays
instruct educated, taught
instruments contracts, legal documents
intentively earnestly, intently
intercourse trade, dealings
inured experienced in, used to
inventions ideas, proposals
invited attracted
javel rascal, worthless fellow
jeopardy danger
jet strut, swagger
juggling conjuring, trickery
junkets sweet dish of curds and cream
jus right, law
just equal
keep no measure fix no limits
kenning about 20–1 miles: as far as the eye can see, especially at sea
kindly naturally
knowledge acknowledge
lading cargo
lanthorn lantern, light
last duration
laud praise
leaded framed
leagues treaties
let hindrance (noun); hinder (verb)

letted hindered, impaired
letters writing
lewd ignorant, untaught
licence permission
licensed freed
lightly casually
like the same
line equinoctial the equator
lines distances
living livelihood
lodestone magnet
looked expected
lot lottery
louting cringing
lubber dolt
lust wish to
lusty full of life
madder a plant yielding a valuable red dye
made away disposed of
manfully bravely, honourably
masculine love homosexuality
mattock tool like an adze or pick
maturations the act of bringing to ripeness
maws inward parts
mean season meantime
mean medium, small
meaner vulgar, of lower class
meats foods
meretricious embracements embraces of a prostitute
merrily in jest
mess a serving of food
meteors any meteorological phenomena
mislike displease
Montera helmet-like cap
mortified made tender by hanging or keeping
motions causes
moved made
moveth to attempts
mulct to punish with a fine
multiplications intensifications
murrain plague, especially of animals
namely especially; by name
naughtiness wickedness, depravity
needeth is necessary
newfangledness new fashions, fads
next immediately

niggish miserly, niggardly
nigh closely related to, near
nitre saltpetre
noisome disgusting, unpleasant
noyous troublesome, vexatious
observation usage
occupieth takes up; interacts; trades; uses
of place of high rank, of authority
offered to expressed an intention to, made as if to
open public
open explain
ordinances decrees
ordnance military materials, artillery
orisons prayers
other others
out of comparison beyond compare
out of fashion unrefined, out of shape, rough
outlands outlying islands, foreign countries
over upper
overblown put to rest
overplus surplus
overrunned trampled down, crushed, ravaged
overthwart across
pale boundary, limit
parcel portion, part
pardy by God!, verily, certainly
parting dividing
pass us surpass us
pass care
patrimony inheritance
patterns models, blueprints, instructions
pennyfathers misers
physic medicine, art of healing
pick a thank slavish fawning
pieces guns
piles pointed stakes or posts
pilled shaved, stripped
pioners miners
pistolets Spanish, Venetian, or Florentine coins
pitied was merciful to, compassionated
planted settled
plat plot, device
platform ground plan

platted plotted

plot location, plot of land

plush rich cloth, of silk, cotton, or wool

policy stratagem, trick; political acumen

poll cut short, lop off

pontifical episcopal

portion dowry, financial gain

postern back

practices of experiments with

practique practice, way of arranging matters

precepts principles

prefer promote

preparations instruments

prescript prescribed, set down

presently immediately

preservative prophylactic

pretenced intended

pretty quite substantial

prevent anticipate our wants

pricked tormented

pristinate original

privy secret, private

probable just, defensible; credible

proof result, harvest

propriety ownership; property; quality

provide prepare

puissance might

pullen poultry

purgings evacuations of the bowels

quailed withered, faded

qualify invest with qualities, to make fit for

quarter-sounds quarter-tones

queans hussies

quoits a game played with discs or hoops

rampire fix, establish firmly

rank foul

ravin robbery, plunder, gluttony

re-edify rebuild, re-establish

rearward rear guard

reculed fallen back, recoiled

reeds Papyrus

registers records

rehearsal retelling

relicts vestiges

remain remnant

removing moving

render give up

represent reproduce

require call in

rested consisted

retainer advisor, consultant

return (noun) side

rings chimes

room place

rot virulent disease affecting liver of sheep fed on moist pasture

rude uncivilized, crude, ignorant, unskilled

run in incur

rush-bucklers swashbucklers

rushes plants with straight stems, like bulrushes

sad dignified, solemn

sallets salads

savours perfumes, aromas

scala coeli stairway, ladder to heaven

scant scarcely, hardly; (verb) stint

science liberal discipline

securely certainly, surely

seen versed, experienced

seething boiling

sensible sensitive

separations extracting separate elements of a substance

serviceable servant-like

set seated

set field battle array

set on set to

several different

shamefastness shamefacedness

sheaths sword sheaths

shelves sand banks

shops places of industry

shrewdly severely, sharply

silly simple

simples things consisting of only one substance (particularly medicinal plants)

simulation pretending to be someone you are not

sindons fine thin linen, used as a wrapper or shroud

skilleth not does not matter

sleight cunning, trick

slenderly weakly, poorly

slides processions of ascending or descending notes

smack in taste for

small less
so that as long as
so as so that; therefore
softly quietly, gently
solemn formal, dignified
somewhat something
sort manner
space time
sparing little
stablished established
stamp seal
stand with agree with
standing still; position; duration
state canopy; ceremony
states statesmen
stay hesitation; state of stability
stayed prevented
stews bath-houses, brothels
stiff-necked unyielding
stirps branch of a family
stomachs dispositions
stonish dull, senseless
strain extract
strait narrow, severe; close
strange foreign; irregular, remarkable
stripes lashes of the whip
strokes blows
strumpets debauched women, harlots
study not don't try
stuff material
subscription seal, signature to a
  document
substantive self-sufficient
suffer allow
suitors petitioners
suits disagreements, legal actions
  against requests
summum bonum supreme good
supported attended
supporters flotation devices
suppositious based on supposition,
  spurious
surely securely
swam floated
swathing swaddling
sweating toiling
sweet fresh, not salt
swimming girdles lifebelts
symbolize agree with, be at one accord
  with

tables a board game, like backgammon
tacklings rigging
take the virtue absorb the properties
tears sap
tedder tether, confines
temper kind, type
tender hesitant
think imagine
threads cloths, fibres
throng crowded
tippet narrow slip of cloth, forming part
  of a hood, head-dress, or sleeve
tipstaff staff with a cap of metal, carried
  as a badge of officialdom
tissued woven, adorned
tissues cloths
together at the same time; continuously
took us off relieved our embarrassment
touch indication
touch-stone basanite, a variety of quartz
touching concerning
towardness inclination
train something which lures someone on
translating transferring
trapped fitted out, decorated
travail labour
traverse screened apartment
tremblings tremolos
trough-wise like a trough
trunks tubes
tun barrel
turn him to deal with, turn his attention
  to
turves slabs of turf
tush exclamation of contempt or
  impatience
unmeet inappropriate
unsearchable inscrutable, unfathomable
uplandish rustic, uncultivated, boorish
use direct knowledge; adopt
vale! farewell!
valiant strong
versions conversions
viands food
victual food
visual visible
vitiate infected, depraved
vitrificated turned into glass
void empty, unoccupied
vouchsafed agreed, bestowed, granted

Glossary

vulgar plebian, common
wanted lacked
ward look-out
waxed well became better
wayfaring travelling
weal well-being
weal-public commonwealth, state or
  body politic
wealthily happily, prosperously
well a worth alas!
well-spring source of perennial supply
whereof from what
whether whichever
whole healthy
wickers twigs used for making things
  like baskets

wile trick
wink at close our eyes to
wiped beside cheated of
withal notwithstanding; likewise, as well
without outside
wittily wisely
workmanship creation
wot knew
wrested strained, twisted
wried contorted
writhen perverted, deflected
writing tables small blocks (of wood) on
  which to take notes
wrought embroidered
yet just the same
yield give

The Oxford World's Classics Website

www.worldsclassics.co.uk

- Information about new titles
- Explore the full range of Oxford World's Classics
- Links to other literary sites and the main OUP webpage
- Imaginative competitions, with bookish prizes
- Peruse the Oxford World's Classics Magazine
- Articles by editors
- Extracts from Introductions
- A forum for discussion and feedback on the series
- Special information for teachers and lecturers

www.worldsclassics.co.uk

American Literature

British and Irish Literature

Children's Literature

Classics and Ancient Literature

Colonial Literature

Eastern Literature

European Literature

History

Medieval Literature

Oxford English Drama

Poetry

Philosophy

Politics

Religion

The Oxford Shakespeare

A complete list of Oxford Paperbacks, including Oxford World's Classics, Oxford Shakespeare, Oxford Drama, and Oxford Paperback Reference, is available in the UK from the Academic Division Publicity Department, Oxford University Press, Great Clarendon Street, Oxford OX2 6DP.

In the USA, complete lists are available from the Paperbacks Marketing Manager, Oxford University Press, 198 Madison Avenue, New York, NY 10016.

Oxford Paperbacks are available from all good bookshops. In case of difficulty, customers in the UK can order direct from Oxford University Press Bookshop, Freepost, 116 High Street, Oxford OX1 4BR, enclosing full payment. Please add 10 per cent of published price for postage and packing.